FIGHTING CORRUPTION IN THE PUBLIC SECTOR

CONTRIBUTIONS
TO
ECONOMIC ANALYSIS

284

Honorary Editors:
D. W. JORGENSON
J. TINBERGEN[†]

Editors:
B. BALTAGI
E. SADKA
D. WILDASIN

FIGHTING CORRUPTION IN THE PUBLIC SECTOR

Jorge Martinez-Vazquez

Javier Arze del Granado

Jameson Boex

*International Studies Program, Andrew Young School of Policy Studies,
Georgia State University, Atlanta, GA, USA*

Emerald

United Kingdom – North America – Japan
India – Malaysia – China

Emerald Group Publishing Limited
Howard House, Wagon Lane, Bingley BD16 1WA, UK

British Library Cataloguing in Publication Data
A catalogue record for this book is available from the British Library

ISBN: 978-0-444-52974-9

Awarded in recognition of
Emerald's production
department's adherence to
quality systems and processes
when preparing scholarly
journals for print

INVESTOR IN PEOPLE

Introduction to the Series

This series consists of a number of hitherto unpublished studies, which are introduced by the editors in the belief that they represent fresh contributions to economic science.

The term 'economic analysis' as used in the title of the series has been adopted because it covers both the activities of the theoretical economist and the research worker.

Although the analytical method used by the various contributors are not the same, they are nevertheless conditioned by the common origin of their studies, namely theoretical problems encountered in practical research.

Since for this reason, business cycle research and national accounting, research work on behalf of economic policy, and problems of planning are the main sources of the subjects dealt with, they necessarily determine the manner of approach adopted by the authors. Their methods tend to be 'practical' in the sense of not being too far remote from application to actual economic conditions. In addition, they are quantitative.

It is the hope of the editors that the publication of these studies will help to stimulate the exchange of scientific information and to reinforce international cooperation in the field of economics.

The Editors

Contents

Preface

Corruption in government, where public officials use their offices for private gain, has a significant negative impact in countries all over the world. In fact, very few governance issues have more of a negative impact than does corruption. This book addresses the problem of how to fight corruption in the public sector. The study presents a comprehensive analysis of corruption that highlights not only the problems, but also potential solutions for a broad range of corruption manifestations in tax administration, government expenditure programs, and other areas of fiscal policy and management. The analysis and discussion is supported and clarified by relevant real-world examples and empirical analysis. In particular, country-specific examples are used to identify key issues and valuable lessons for reducing corruption.

We have benefited from financial support from the US Agency for International Development for prior work under contract to Development Alternatives, Inc. and Georgia State University that was important in producing this current study. We also would like to thank Mark Gallagher and several reviewers for helpful comments and Attasit Pankaew, Riatu Qibthiyyah, and Juan Luis Gomez for helping us to get this volume ready for publication.

Jorge Martinez-Vazquez
Javier Arze del Granado
Jameson Boex
Atlanta, October 2006

List of Figures

List of Boxes

List of Tables

CHAPTER 1

Corruption, Fiscal Policy, and Fiscal Management

When I personally arrived, I was told that you did not talk about the "c" word. I said, "what is the 'c' word?" ....He took me quietly to a corner to explain to me that the "c" word he had whispered to me was "corruption" and that you did not mention the word "corruption" because the Bank is not a political organization. Corruption, he said, dug deep into politics and we should stay out of it.

James D. Wolfensohn, President, The World Bank Group, Athens, Greece[1]

For many years the issue of corruption has, to some extent, been downplayed by governments, international organizations, and policy experts. This is true because, first, corruption was considered a cultural and political issue; and second, because measuring corruption, much less getting rid of it, was perceived as nearly impossible. Thus, elimination of corruption was not usually an economic objective of development reforms. Instead, it was taken as part of the nature of a country, as exogenous perhaps as its geography. However, times have changed. Frustration with the lack of effectiveness of traditional approaches to development and the recognition that institutional development and good governance practices play a fundamental role in economic development have led to increased attention given to corruption. Many studies that assess corruption and discuss how to address it are already available, as shown here below, and the number is growing rapidly. Furthermore, there is no remorse about exposing these issues, but rather there is a growing eagerness to discuss them openly at national and international levels.

Besides general development issues, the growing interest in corruption is a result of several factors. First, the negative consequences of corruption on poor countries are evident. International Financial Institutions (IFIs) cannot afford to ignore this problem anymore as most development aid and antipoverty strategies are predestined to fail if those resources are diverted by corrupt domestic administrations. Thus, IFIs have started to address corruption as a fundamental component of their development programs. Besides IFIs, many other non-governmental, bilateral and

---

[1] Remarks at the Fourth Annual Conference of the Parliamentary Network on the World Bank. March 9, 2003.

international organizations have also taken an active role in the fight against corruption.

Second, one tangible result of the engagement of the aforementioned institutions was the collection and dissemination of objective data, which opened possibilities of research previously impossible. This availability of data was coupled with the application of new measurement techniques, which made possible the construction of broad datasets of cross-country measurements of corruption. The growing number of studies using these measurements, in turn, has provided further incentives for institutions to extend their measurements from general indicators of corruption to several indicators of specific types of corruption. As stated by Kaufmann (2003), data on corruption has helped to debunk old myths and to 'desensationalize' the topic of corruption, making it an objective topic of dialogue. One of the myths the recently developed data sets on corruption have put in question is the belief that only developed countries can attain low levels of corruption. As discussed further below, data shows that some developing countries have reached levels of sound governance and corruption control comparable to those of most developed countries.

Third, there is a growing consensus that issues such as poverty and corruption are part of a global phenomenon, and as such, affect all countries without exceptions. The close interconnection of these issues among countries is more and more apparent. Illnesses and diseases such as AIDs, for example, do not discriminate among countries or regions based on race, religion, geographic location, or per capita income. As a result, containment in countries that are more affected is necessary to prevent uncontrolled global spread. Similarly, poverty leads to social distortions and discontent, which in turn are translated into migration patterns of unemployed populations toward industrialized countries. Political instability and weak rule of law also spread to the international community in several forms, such as organized crime, drug trafficking, and terrorism. The realization that corruption is a global phenomenon makes it clear that the fight against corruption is not an issue of international aid, but rather a matter of global subsistence.

However, the growing interest and increasing number of studies of corruption, does not suggest the existence of easy solutions to serious problems affecting the social, legal, and economic dimensions that have an effect on corruption. Analogous to most structural policy issues, the experience indicates that there are no unique solutions, but rather that fighting corruption requires the application of a wide range of strategies and the recognition of the unique cultural and historical characteristics of a county. Yet, despite the complexity of anticorruption policy design, anecdotal cases of success suggest that corruption is neither part of a predetermined destiny nor is necessarily ingrained in some cultures, but rather corruption is an issue that can be addressed, and fighting corruption is possible and worth doing.

Corruption manifests itself in innumerable areas, in various and complex forms and interactions. Corruption has dominated in the fiscal arena. Although often unintentionally, fiscal policies sometimes facilitate corruption in the private and public sectors, as a result of the ways governments collect and spend resources. The relationships between corruption and fiscal policy can be simple and direct but also subtle and complex. These relationships can vary significantly from country to country. In some cases, the public sector its public servants an incentive to be corrupt. For instance, poorly compensated public servants have powerful financial incentives to search for additional sources of income, including through bribes or extortion if necessary. Likewise, if ethic standards are equivalent in two countries, there will be more corruption in the country where it is easier to conceal that a bribe was paid, for example, due to a much more complex tax structure. Poorly designed expenditure programs and budget processes may also give individuals or firms opportunities or incentives to bribe public officials or to perpetrate other frauds. Other corrupt practices are internal to the public sector itself. Corruption can result from acts by politicians or senior policy makers; tax administration and customs officials; or those entrusted with contracting or delivering government services.

In summary, there are countless types of corruption and many distinctions can be made based on the dynamics of the act (i.e., unilateral, multiparty), the agents involved (i.e., high-level officials, low-level officials, private agents), the size of the corrupt act (grand corruption or petty corruption), the budgetary functions affected (i.e., expenditures, revenues), the nature of the determinant involved (i.e., structure of incentives, institutional opportunities), and so on. One main conclusion of this study is that all types of corruption – including fiscal corruption – are detrimental, in different degrees, to the fundamental role of government to provide a stable economic framework, generate economic growth, and improve general welfare.

1.1. Overview of this study

The relationship between fiscal policy and corruption has been discussed extensively in the economic literature. The lessons learned in relation to fiscal policy and corruption seem to be separated according to their specific focus, analytical framework, and discipline of study.[2] There is also a gap between qualitative and quantitative studies in corruption. While

---

[2] On the basis of over 4,000 publications on corruption, Transparency International (2001) reports that the distribution of subject areas is: Politics and Public Administration 74 percent, History 10 percent, Law and Judiciary 9 percent, Economics 4 percent, Ethnographic and Cultural 2 percent, and Business and Ethics 1 percent.

qualitative research is typically based on broad and general discussions of the nature and consequences of corruption, quantitative studies are usually focused on cross-country comparisons.

This study seeks to assess the current state of knowledge and contribute to our understanding of how fiscal policies and management interact with corruption issues by integrating concrete and practical issues with theoretical and quantitative analysis of their nature and consequences. This study presents a comprehensive analysis of corruption that not only points out the problems, but also potential solutions for a broad range of fiscal policy and fiscal reform issues. Our analyses and discussions are supported and clarified by relevant real-world examples and empirical analysis. In particular, country-specific examples prove to be quite useful to identify key issues or valuable lessons in minimizing corruption. The study is organized as follows.

- The remainder of this chapter starts by presenting an overview of the issues involved in corruption, the current state of anticorruption commitment, and the definition of corruption used in this study.
- Chapter 2 presents a theoretical framework of the economics of corruption by addressing several issues. First, we present corruption as an economic phenomenon arising as the product of individual conscious decisions within a given institutional environment. Second, we discuss the methodological challenges regarding the measurement of corruption, as well as currently available measurement sources. Third, we review the current state of knowledge regarding the costs that corruption imposes on society.
- Chapter 3 presents a region-by-region overview of dominant corruption issues around the world.
- Chapter 4 describes the forms that corruption might take (within and around the public sector) as a result of poor fiscal policy and fiscal management practices. This description and categorization of the different forms of corruption constitutes the first necessary step to identify policy issues and suggest remedies. The analysis is focused on three fiscal areas: expenditures, revenues, and the quasi-fiscal sector. The discussion also identifies the determinants of corruption within these areas by making the distinction between those factors affecting incentives and those affecting opportunities for corruption.
- Chapter 5 presents potential solutions based on practical anticorruption policies and reforms for each of the issues identified in the previous chapter.
- Chapter 6 provides an in-depth case study describing policy responses to fiscal-related corruption in Tanzania.
- Chapter 7 presents some concluding thoughts on how to address the problem of corruption through reforms of fiscal policy and fiscal management.

1.2. Defining corruption

Numerous definitions for the term "corruption" have been proposed and cited in the academic research and policy-relevant literature on corruption. The Oxford English Dictionary, for example, defines corruption as "the perversion or destruction of integrity or fidelity in the discharge of public duties by bribery or favor". Yet other definitions of corruption stress the role of the participation of public agents such as public officials, bureaucrats, legislators, or politicians. Perhaps the most widely cited definition of corruption in the public sector – and the one used in the current study – denotes corruption as:

"The abuse of public office for private gain."

Public office is abused for private gain when an official accepts, solicits, or exhorts a bribe. It is also abused when private agents actively offer bribes to circumvent public policies and processes for competitive advantage and profit. Public office can also be abused for personal benefit even if no bribery occurs, through patronage and nepotism, the theft of state assets, or the diversion of state revenues. (World Bank, 1997, p. 8)

Alternative definitions of corruption include "the degree misuse of public power for private benefit",[3] and "the likeliness to demand illegal payments in high and low levels of government". However, as shown in subsequent chapters, not all types of corruption involve direct monetary payments, as government officials may receive more subtle benefits from corrupt activities, such as political support. Public officials may demand bribes to do what they are supposed to do anyway (i.e., the so-called "speed or grease money") or accept bribes to do what they are not supposed to do, such as overlook the underreporting of tax liabilities (see Bardhan, 1997).

Despite being immoral and illegal, "speed money" types of corruption are widely perceived as less harmful to an economy than certain other types of corruption that involves payments for the execution of illegal activities. The negative effects of speed money are, at best, ambiguous to many. Some studies even have suggested that this type of corruption has positive effects, because they represent an incentive for public officials to work harder and/ or to recognize the different opportunity costs of time for different individuals.[4] As a result, speed money corruption is not usually addressed as a main topic in the fiscal policy debate.

---

[3] This type of formulation, with some variations, is used in several surveys to measure corruption across countries. Some examples are the surveys generated by the World Economic Forum (2003) (Global Competitiveness Report) and the Business Environment Risk Intelligence/Business Risk Service.

[4] Among many studies along these lines are the following: Leff (1964); Huntington (1968); Mauro (1995); Mookherjee (1997); Bardhan (1997); and Fjeldstad and Tungodden (2003). However, these arguments have also been highly criticized by other studies, such as Kaufmann (1997) and Doig and Theobald (2000).

Although corruption affects many areas of the public sector, this study focuses exclusively on the fiscal dimension of corruption, which may be called "fiscal corruption". Fiscal refers to all issues pertaining to public resources, taxation, and spending policies. Hence, fiscal corruption encompasses all types of corruption pertaining either to tax administration or spending policies, including tax evasion and customs fraud, tax administration corruption, corruption in service procurement, and so on. We specifically do not focus on non-fiscal types of corruption, in which public officials abuse their public powers for private gain outside the realm of fiscal processes (such as law enforcement officials extorting bribes from motorists under the pretext of alleged traffic violations). With this caveat, we note that for brevity in much of the following discussions, "fiscal corruption" will be referred to simply as "corruption".

It is important to note that, given the definition used in this book, a public official must be involved for corruption to take place. After all, it is the abuse of official power that constitutes corruption. This important distinction is relevant to connections between corruption and certain other issues, for example, the relation between tax evasion and corruption. While taxes may be evaded unilaterally by a taxpayer, it is likely that in many instances tax evasion is related to some form of corruption. Thus, most factors that have an impact on tax evasion (such as high levels of taxation) have also at least an indirect effect on corruption. While this study aims to analyze the effects of the fiscal structure and fiscal reforms on corruption, in many cases non-fiscal factors also need to be considered in order to reduce fiscal corruption.

1.3. Corruption around the world

It is widely known that corruption manifests itself in a variety of forms within and across countries. What was not known before the recent "data revolution" in the corruption literature was the severity of corruption across countries, or the existence of patterns in the distribution of corruption. Data across countries reveals that most developing and transitional countries have (or more correctly, are perceived to have, since all key measures of corruption are currently based on opinion surveys) the highest levels of corruption (Figure 1.1). Indeed, corruption tends to be more of a poor country disease: the correlation coefficient between the Transparency International's (TI) Corruption Perception Index (CPI) and Gross Domestic Product (GDP) per capita for a sample of 89 countries for 2001 is 0.85.

However, as mentioned previously, data on some developing countries also demonstrates that low levels of income do not necessarily imply high levels of corruption. "*Countries like Botswana, Chile, Costa Rica, and Slovenia, which have curtailed corruption to levels comparable with those of many wealthy industrialized countries, challenge the popular notion that a country needs to become rich in order to address corruption*" (World Bank,

Figure 1.1.   Patterns of corruption around the world, based in Transparency International Corruption Perception Index (2003)

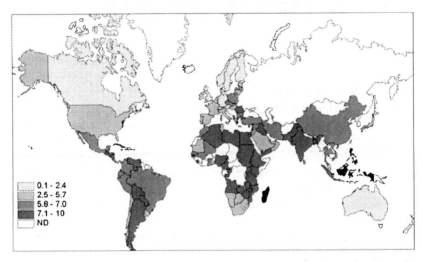

Note: Corruption data from Transparency International (2003). The Corruption Perception Index is recoded as: 0 = highly clean, 10 = highly corrupt, N.D. = no data available.

2003). The new rhetoric is that the quality of governance of a nation is the factor that plays the main role in its ability to deter corruption. Governance is likely to be weak while countries are reforming their market structures or engaged in deep structural reforms. This observation may support the alternative contention that there is a link between fiscal reform and corruption; however, there is no evidence for this argument. Furthermore, there are reasons to believe that the origins of corruption are not the reforms themselves, but rather that corruption may result from poor policy implementation. While the geography of corruption may be influenced by determinants such as the institutional, economic, and fiscal structure of a country, other characteristics such as cultural and social customs may also be prevalent.

1.4. Stakeholders in the fight against corruption

Many institutions and actors have taken proactive roles in the fight against corruption. Domestically, advocacy for greater transparency and surveillance are increasingly undertaken by civil society organizations, media, and several types of anticorruption agencies; many of these are further discussed in consequent chapters of this study. Externally, anticorruption efforts have been supported, on several different grounds, by International Finance Institutions, Multinational Organizations of various types, and non-governmental organizations (see Box 1.1).

Box 1.1.   Fighting corruption: the role of International Finance Institutions, bilateral and multilateral donor organizations, and NGOs

During the past decade the problem of corruption has received increasing attention by international finance institutions, multilateral donors, and NGOs. Often the problem of corruption is addressed by these institutions in the context of the broader issue of good governance.

In the case of the World Bank, the strategy for combating corruption has been based on four pillars: (a) strong policy of fraud prevention in own financed projects and programs, (b) support of countries that request help in fighting corruption, (c) preventing corruption inside the Bank's analysis and lending decisions, and (d) supporting international anticorruption efforts (World Bank, 2003). In addition, the World Bank includes anticorruption policies as a component in many of its economic reform lending operations, with more than 40 percent of the Bank's lending operations including public sector governance components (World Bank, 2004a). In addition, the World Bank has a special team devoted to do research and provide advice on "Governance and Anticorruption" issues. This team has a special section in the Bank's Website, which offers to interested parties a wide range of resources, including the Bank's publications, research papers, and reports on corruption issues, newsletters archives, and interactive datasets.

The International Monetary Fund (IMF) is also addressing corruption issues through its technical assistance and financial support activities. One of the IMF's steps to promote transparency and accountability in government is the development of standards and best practice codes such as: "*The Code of Good Practices on Fiscal Transparency*" and "*The Code of Good Practices on Transparency in Monetary and Financial Policies*". IMF's anticorruption initiatives also include the development of reports and assessments that reveal weaknesses of the financial sector and lack of observance of international standards. Some examples are the Report on the Observance of Standards and Codes, the Financial System Stability Assessments, and the Financial Sector Assessment Program. Others are mentioned in the IMF's website (www.imf.org) under the menu selection "IMF and Good Governance".

The United Nations (UN), the Organization for Economic Co-operation Development (OECD), and the Organization of American States (OAS) have taken important steps in relation to fighting corruption in international transactions (i.e., transnational bribery). One of the most important steps forward in this area has been the signing of the *United Nations Convention Against Corruption* by leaders of nearly 100 countries (December 2003). This document addresses issues such as bribery, embezzlement, misappropriation, money laundering, protection of whistle-blowers, and makes explicit the intention of cooperation among countries in combating corruption. This is the first document of its kind since it encompasses countries of all different regions in the world. Predecessors of this type of convention are the *Inter-American Convention Against Corruption,* an initiative of the OAS signed by American countries in 1996, and the *Convention on Combating Bribery of Foreign Public Officials in International Business Transactions,* an initiative of the OECD, which entered into force in February 1999. Moreover, all of these institutions fund a variety of anticorruption programs and offer a wide range of information and other type of anticorruption resources on their websites.

The European Union (EU) has also strengthened anticorruption efforts with the signing of the *Convention on the Fight Against Corruption Involving Officials of the European Communities* in 1997, and the technical cooperation and support for anticorruption issues provided by institutions such as the European Court of Auditors, the European Organization of Supreme Audit Institutions, and the European Ombudsman.

Bilateral donor agencies, such as USAID, DFID, DANIDA, and Regional Development Banks, such as the Inter-American Development Bank (IDB), and the Asian Development Bank (ADB), African Development Bank (AFDB) have also developed their own anticorruption strategies and funded different types of anticorruption programs around the world. For example, USAID has been a leading institution fighting corruption with programs as diverse as financial management improvement in Latin America, to conflict of interest legislation in Georgia, and judicial system reforms in Russia (USAID, 2000). Some important documents produced by USAID on the topic of corruption and anticorruption activities include, *A Handbook on Fighting Corruption* (USAID 1999) as well as a number of USAID Technical Publications in relevant governance areas. All these documents are available from the USAID website.[5]

---

[5] On USAID's website (www.usaid.gov), follow the menu selection: Our work, Democracy and Governance; Technical Areas, Anticorruption

NGOs increasingly are being recognized for their active participation in combating corruption. In particular, the international NGO Transparency International (TI) has been a leader with its efforts in the collection of data on corruption across countries, publishing them in widely available sources, such as the Corruption Transparency Index and the Bribe Payers Index (both of which are further discussed in Chapter 2 of this study). TI's "national chapters" in more than 85 countries represent a leading initiative for corruption awareness and a source of practical anticorruption strategies. TI also provides a wide variety of literature on its website including anticorruption guides, toolkits, and best practice source books. In particular, the Global Corruption Report (available for years 2001, 2003, and 2004) is a useful tool of discussion that gathers country and regional experiences and reports anticorruption progress around the world. Other NGOs that have made significant contributions in this area are the International Chamber of Commerce and Global Transparency.

Sources: Various technical reports referenced in the text, and documentation posted on institutional websites.

1.5. Concluding remarks

This book contributes to our knowledge on the issue of corruption in a fundamental way. Most of the current literature has focused only on some limited aspects of the interaction between fiscal policy, fiscal management, and corruption. This book provides a comprehensive overview of corruption with several features: (i) it identifies the conceptual and practical driving factors for corruption: motivations and opportunities; (ii) it covers the different forms of corruption: administrative and political corruption; (iii) it examines corruption in all important areas of fiscal policy and management: public expenditures, fiscal management and budgeting, taxes and other public revenues, and the quasi-fiscal sector; and (iv) it identifies successful policy responses, piecemeal and programmatic, for the different forms of fiscal corruption.

The responses reviewed are not limited to those in fiscal policy reform, but rather extend to other policy dimensions such as fiscal management (institutional and organizational structures of the fiscal apparatus), legislative reform, as well as the role of the parliament, the judiciary, and civil society.

CHAPTER 2

The Economics of Corruption

The previous chapter noted that corruption is a universal phenomenon, and that it exists – albeit to a greater or lesser extent – in every country in the world. What explains the general presence of corruption in developing, transition, and developed countries? This chapter explores the factors that influence the decision of public officials to engage in corrupt acts. We use economic concepts to model the corruption decision because *"whenever alternatives exist, life takes on an economic aspect"* (Mundell, 1968).

This chapter is organized as follows. Section 2.1 conceptually classifies the factors that determine the degree of corruption in two groups: motivating factors and windows of opportunity. Based on this classification, Section 2.2 develops a basic economic model of corruption that shows the theoretical impact of motivation and opportunities on the level of corruption. Section 2.3 considers how to determine the optimal amount of resources that should be allocated to corruption controls. Section 2.4 considers how policy experts and analysts have sought to measure corruption. Finally, Section 2.5 explores some theoretical and empirical issues related to the measurement of the costs of corruption (Section 2.5).

We need to recognize that, although corruption is a distinct issue within public finance and economics, corruption is closely linked to several other policy issues, including tax evasion and crime. The key distinction between tax evasion and corruption is that, whereas tax evasion is by definition perpetrated by a taxpayer, corruption by definition involves public officials. At the same time, the economics of corruption is closely related to the economics of crime; after all, corruption is a crime of self-enrichment by public officials, which is perpetrated either at the expense of the users of government services or at the expense of the public treasury. As with all crimes, those involved in have obvious reasons for secrecy. However, in the case of corruption, the perpetrator generally exercises some degree of state power over the victim. This issue makes corruption a particularly complex problem to study.

2.1. Motivation versus windows of opportunity

Some studies of corruption assume that the degree of corruption in a country is predetermined or exogenous. Although this assumption might be convenient for certain research purposes, this is a simplifying assumption regarding the nature of corruption and corrupt government officials. Most economic studies, however, do not regard the existence of corruption as exogenous; instead, corruption is considered an economic choice made by public officials. There are no economic reasons to believe that the nature of an individual predetermines that he or she is a "saint or a sinner".[6] Given the universal nature of corruption, the following analysis begins with the assumption that every individual may choose to engage in – or may choose not to engage in – corrupt acts under particular circumstances.

Something that is starting to be recognized in the corruption literature is the distinction between two categories of contributing factors to corruption: first, elements that affect the motivation or incentives of agents to engage in corruption, and second, elements that create windows of opportunity for corrupt activities (Klitgaard, 1989; World Bank, 1999).[7] We should acknowledge that this distinction may be at times somewhat unclear since incentives and opportunities are interdependent in the corruption decision and cannot fully be separated into completely independent dimensions. Nevertheless, this division provides a useful simplification of a complex system of interactions among these factors. A comprehensive and successful anticorruption policy requires addressing not only the motivations for corruption, but also the opportunities for corruption, which provides the institutional framework within which politicians and bureaucrats make their decisions.

> Although corruption may be perpetrated by individuals, it takes place primarily within an institutional context. However, people, not institutions engage in corruption. (Kpundeh, 1997, p. 4)

Following this rationale, the subsequent discussion draws a distinction between causes of corruption depending on whether they affect the motivation of individuals, or the opportunities for corruption. On one hand, we consider factors that affect the "willingness" of individuals to engage in corruption as part of the motivation issue. When several government officials are faced with the same opportunity for corruption, why are some government officials motivated to engage in the corrupt act, while the others are not? Part of the answer to this question lies in the potential "price" faced by individuals, as for example, the enforcement of penalties for corruption. Penalties are undoubtedly important deterrents (i.e., a negative motivation) for corruption: as penalties increase, the costs (if caught) for officials that are considering the possibility of engaging in

---

[6] Genetic predisposition for crime is outside the scope of this study. Those interested in this line of reasoning may find it useful to review Brennan *et al.* (1996).

[7] The terminology used in the literature varies across studies. For instance, policy responses associated with factors referred to in this study as motivations or incentives are classified as in other studies as *preventive* strategies, whereas policy responses to factors described here as windows of opportunity are referred to in other studies as *enforcement* mechanisms.

corruption also increase. Since penalties are by nature imposed after the detection of illegal behavior, penalties are clearly not capable of eliminating the opportunity for corrupt activities. Instead, penalties are designed to have an impact on individuals' incentives.

On the other hand, even though public servants may have an incentive to engage in corrupt acts, the opportunity may simply never arise. The factors that affect a government official's "ability" to engage in corrupt activities (for instance, whether there are institutional controls, such as personal oversight, that prevent government officials from engaging in bribes) are considered part of the "window of opportunity" for corruption.

This distinction may be further clarified with the help of basic economic theory. Even when the "prices" or incentives for corruption are right and there is a demand for corruption, individuals willing to partake in corruption can only succeed if the opportunity is offered. For instance, while factors that affect tax collectors' motivations affect the demand for corruption, corruption is only consummated where there is a supply of opportunities provided by taxpayers willing to offer bribes. The importance of making this distinction goes beyond theoretical elegance. Understanding the nature of the problems raised by corruption is particularly useful to clarify the types of policy response that are needed to address the specific problems. As we see in the sections below, the distinction between incentives and opportunities is of pivotal relevance when designing anti-corruption policy.

2.2. A conceptual model of corruption

A considerably large number of theoretical studies on political economy have focused on the underpinning determinants of corruption and its interaction with institutional and economic factors. Several recent studies, such as Jain (2001) and Aidt (2003), offer good discussions of the approaches used in the past. The following discussion builds on a study by Jain (2001), who sets out a useful categorization of the many types of corruption models found in the literature. Conceptual and theoretical studies of corruption can be roughly categorized as follows:

(i) *The agency model of corruption.* Agency models have been widely used in political science and economics of crime. The discussion in agency-type models centers on the factors affecting the agents' decision to partake in corruption. A distinction can be made among these models regarding on how they define the 'agent'. One group of models follows Becker (1968) and Becker and Stigler (1974) in defining lower level public official or bureaucrats as the agent, and higher level government officials as the principal. These models focus on the determinants of bureaucratic corruption by examining determinants of public officials' decision on principal–agent type of model, where public employees

weigh the return of corruption against public wages level, the penalty
and the probability of being detected (e.g., Becker and Stigler, 1974;
Banfield, 1975; Klitgaard, 1988, 1991; Andvig and Moene, 1990; Flatters and Macleod, 1995; Chand and Moene, 1997; Van Rijckeghem and
Weder, 2001; Acconcia *et al.*, 2003). This modeling works under the
implicit premise that the higher level of government acts as if it were
ruled by a benevolent principal aiming to motivate agents to be honest.
This model setup has been widely cited and served as a foundation for
empirical research and policy design to combat administrative, bureaucratic, or petty corruption.

A second branch of agency models internalizes higher levels of government into the analysis by assuming that legislators are, either agents
themselves or non-benevolent principals. High-level government officials –
represented by legislators or elected public officials – institute or manipulate existing policy and legislation in favor of particular interest groups –
from the private sector or units of lower bureaucracy competing for higher
budgets – in exchange of rents or payments.[8] In this type of model, legislators weigh the personal gains from being reelected against the gains
they could receive from corrupt transactions. Factors affecting this decision include campaign-financing mechanisms, information available to
voters, and so on. The contract enforcement is determined by the democratic and political institutions, including the ability of citizens to vote out
corrupt legislators, the degree of political contestability, electoral systems,
and other democratic institutions. Examples of these type of model include: Rose-Ackerman (1978), Andvig and Moene (1990), Grossman and
Helpman (1994), Flatters and Macleod (1995), Chand and Moene (1997),
Van Rijckeghem and Weder (2001), and Acconcia *et al.* (2003). The conceptual setup offered by this second group of models is better suited to
analyze state capture or political corruption.

(ii) *The resource allocation model.* Applications of these models build on
     game theory and oligopolistic competition analyses to explain com-
     petitive rent seeking among firms or bureaucracies competing for
     budgets under a variety of premises. Typically, the number of players,
     the relations of cooperation among them, the level of bribes, and the
     magnitude of the rent available for capture are relevant factors in the
     analysis (e.g., Linster, 1994; Paul and Wilhite, 1994; Kaufmann and
     Wei, 1999)

---

[8] Reinikka examines how 'leakages' on education spending in route increase with regions
income. An explanation may be that regions with higher income; usually those also with
higher lobbying power; are allocated higher budgets by the central government in exchange of
a share of the leakage of these funds.

(iii) *Corruption in internal markets.* These models examine the system of interrelations among different levels of bureaucracy within the government apparatus. These studies develop under the premise that corrupt officials "buy" lucrative positions subject to complex internal markets dynamics (e.g., Wade, 1985; Bliss and Di Tella, 1997). Where such markets are developed, all participants have strong interests in maintaining a organizational status quo and the government structure is characterized by systemic corruption.

(iv) *Level, persistence, and equilibrium of corruption.* These studies aim to explain the nature and dynamics ruling the equilibrium level of corruption within a society. Results suggest the existence of multiple equilibria, depending on the number of corrupt officials and the characteristics of the political systems in place (e.g., Bardhan, 1997; Rose-Ackerman, 1999; Martinez-Vazquez *et al.*, 2006).

(v) *Structure of government institutions, decentralization, and corruption.* A broad number of studies focus on the effects that government structure and political decentralization have on corruption levels and corruption distribution (i.e., centralized vs. decentralized corruption). The factors considered in this type of analysis include the degree of central government's control of lower level agencies on a hierarchical government, the degree of monopoly power over corruption transactions, the number of regions, the number of power groups, and the degree of mobility of entrepreneurs (Shleifer and Vishny, 1993; Ahlin, 2001; Waller *et al.*, 2002). There is a fine line dividing theoretical models that focus on the effects of intergovernmental relations on corruption and those that analyze the decentralization of corruption within a multitier hierarchy from an "industrial organization of corruption" type of framework (Reja and Tavitie, 2000). In the latter group a distinction is made between "top–down corruption" – where corrupt high levels buy lower levels by sharing a portion of gains – and "bottom-up corruption" – where low level officials share their own collected bribes with superior levels to avoid detection or punishment. In principle a highly centralized government may have a well-decentralized structure of corruption. Tirole (1986), for example, has suggested analyzing the topic by means of a three-tier principal–supervisor–agent model (Guriev, 1999). This extension of a conventional principal–agent model enables making some inferences regarding the type of corrupt relations that could evolve under multiple levels of government. Results form three-tier models of the type principal–supervisor–agent are varied and depending on the parameters of the model, the complexity increases even more when four-tier hierarchies are modeled (Bac and Bag 1999; Carrillo 2000).

Drawing on results from conventional industrial organization theory, Shleifer and Vishny (1993) conclude that decentralization is likely to increase corruption. In their model, government bureaucracies and agencies act as monopolists selling complementary government-produced goods, which are legally required for private sector activity. According to this model, bureaucracies act like a join monopoly under centralized corruption, whereas under decentralized corruption bureaucracies behave as independent monopolies. When bureaucracies act as independent monopolies, they ignore the effects of higher prices on the overall demand for a good and hence drive up the cumulative bribe burden.

Waller *et al.* (2002) define decentralized corruption as a system in which higher level officials collect a fixed amount of bribe income from each of the bureaucrats that take bribes, without mandating the bribe size that the bureaucrats charge. In a centralized system, on the contrary, bribe size is determined by the higher level of government, which collects bribes from bureaucrats and redistributes them after keeping a share. Waller *et al.* posit that decentralized corruption leads to lower levels of total corruption in the economy (lower spread), higher levels of bribe per entrepreneur (higher depth), and a smaller formal sector vis-a-vis a centralized corruption equilibrium. Yet, these results vary widely for specific 'regimes' in the model – when given parameters satisfy key conditions – for instance, for high-enough wages and monitoring systems centralized corruption may reduce total corruption and expand the formal economy.

Three recent studies have shed additional light on the relation between decentralization and corruption. While previously discussed studies centered on the organizational structure of corruption, Ahlin (2001) takes a different approach by concentrating on the alternative effects of different types of decentralization. In his model, a country is divided in regions containing a given number of independent power groups. Bureaucratic decentralization affects the political organization in a region by increasing the number of power groups or bureaucracies, while the number of jurisdictions captures the degree of regional decentralization (i.e., a unique region and bureaucracy would reflect the maximum degree of centralization). Ahlin's results suggest that corruption is determined by mobility of economic agents across regions. Under the assumption of no interregional mobility, corruption increases with the degree of bureaucratic decentralization and is independent on the degree of regional decentralization, whereas in the case of perfect interregional mobility corruption decreases with regional decentralization and is independent of bureaucratic decentralization. A key intuition of the model is that bureaucracies fail to internalize the costs that increasing their bribe-charges imposes to other bureaucracies. This argument had also been put forward by Shleifer and Vinshy (1993).

Arikan (2004) adopts a tax-competition framework to analyze decentralization and corruption. In Arikan's model, corruption is measured as the proportion of tax revenue appropriated by bureaucrats, whereas decentralization is captured by the number jurisdictions competing for a mobile tax base. Local governments decide on the levels of tax rates and corrupt earnings in order to maximize a weighted sum of corrupt earnings and citizen's utility. Arikan's results suggest that higher decentralization leads to lower levels of corruption.

Bardhan and Mookherjee (2000) focus on the determinants of capture of the democratic process and conclude that the extent of relative capture is ambiguous and context specific. They find that the extent of capture at the local level depends on the degree of voter awareness, interest group cohesiveness, electoral uncertainty, electoral competition, and the heterogeneity of interdistrict income inequality.

In all, conventional conceptual models reveal that the extent of relative capture is dependent on a wide range of conditions and so, conclusions are undoubtedly context specific. Given the complex nature of the phenomenon of corruption and its relationship with decentralization is unlikely that this relationship could be explained by a "one size fits all"-type of analysis tool.

(vi) *New Public Management and New Institutional Economics.* The policy debate on New Public Management (NPM) is predominantly focused on the analysis of actor-centered reform and accountability for results. It is commonly argued that NPM leads to a more decentralized structure of governance by promoting reforms toward devolution of service delivery, contracting out, purchaser–provider split, and greater competition. Thus, as a conceptual basis, decentralization overlaps with NPM in their emphasis to foster greater accountability to citizens. Yet, under the conventional rhetoric of decentralization, accountability is enhanced by voice and exit mechanisms and the local governments' ability to tailor decision-making to local needs, while it places less emphasis than NPM on the role of the private sector and mechanisms of accountability for results. On a recent study, Shah and Mathew (2003) suggests that an approach of citizen-centered local budgeting, which per se implies a given extent of local decision-making authority, may improve local governance by enhancing accountability and responsiveness at the local level.

There are two main arguments suggesting that NPM could lead to corruption-enhancing effects as opposed to greater accountability. First, it has been argued that greater competition on the tendering for service delivery, automatization, and separation of purchaser from providers has led to increases in rent-seeking behavior and possibilities for corruption (Batley, 1999; Von Maravic, 2003). A second argument suggests that opportunities for corruption are greater under decentralized management due to weaker supervision from higher levels and the inadequacy of mechanisms to exert controls over decentralized agencies (Scharpf, 1997). The latter line of thought, however, focuses exclusively on the loss in horizontal accountability while it does not address the potential gains from enhanced vertical accountability.

The New Institutional Economics (NIE) is a conceptual framework that has encompassed part of this debate. The NIE approach advocates for the inclusion of institutionalism to the rational choice analysis of corruption (Von Maravic, 2003; Lambsdorff et al., 2005). The analysis of decentralization and corruption under the NIE perspective is complex due to the broad scope and implications of the NIE perspective. Hence, it is important to identify and clarify some of the arguments over which NIE is built upon. This discussion may be organized along the following themes:

Transaction costs. Norms and institutions determine the way in which individuals interact socially and economically. In absence of such arrangements these interactions would imply, undoubtedly, higher transactions costs. Hence, institutional arrangements are designed formally, or evolve informally in order to minimize those transaction costs. Moreover, 'conditional situations' characterizing corrupt transactions, such as secrecy, raise the possibility of opportunism increasing corruption transactions costs above that of legal transactions (Pechlivanos, 2004; Graeff, 2005; Lambsdorff *et al.*, 2005). The NIE defines corruption as a contractual relationship, and as such, is affected by both a system of motivations and transaction costs. Following this line of thought, Lambsdorff *et al.* note that in fighting corruption from a NIE perspective policymakers should aim to "encourage betrayal among corrupt parties, to destabilize corrupt agreements, to disallow contracts to be legally enforced, to hinder the operation of corrupt middlemen and to find clearer ways of regulating conflicts of interest." An important issue is how does decentralization affect transaction costs and the preconditions involved on the terms of the corrupt agreement? One possible argument is that ex ante (building a 'relationship' drafting, negotiating, and safeguarding an agreement) and ex post transaction cost (costs aimed to secure commitment) decrease with decentralization as the higher levels of the bureaucracy chain come closer to citizens, and the number of layers involved in the negotiation is reduced. By reducing the transaction costs associated with corrupt transactions, decentralization would lead to higher levels of corruption. This argument is consistent with one put forward by Tanzi (1995), who posits that the increase in personal contacts associated with decentralization increases corruption levels.

The holistic view of the interrelationship among institutions. The NIE approach stresses the importance of examining institutions while studying corruption. As noted by Brock (2002, p. 1) "when institutions work well, they can be largely ignored for economic analysis and standard neoclassical arguments remain valid. However, when institutions work

**Table 2.1.   Transparency International's Corruption Perception Index:
perceived corruption in selected countries (2003)**

Top ten most corrupt countries		Top ten least corrupt countries	
1. Bangladesh	8.7	1. Finland	0.3
2. Nigeria	8.6	2. Iceland	0.4
3. Haiti	8.5	3. Denmark	0.5
4. Myanmar	8.4	4. New Zealand	0.5
5. Paraguay	8.4	5. Singapore	0.6
6. Angola	8.2	6. Sweden	0.7
7. Azerbaijan	8.2	7. Netherlands	1.1
8. Cameroon	8.2	8. Australia	1.2
9. Georgia	8.2	9. Norway	1.2
10. Tajikistan	8.2	10. Switzerland	1.2

Source: Transparency International (2003), corruption data from Transparency International.
Corruption Perception Index is recoded as: 0 = highly clean, 10 = highly corrupt.

poorly, they must be considered explicitly." Moreover NIE places particular emphasis on considering the corruption phenomenon from a
holistic perspective. This line of thought is also supported by this study.
In this context, decentralization is viewed as a component of an overall
system, which may only serve to effectively reduce corruption once a fair
level of overall governance is reached (see Table 2.1).

Path dependency and dynamics aspects of corruption. The NIE perspective has also supported the argument that once a corrupt transaction
is undertaken, future corrupt activities become increasingly more
likely. That is, corrupt activities reinforce themselves until becoming
established institutions as they are, allegedly, subject to 'increasing
returns or a positive feedback' (Della Porta and Vannucci, 2005). The
NIE emphasizes the role of established institutions – formal and informal rules – as well as the role of norms of behavior and cultural factors
in defining a path of action that once is initially developed is hard to
change.

2.2.1.   Principal–agent model of corruption

Before we discuss the elements and determinants of corruption in terms of
real-world examples, we think it is helpful to develop a simple, conceptual
model of corruption. Our motivation here is not to develop or extend the
literature so to arrive at new theoretical conclusions, but rather to introduce a common basic framework of analysis for the entire volume.[9] The

[9] The model developed here relies on a basic framework that combines part of models from
Becker and Stigler (1974), Chand and Moene (1997), and Van Rijckeghem and Weder (2001).

goal of the model is to sufficiently simplify reality in order to provide a useful framework to analyze the interaction between possible contributing factors and observed levels of corruption.[10]

The material presented herein simplifies reality with the objective of shedding some light on the interactions among a number of factors and observed levels of corruption. In this type of economic model, the "agent" (e.g., any public employee, such as a tax collector) is hired by a "principal" (e.g., a chief officer, policymaker, high-level bureaucrat, or ultimately the government) to interact with the government's "clients" (e.g., the taxpayers). In the model the principal is assumed to be non-corruptible and thus is also known as a "benevolent principal".

Modeling the motivation for corruption. A basic assumption of the model is that government officials seek to maximize their income (or more accurately, the expected value of their income) when deciding whether or not – and to what extent – to engage in corruption. The analysis developed in this section establishes a general or "baseline" model of corruption, which may be modified as needed in order to be applied to specific cases of corruption.[11] This basic framework yields some basic relationships that, although intuitive, do not necessarily represent the only possible (or even the best) way of modeling the corruption decision.[12]

The subject of study of the conceptual model is a government official who gets to determine whether to engage in corruption, and if so, the number of corrupt acts, C. In making his or her decision of whether or not to engage in corrupt acts, we assume that he or she will weigh his or her official income (guaranteed when $C = 0$) with the expected value of his or her income if he or she engages in corrupt acts (i.e., when $C > 0$). When $C > 0$, the expected value of income weighs the benefits received if corruption is not detected with the expected costs and benefits if caught). Of course, in order to assess the expected benefits and costs, the public official will take into account the expected probability of either event (not getting caught or getting caught) occurring. As such, P can be defined as the probability of being detected in one corruption act, then the official's total probability of detection is equal to this probability times the number of

---

[10] For a review of other models of corruption see Jain (1998, 2001).

[11] Further examples of theoretical analysis of this topic are Andvig and Moene (1990), Flatters and Macleod (1995), Acconcia *et al.* (2003), Chand and Moene (1997), Van Rijckeghem and Weder (2001).

[12] For illustrative purposes, the model developed here seeks to maximize the expected income of the public official. However, economics students realize that individuals are typically presumed to maximize their utility rather than income. A more complete model would consider maximizing the expected "utility" (satisfaction or happiness) in modeling the corruption decision, along the lines, for example, with Alm (1998). The income maximization model is chosen in order to preserve the simplicity of the discussion for the non-economist reader.

corrupt acts in which the individual has participated (PC).[13] The expected income (I) for the government official *in case he or she engages in corruption and does not get caught* may be defined as:

$$E(I|\text{not caught}) = (1 - P \cdot C)(C \cdot B + W_g)$$

where W_g represents the public wages received by the government official and B is the amount of personal gain (for instance, the size of the bribe) received by the government official per corruption act. CB is therefore the total amount of additional resources potentially received from corrupt acts. The source of the personal gain (i.e., whether the gain is from outright theft of public funds, a bribe from evading taxpayers, fraud in the tender process, or extortion of public service user) is inconsequential to the basic model.

Of course, if the public official gets caught perpetrating corrupt acts, he or she will face the associated costs of corruption, which may include job dismissal and other penalties, such as jail time or fines. In addition to the direct monetary costs associated with being detected, if dismissed or jailed, the public official must consider the loss of his or her public wage as a cost. However, if dismissed (but not jailed) he or she may be employed in the future by the private sector, thereby only considering the differential between the public (W_g) and private wages (W_p) as a cost $(W_g - W_p)$. Thus, the greater the private sector wages relative to public wages, the lower the relative cost of dismissal from the public sector.[14] Let us further assume that F represents the monetary total amount of fines and penalties (including potential jail time).[15] The overall expected income for a corrupt official *in case he or she engages in corruption and gets caught* can be written as:

$$E(I|\text{caught}) = (P \cdot C)(W_p - F)$$

---

[13] We make the simplifying assumption that P is constant. In fact, it may be the case that the marginal probability of getting caught in corrupt acts increases with the number of corrupt acts that the official engages in.

[14] Notice that if private wages are higher than public ones the cost of being dismissed by the public sector becomes negative, which actually signifies a gain.

[15] If jail terms are applied as penalties for corruption then the private wage should be considered negative as it measures the opportunity cost of time spent in prison plus the cost of lost freedom per year. An optional specification could include an "anguish cost" or the psychological costs associated with the possibility of being caught or those that result from a "guilty conscience" from engaging in activities the individual considers immoral or dishonest. This cost could increase in proportion to the number of corruption acts (C). Many other permutations could be modeled, such as the relation between the anguish cost and the degree of risk aversion of the individual, or whether the total amount of anguish costs should be decreasing in the number of corrupt acts. We avoid these issues in order to maintain the tractability of the argument.

The official's overall expected income equals the sum of the expectations under both scenarios:

$$E(I) = (1 - P \cdot C)(C \cdot B + W_g) + (P \cdot C)(W_p - F)$$

Public officials choose their optimal value of corruption (C^*), that is the value of corruption that maximize their expected income. Note that if the official would decide not to engage in corruption ($C^* = 0$), the expected income is equal the public sector wage (W_g). This observation is useful to emphasize that a public official would only consider engaging in corruption ($C^* > 0$), if the expected income at that level of corruption is higher than his/her current wage in the public sector $E(I|C^*) > W_g$.[16] An equation of this nature was used by Becker and Stigler (1974) to note that corruption could be controlled if the level of public wages is high enough. It is also useful to note that if probability of being detected in a corruption act is zero ($P = 0$), say due to a coalition between the monitoring agent and the official being monitored, expected income equals $E(I) = CB + W_g$. It is straightforward to note, from this last equation, that any positive value of corruption would increase expected income regardless of the level of public wages. This realization is important in order to highlight the interdependence between wage levels and detection probabilities in controlling corruption levels.

A rational individual optimizes his decision to get involved in corrupt acts, or not, and if so, by how much, by equating the marginal benefit from further corruption to the marginal cost of that additional corruption.[17] Given the simplicity of the equation and the signs of each variable, many theoretical conclusions may be derived from this model. The level of corruption that a public officer is motivated to engage in will be higher when:

- Public sector wages are lower (i.e., an absolute wage effect).
- The difference between private and public wages is greater (i.e., a relative wage effect).
- The level of personal gain is higher (e.g., the higher the bribe offered).

---

[16] As noted before, this simple model is framed in terms of monetary values, as opposed to utility. If utility is introduced to this analysis, the decision of whether to engage in corruption or not would also depend on the degree of risk aversion of the individual. That is, for any given combination of salary and expected income from corruption, individuals that are more averse to risk will be less likely to engage in corruption than individuals who are risk lovers. Ignoring this issue allows us also to avoid further considerations regarding the functional form of the utility function (e.g., constant risk aversion, relative risk aversion, or hybrids). However, the main conclusions of the expected income model are consistent with the expected utility models.

[17] Mathematically, in order to reveal the marginal effects that each of these variables has on the optimal amount of corruption, we know that the first-order necessary condition for an optimal solution is that the first derivative of the equation with respect to C should be equal to zero at the optimum.

- The probability of detection (P) is lower.
- The amount or monetary value of the penalty is lower.

The validity of these conclusions or hypotheses about the motivations of corruption must obviously be tested by empirical analysis. Most of these empirical issues are discussed in Chapter 4.

Modeling the opportunities for corruption. The analysis up to this point has strictly modeled the motivation for corruption, and simply assumed the possibility or availability of opportunities for personal gain (equal to B) for the potentially corrupt public official. At this point, we wish to expand the basic model to include not only the motivation to engage in corruption, but also the opportunity for corruption. Klitgaard (1995) presents a useful and simple representation of the factors affecting opportunities for corruption. This perspective focuses on corrupt systems rather than on individuals, but suggests broadly that three key factors affect the opportunity for corruption, notably the financial discretion or control yielded to government officials (D), the monopoly power of public officials (M), and the accountability to which public officials are subjected (A).

The level of discretion could be measured by the amount of financial trust or control that the public official is accorded. A cynical view of the amount of discretion D is that it constitutes the base amount for potential corruption. For a tax collector, the amount of discretion is the amount of tax collections that he or she could "let slip through the fingers" when properly motivated. Likewise, for a headmaster, the level of discretion might be equal to the value of school books or other resources that he or she has been provided for distribution to students, which may be embezzled or for which the headmaster may require illicit payments. Each of the other factors (monopoly and accountability) can be represented as a scalar between zero and unity; complete monopoly power by the public official would be represented by one, while the absence of monopoly power would be represented by zero. Inversely, the presence of accountability mechanisms could be represented by zero, whereas the absence of accountability mechanisms could be reflected by $A = 1$. Based on this perspective, we can specify the opportunity for personal gain (B) as a function of D, M, and A, so that

$$B = (M \cdot A)D$$

The greater the level of financial discretion a public official is given, the greater his or her window of opportunity to extract personal gain through theft, bribes, or other corrupt acts. The size of the window is institutionally determined by the degree of monopoly control over the resources as well as the accountability and oversight to which the public official is subjected.

How do individual decisions to engage in corruption relate to the opportunities of corruption? Since we established a positive relationship between the amount of potential personal gain (B) and the degree of corruption, given the above formulation of potential personal gain (the window of opportunity), it is clear that anticorruption policy should focus on decreasing the amount of monopoly power of public officials, while increasing their accountability. The government may also wish to reduce the financial discretion of public officials. Chapter 4 of this study discusses factors that could be added to this equation of opportunities. In fact, in that chapter we unbundle opportunities for corruption into different forms: by whether the opportunity manifests itself on the revenue or expenditure side of the budget, and by the agent for corruption (i.e., political corruption or bureaucratic corruption).

Conceptually, it is possible to portray two policy scenarios to fight corruption. In the first scenario, the corruption containment strategy is based on a strong control of opportunities, while maintaining a weak structure of incentives. This type of anticorruption approach is unlikely to be successful due to the pressure of a large number of individuals motivated to break the system of control. The second possible anticorruption strategy may be based on a strong control of motivation (incentives) while downplaying control over opportunities. Once again, such anticorruption policies are likely to fail since those agents who would not have incentives otherwise feel tempted by the ease with which corrupt gains are made. While aggressive control of either one of these dimensions may reduce corruption in the short run, a sustainable and comprehensive strategy against corruption should address both incentives and opportunities for corruption.

2.3. The economics of corruption control

One fundamental question in anticorruption policy design is *how much should be spent to fight corruption?* Although from a moral standard the optimal corruption may be equal to zero, from an economic and budgetary point of view the costs of prevention or reducing corruption to zero may be too high (if not infinite). This is evidenced by the fact that some corruption occurs even in the most developed, "uncorrupt" countries. The amount of corruption that is optimal for a society may be determined by comparing the costs of preventing corruption with the costs that corruption imposes on society.

Many instruments and mechanisms may be devised to affect incentives and opportunities for corruption (as discussed in Chapter 4) and most of these reforms are costly. Increasing accountability usually requires, among other things, the implementation of monitoring systems, which imposes a cost to the government. Similarly, reducing the monopoly power and individual discretion of public employees in government decisions requires tightening legislative and regulatory frameworks and introduction of non-discretionary rules, which can result in a more bureaucratic approach to

Figure 2.1.   Socially optimum amount of corruption

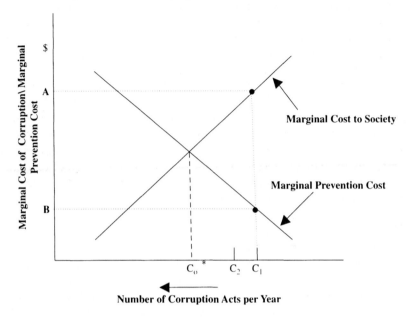

government administration. The total cost of the measures implemented to counteract corruption can be labeled as *corruption prevention costs.*

The general trade-off between the marginal cost of corruption to society and the marginal prevention cost is illustrated in Figure 2.1. If corruption is measured by the numbers of corrupt acts per year, the cost of reducing corruption at the margin should be expected to be lower at an initial high level than at an initial low level of corruption. That is, the cost per unit of reducing the number of corrupt acts per year from, say, 200–170 cases is lower than the cost of achieving a reduction from 50 to 20 corrupt acts per year, although in both situations acts of corruption are reduced by 30 cases. The rationale for this is that the most visible types of corruption are less costly to detect and are also the first to be detected by anticorruption policy. The remaining cases are more complex and requiring more sophisticated mechanisms of detection, greater monitoring capacity or even structural reforms and, thus, the use of more resources. Consequently, the marginal prevention cost (the cost of prevention of one additional unit) is negatively sloped (Figure 2.1).

On the contrary, one could posit that the greater the accumulated level of corruption, the greater the marginal cost to society of one additional unit of corruption. While a low level of corruption will have a limited impact on the economy (for instance, economic growth), the inefficiencies and costs to society associated with increasing levels of corruption (possibly beyond a certain threshold) tend to compound each other and cascade the economic costs of corruption.[18] Thus, as shown in Figure 2.1, the marginal cost to society has a positive slope. Unlike the costs of prevention, which can be gathered from government spending records, the economic costs of corruption to society are much harder to measure and may never be exactly known. Section 2.5 presents a more detailed discussion on estimating the costs of corruption.

Figure 2.1 suggests that resources should be spent on corruption prevention as long as the cost imposed on society by an additional unit of corruption is greater than the cost of prevention of that corrupt act. Consider, for instance, a reduction from level of corruption C_1 to level C_2 in Figure 2.1. The marginal cost to society of this unit of corruption is represented by the monetary value A, while the cost of prevention of that unit is represented by the monetary value of B. Since the value of A is higher than B it would be economically rational to reduce corruption from level C_1 to C_2 and all the way to level C_0. The amount of corruption optimal for society is at C_0 at which the costs of preventing the last unit of corruption equal the costs that this unit of corruption imposes on society.

Why does this type of analysis matter? Analyzing the factors that affect incentives and opportunities for corruption shows us where to target anticorruption policy and how to best spend resources on corruption control. Quantifying corruption levels and the costs that corruption imposes on society is crucial in order to determine which corruption target levels are acceptable and how much to spend on corruption prevention. In practice, however, as discussed in the remainder of this chapter, both the level of corruption and the economic costs of corruption are particularly difficult to measure.

2.4. Quantifying corruption

In Chapter 1 of this study we stated the definition of corruption to be used in the rest of the study as "the abuse of public office for private gain". In Chapters 3 and 4 of this study we will describe and provide examples of the many forms fiscal corruption can take in the public sector, both in relation to tax administration as well as government spending policies. Here we discuss issues related to the measurement of corruption.[19]

Why measure corruption? Despite many of the difficulties of measuring corruption, governments need to know the true extent of corruption in

---

[18] In a sense there is a parallel between the cost of corruption and the excess burden costs related to distortions introduced by taxes. For the latter, we know that excess burden losses grow exponentially with the tax rate (Harberger, 1962). See Section 2.5 for a more detailed discussion of the economic costs of corruption.

[19] See also Jain (1998) for a collection of studies reviewing the measurement of corruption and its economic analysis.

their economies. Corruption measures (such as corruption perception surveys) often not only provide a benchmark measurement of corruption that can be used to assess the effectiveness of anticorruption policies and institutional reforms, but they can also identify key sources of corruption and thus the need for reform in these areas.

How to measure corruption? Measuring corruption is quite challenging, as noted in the evolving literature on this topic. The biggest challenge faced in the measurement of corruption is obviously the illicit nature of the activity. Neither the corrupt official, nor the accomplice (for instance, an evading taxpayer), nor the victim of corruption (e.g., an extorted user of government services) has an incentive to reveal the corruption, either for apparent self-serving reasons (such as detection of tax evasion) or for fear of retribution. We should recall that corruption is different from regular crimes because the perpetrator of corruption has a degree of state power.

There are several approaches to measuring the extent of corruption. A first approach, employed in some studies, simply relies on anonymous questionnaires or surveys to elicit self-disclosure of corruption. Of course, this approach is prone to significant underreporting of corrupt acts. A second approach surveys not the incidence of corruption directly, but rather the *perception* of corruption within the business community. A third approach analyzes data on corruption prosecutions within a period of time. A fourth approach seeks to measure corruption through its correlation with other hard indicators such as non-compliant economic behavior (e.g., the level of tax evasion or the size of the shadow economy in a country), or by the difference between budgeted capital spending and field assessments of public infrastructure value. Further details of survey-based and non-survey-based estimations are discussed in the following subsections.

An additional challenge in the measurement of corruption is not in the methodology employed to measure corruption but rather in the nature of the object of study itself: corruption. What should be measured ought to be answered before raising the question of how it should be measured. Given the definition of corruption used here, the answer to the first is that the degree of misuse of public power for private benefit does not imply any one unit of measurement. Should corruption be measured by the number of corrupt acts, the monetary value of bribes received, the amount of resources embezzled, the reduction of economic growth caused by corruption, or by the efficiency loss associated with the level of corruption? There is no unique answer for this question, probably because each and all of these dimensions are indeed relevant and efforts should be made to measure all of them (in their respective units).

Additionally, which specific type of corruption is any given measure capturing? It must be acknowledged that corruption is a multidimensional problem, manifesting itself in multiple and complex sets of relations between the state, its institutions, the private sector, and civil society. The fact that there are several types of corruption is perhaps one reason corruption received relatively little attention in the policy research literature before the 1980s: it is difficult to address in a systematic way a concept embracing so many forms and involving so many dimensions. Fortunately, the more recent availability of (more or less) systematic measurements of corruption has led to a more open discussion of these issues and much more is starting to be known about it.

Can all of the dimensions of corruption be collapsed into one unique measurement? The answer is yes, but this composite index in general will not be a particularly useful indicator for anticorruption policy design. As discussed below, some surveys have started to unbundle the concept of corruption by including questions that reflect specific forms of corruption.

2.4.1. *Non-survey-based measurements*

As noted earlier, the measures of corruption can be divided in survey-based and non-survey-based techniques. Among the main candidates of non-survey-based measurements for corruption we can mention (i) prosecution records, (ii) economic-based indicators, and (iii) estimations of the underground economy.

The first possible measure of corruption is based on the number of prosecutions of corrupt cases, or convictions. One source of this type of data is the criminal justice data collected by the United Nations Crime Prevention and Criminal Justice Division (see Fisman and Gatti, 2002b).

The number of prosecutions of corruption cases in court, or convictions may be particularly useful as a benchmark of corruption control within a given country. This index would not only measure the prevalence of corruption but would also reflect the effectiveness of monitoring mechanisms, and the probity of the judicial system (since because of corruption itself, true corruption cases sometimes end up not being prosecuted). However, using this indicator for analysis across countries will be biased due to differences in the criminal justice systems across countries and differences in legal definitions of corruption.

Yet, even if the number of corrupt acts could be precisely measured, is the number of acts what really matters? The answer to this question depends on whether the unit of measurement is the monetary value involved in corrupt transactions or the frequency of the violation. Probably there are reasons to believe that both of these matter. While the monetary amount involved in corruption reflects to some degree the cost to society, the frequency of the violation reflects how weak the anticorruption control and monitoring systems are. Rose-Ackerman (1999) argues that when corruption is entrenched in a county, the number of corrupt acts tends to decrease as they are substituted by fewer (but possibly larger) "deals" at the policy-making level.

An additional dimension that may be of interest besides the number of corrupt acts or the monetary value of the transactions involved is the degree of "corruptness" of the act. Del Castillo (2002) appropriately states that a country in which relatively harmless corruption is practiced widely and openly may receive a higher corruption perception score than a country in which fewer corrupt acts may have much more serious economic and social consequences. For instance, payment of a small "incentive" to expedite a housing construction permit through a long queue may be less harmful socially and economically than, say, repressing a report of chemical industrial contamination which could affect the health of a large population. However, measuring the harm corrupt acts do to society is very complicated. Besides, some may contend that the harm done is irrelevant from the policymaking standpoint. This issue is analogous to the treatment of crime; any given murder is usually not treated differently depending on the number of children left orphaned by the victim.

In contrast to measures of corruption based on a count of prosecution records, other measures of corruption proposed in the literature are based on "hard" economic variables. This approach assumes that the patterns of certain relations among observable economic variables may reflect the existence of unobservable corruption. For example, due to the close relationship between tax revenues, tax evasion, and corruption, some studies considered quantifying the degree of fiscal corruption across countries by comparing the ratio of potential tax yield to actual tax collections (Chand and Moene, 1997). This is in line with the methodology used by some theoretical studies to model corruption. Huang and Shan-Jin (2003), for example, study the effects of corruption in monetary policy. In their theoretical model, corruption is introduced as a fraction measuring the percent of government tax revenue that "leaks" to corruption. However, this kind of measurement can be biased by exogenous factors and can easily be misinterpreted. For instance, a low ratio of potential tax yield to actual tax collections may be a result of ineffective tax administration rather than a result of corruption.

Golden and Picci (2005) suggest an alternative measurement. These authors propose the use of the difference between a measure of the physical quantities of public infrastructure and a measure of the value of public capital.[20] Their rationale is to measure the difference between how much is reflected in the budget, as spent in public infrastructure, and the actual value embedded in the final product. This difference reflects all factors that are not capitalized in the value of the infrastructure in question. These are the administrative costs of managing the project as well as planning costs.

---

[20] As discussed in Chapter 4, this basic approach is also the foundation of Public Expenditure Tracking Surveys (PETS).

After controlling for differences in the construction cost among regions and inflation, the ratio of resources spent for administrative purposes should exhibit some degree of stability among regions and comparable projects. Golden and Picci (2005) create this measure for a total of 20 regions in Italy. However, the feasibility of a dataset needed to quantify this measure across countries is clearly in question.

The estimation of the underground (or shadow) economy provides an additional, alternative for measuring corruption. For instance, Schneider (2003) estimates an index of the shadow economy across 110 countries for 1990, 1995, and 2000. Although there is conceptually a clear link between fiscal corruption and the size of the underground economy, the validity of using underground economy estimates as a measure of fiscal corruption is questionable. The problem with this approach is that the informal economy (i.e., informal household economy, informal productive activities, and crime) encompasses activities that may not directly related to corruption (as defined in this study), since they do not entail the participation of public agents. If nothing else, measurements of the size of the underground economy could be used to compare and contrast with corruption estimates obtained from other sources. In general we should exercise caution if survey data reveals a low level of corruption in a country in which other sources suggest the existence of a large underground economy.

2.4.2. Measuring corruption using perception surveys

The number of sources of survey data on corruption has grown in recent years as more researchers and institutions have started to develop different indicators of corruption across countries. A distinction may be drawn between two types of measures. While most sources present results from surveys conducted by their own organizations, others have focused on creating aggregate indexes by pooling information from different surveys. In the next few paragraphs we discuss two aggregate indexes, which have played an important role and have received considerable attention in the economics literature.[21]

The Corruption Perception Index from Transparency International. TI's CPI is perhaps the most widely known and referenced measure of corruption available. The TI index is available for years 1995–2003. The index is constructed based on perception surveys of business people, academics, and risk analysts about the extent of corruption in a list of countries. This index is computed by averaging scores of a group of surveys in each

---

[21] For a review of "own collected survey sources" (not aggregated) measurements of corruption, see the subsection on "Data and Research" in Global Corruption Report (Transparency International 2001) and Kaufmann *et al.* (2003).

country and ranges between 10 (highly clean) and 0 (highly corrupt).[22] A detailed description of the survey sources used for the computation of the index is presented in TI CPI's framework document on a yearly basis, the latest one being Lambsdorff (2003).[23] Treisman (2000) and Gurgur and Shah (2000) also present summary information on the underlying surveys and number of respondents. Table 2.1 contains an overview of the most and least corrupt countries based on TI's most recent CPI.

Currently, the TI's CPI averages the scores from 13 surveys for countries on which all survey sources are available, while a minimum of three surveys is required for each country to be included in the ranking.[24] Some researchers have argued that this index suffers from a systematic bias since the estimation is less reliable for countries with the lowest number of surveys (Golden and Picci, 2005). Since the countries with lowest number of surveys are usually the less developed countries, the index tends to be less reliable precisely where corruption is more of a serious problem. On the other hand, the alternative aggregated index of corruption available, estimated by Kaufmann, includes countries for which there are fewer than three surveys available. It must be noted that these two indexes are not perfectly comparable because they use different methodologies to aggregate data. While Kaufmann's index is based on an unobserved component aggregation methodology, the TI perception index is based on a simple average of rescaled scores.

The TI CPI has been increasingly used for cross-country comparison studies.[25] Additionally, TI also estimates the Bribe Payers Index aimed to assess corruption in an international context. This survey is designed to evaluate the effects of the OECD Antibribery Convention. In the Bribe Payers Index, executives of leading exporting countries are asked to estimate "*how likely companies from the following countries are to pay or offer bribes to win or retain business in this country.*"

Kaufmann's Corruption Index. Kaufmann et al. (2003) have developed six governance indicators based on several available survey data sources. In addition, with these six indicators Kaufmann et al. (2003) compute a composite measurement of corruption, which they label "Control of

---

[22] Many of the empirical studies that have used this database have recoded the data to reflect the highest level 10 as highly corrupt. This is because otherwise the index would seem to be measuring levels of probity rather than corruption.

[23] The framework document includes information regarding the groups of respondents surveyed in each case, the subjects asked, the number of replies, the methodologies employed to standardize the data, and the precision of the estimates.

[24] The number of sources is actually presented as 17 by Transparency International (2003). This is because the data from sources that conducted surveys in multiple years are counted as different sources.

[25] The first study that used this index appears to have been Mauro (1995). Subsequently, the TI index has been used by many other empirical studies of corruption.

Table 2.2. Kaufmann's Corruption Control Index: perceived corruption in selected countries (2002)

Top ten most corrupt countries		Top ten least corrupt countries	
1. Equatorial Guinea	−1.89	1. Finland	2.39
2. Haiti	−1.70	2. Singapore	2.30
3. Iraq	−1.43	3. New Zealand	2.28
4. Congo, Dem. Rep. (Zaire)	−1.42	4. Denmark	2.26
5. Myanmar	−1.37	5. Sweden	2.25
6. Afghanistan	−1.35	6. Iceland	2.19
7. Nigeria	−1.35	7. Switzerland	2.17
8. Laos	−1.25	8. Netherlands	2.15
9. Paraguay	−1.22	9. Canada	2.03
10. Turkmenistan	−1.21	10. Luxembourg	2.00

Source: Kaufmann *et al.* (2003).

Corruption". Since the Corruption Control Index is normalized by its mean, the measure ranges roughly from −2.5 (least control over corruption) to +2.5 (greatest control over corruption). The index is available for 202 countries and for the years: 1996, 1998, 2000, and 2002.[26] Table 2.2 contains an overview of the most and least corrupt countries based on Kaufmann's most recent Corruption Control Index.

As mentioned, the Corruption Control Index is similar to the TI index in that it is based on weighting of different corruption indices or ratings. However, Kaufmann *et al.* (2003) apply an extension of the "unobserved component methodology" (UCM) to arrive at the corruption index, as opposed to the simple average of rescaled survey scores used for the TI index estimation.[27] The Kaufmann *et al.* (2003) study compares their Corruption Control Index to the TI index by employing their UCM methodology to the TI data. They find that TI's simple average reports smaller standard errors for countries with few survey sources, which leads this index to overstate its precision over those countries.[28] Another difference between the two measures of corruption is that TI uses information from different years as separate data sources while the Kaufmann index only includes data sources from one single year.

---

[26] Their study and the full dataset are available on the World Bank website (www.worldbank.org).

[27] In particular, in the UCM, observed data are expressed as a linear combination of country-specific unobserved governance.

[28] This indicates that if those countries are included in the index, the unobserved components methodology would produce better estimates of precision. However, for the number of sources and countries used by the TI index, the benefits in efficiency gain of using a UCM, as opposed to a simple average, are small.

Table 2.3. Sources of Transparency International Corruption Perception Index (2003) and Kaufmann et al. (2003) control of corruption

Source and name of survey	Transparency International Corruption Perception Index (2003)	Kaufmann *et al.* (2002)
Columbia University/State Capacity Project	1	5
Global Insights DRI McGraw-Hill/Country Risk Review	X	1
Economist Intelligent Unit/Country Risk Service	1	1
Political Risk Services/International Country Risk Guide	X	1
Business Environment Risk Intelligence/ Qualitative Risk Measure in Foreign Lending	X	1
World Markets Research Center/World Markets Online	1	1
Afrobarometer/Afrobarometer Survey	X	1
World Bank/Business Enterprise Environment Survey	1	5
World Bank/Country Policy and Institutional Assessments	1	1
World Bank/World Business Environment Survey	2	X
Business Environment Risk Intelligence/ Business Risk Service		1
Freedom House/Nations in Transition	1	1
World Economic Forum (2003)/Global Competitiveness Report	5	11
Latinobarometro/Latinobarometro Survey	X	1
Institute for Management and Development/ World Competitiveness Yearbook	2	1
Information International/Survey of Middle Eastern Business People	2	X
Political and Economic Risk Consultancy/ Asian Intelligence Issue	1	X
PricewaterhouseCoopers/Opacity Index	1	X
A multilateral development bank/Survey	1	X
Gallup International/Corruption Survey	1	X

Note: Number of questions used from each source is cited in parenthesis. An X means that the source is not used in the construction of that index.
Source: Transparency International (2003) and Kaufmann *et al.* (2003).

Table 2.3 lists both the sources used to compute TI CPI for year 2003 and the sources used by Kaufmann *et al.* (2003) for the estimation of the "control of corruption index" for year 2002.

Shortcomings of perception-based surveys. A first shortcoming of both aggregate indexes of corruption (TI and Kaufmann) is that they measure corruption as a one-dimensional concept despite the fact that many of the survey questions reflect the prevalence of different varieties of corruption. Although useful for some general purposes, the composite index measures are not particularly useful for the design of anticorruption strategies. This is because general knowledge that a country is corrupt does not help to identify specific targets for reform, such as political corruption or administrative corruption. However, some of the new corruption surveys available for research make it possible to unbundle different dimensions of corruption, offering greater insight for analysis, and for the design of reform strategies. The first generation of surveys available focused largely on indicators of administrative corruption, with questions such as: "How common is it for firms to have to pay irregular additional payments to get things done?" or "What is the frequency of bribing?". Newer surveys include questions useful to measure the extent of political corruption. For instance, the *World Business Environment Survey* (WBES) conducted by the World Bank contains the following question: "How often do firms make payments to influence the content of new legislation?" Other sources such as the *State Capacity Project* by Columbia University also include questions such as: "To what extent do the countries' primary political decision makers engage in patterns of nepotism, cronyism, and patronage?"

The existence of information particular to specific types of corruption allows the study of different patterns of corruption across countries and regions. For example, studies such as Hellman *et al.* (2000) and World Bank (2000a) have used a subcomponent of the WBES for an in depth study of corruption in 20 transitional countries.[29] Such research is particularly useful to target anticorruption policies toward the areas of corruption that cause the most serious problems.

In addition to their unidimensional nature, survey-based corruption measures are often criticized on the grounds of their inability to capture actual levels of corruption. Instead, survey measures reflect individuals' perceptions of the frequency of corrupt acts. Moreover, these measures typically do not provide any information on the monetary values involved in these activities. On the other hand, information quantifying the amounts of corruption is hardly available elsewhere.

Can individuals' perceptions and opinions of how corrupt a country is to be used for scientific analysis? The answer to this question depends on how this measurement is affected by different types of bias. One of the first concerns regarding the validity of corruption survey data is that individuals may have a tendency to overestimate or underestimate corruption,

---

[29] This subcomponent is the *Business Environment and Enterprise Performance Survey* (BEEPS), conducted by World Bank, the European Bank for Reconstruction and Development (EBRD), the Inter-American Development Bank, and the Harvard Institute of International Development. The first round covers 20 transitional countries during the period 1999–2000, while the second round, conducted in 2002, covers 27 countries.

based on their attitudes, interests, experiences, and background. This type of bias is known as perception bias. That is, certain individuals (or groups) have a tendency to complain while others are inclined to take a more favorable view of the same set of circumstances. Statistically, perception bias will not affect the overall results as long as the direction of the perception bias is uncorrelated with the respondents in the group. While it is difficult to believe that institutions applying the survey would intentionally choose one or the other group of respondents, respondents' perceptions may be affected by the surrounding environment and the type of activities that respondents are involved with.[30]

Another concern often raised in the literature is *whose* perceptions of corruption survey does information actually reflect (e.g., see World Bank, 2000a)? Some concern is raised because most survey respondents are not national civil society or local businessmen, but rather foreign experts or international business executives. However, this type of problem seems to have mostly affected the first generation of corruption perception measures; for example, this is the case of TI's CPI. Although foreign respondents still represent the highest percentage of respondents used, more current indexes are starting to remedy this problem by gathering survey data from a more diversified base of respondents.

An additional possible source of bias is related to the ideological tendencies of institutions compiling the data. For instance, institutions that have rightist or leftist political views may consciously or unconsciously favor governments or regimes that have similar ideologies. However, the high correlation among the estimated indexes from different sources would imply that these ideology biases, if they exist, are common to all these data collecting institutions (Kaufmann *et al.*, 1999).[31] This same study applies

---

[30] Individuals are defined by Rosten (1968) as those that tend to *kvetch* (complain) and those that tend to *kvell* (beam with pride or pleasure), respectively (Hellman *et al.*, 2000). In empirical analysis, perception biases can be controlled by what Kaufmann *et al.* (1999) define as 'kvetch control independent variables' – perceptions of government performance or public goods that are commonly faced by all firms within a country, such as the extent of government efficiency or the quality of public works. Recently, Olken (2006) used data from villages in Indonesia to examine the accuracy of beliefs about corruption against a more objective measure of "missing expenditures" in particular projects. He finds that villages' beliefs contain information about corruption but also that there were important systematic biases in corruption beliefs.

[31] Besides the high level of correlation among surveys from different types of respondents (i.e., local businessmen, foreign businessmen, regular citizens, expatriates), the results obtained with different methodologies (Treisman, 2000; Gurgur and Shah, 2000; Kaufmann *et al.*, 2003) are also quite similar. Thus as Treisman (2000) also points out, if these survey measures are indeed biased, these perception biases have to be widely shared across different groups of respondents. Nevertheless, Batra *et al.* (2003) raise concerns regarding alternative uses of survey perception data due to perception biases revealed by the use of kvetch controls variables.

regression analysis to test for the presence of ideological bias. The empirical result obtained provides evidence for the hypothesis of ideological bias for only one of the survey sources. In addition, the magnitude of the ideological bias for this source was rather small.

Additional distortions of individuals' perceptions may arise from the nature of political corruption, as corruption at high levels of government (alternatively referred to as political corruption, grand corruption, or state capture) can be harder to observe directly. Thus, unless exposed publicly by political opponents, the media, or watchdog groups, the perception of political corruption is likely to be less accurate. On the contrary, petty corruption is often observed or even "experienced" first-hand by the ordinary citizens even if it is not publicly disclosed or unveiled. Thus, if corrupt politicians succeed in hiding their corrupt actions, civil society or the private sector may never perceive it. As such, the degree of this type of bias across countries will depend on the ability of politicians to conceal such corruption, or analogously, on the inability of countries' political, judicial, or civil society institutions to hold their politicians accountable. As a result, it is possible that a country with moderate political corruption but a good ability to detect this type of corruption will be perceived as highly corrupt while other countries with high levels of political corruption but in which this type of corruption is seldom detected or exposed may be perceived as less corrupt.

All in all, survey data appears to provide reasonably valid indicators of corruption levels. Although it is much needed, little progress has been made to date to complement survey data with the collection of "hard" objective data on corruption that are verifiable. As a result, for the near future, information on corruption will continue to come from survey data sources.

2.5. The costs of corruption

The costs that corruption imposes on economies and societies are conceptually numerous, but in practice these costs are often difficult to measure. At first glance, it might appear that the only impact of corruption is that it redistributes economic resources, albeit in an unsystematic and potentially distorting way. While in some cases corruption may increase the income of poorly paid public employees, in others it transfers resources from the poor to the rich and privileged (Gupta *et al.*, 1998). Furthermore, as Gould and Amaro-Reyes (1983) point out, individual gains resulting from corruption are unlikely to be reinvested in the productive sector of the economy. Often, the proceeds from grand corruption are transferred to foreign bank accounts resulting in a leakage of domestic capital without any further resource redistribution.

Earlier studies of corruption had advanced the idea that corruption does not represent a cost but rather it may increase efficiency by "greasing the wheels of the economy." (Leff, 1964; Huntington, 1968; Bardhan, 1997) However, this contention has been generally rejected by more recent students of corruption. The current consensus in this literature indicates that corruption is distorting and inefficient.

Corruption has a wide array of effects beyond the redistribution of monetary amounts during the corrupt transaction or the "speed money" effect in public transactions. One area in which the burden of fiscal corruption is quite tangible is in the delivery of public services. Corruption decreases the efficiency and raises the price of public services through several different channels. First, fiscal corruption in its various forms decreases the total funds available to finance public goods and services. For instance, Transparency International (2004) lists estimates of the resources directly embezzled by high-level political leaders, which are therefore no longer available for public services. Second, corruption in the procurement of productive inputs raises the price of publicly procured inputs and increases the costs of public services. Anecdotal evidence indicates that corruption in the public sector can increase the costs of services by 30–50 percent (Wade, 1982; Manzetti and Blake, 1996; Langseth *et al.*, 1997). Third, to the extent that fiscal corruption takes the form of a user fee, it raises the effective price of government services even further. While taxpayers already pay taxes to support the provision of public services, they are commonly forced to pay additional bribes in order to actually receive these services (Transparency International, 1997). Fourth, corruption distorts the allocation of public resources. Mauro (1998), for example, finds that corruption decreases the ratio of health and education spending to Gross Domestic Product (GDP) while other studies find that corruption increases military spending (Gupta *et al.*, 2001). It is difficult to believe that these induced shifts in the composition of public expenditures will enhance the public's general welfare. Fifth, corruption may decrease the quality of public services (Gould and Amaro-Reyes, 1983).

The simplest economic illustration of fiscal corruption is to consider it as an extra cost imposed on households and firms in the purchase of publicly provided services, with very similar effects to those introduced by a tax in the market for a private good. In this example, we assume the corrupt act takes on the form of a direct monetary payment (i.e., a bribe) in order to gain access to a government service. The bribe acts as a "corruption tax" on each unit of government services, which increases the overall cost of receiving public services and more broadly increases the cost of doing business, as public services and public infrastructure are important inputs in private production. Graphically, this is the case illustrated in Figure 2.2; the supply curve is shifted upward as a result of the "corruption tax".[32]

---

[32] Alternatively, corruption can be illustrated as an increase in the costs to households and households of obtaining government services, thereby lowering the postcorruption demand for public goods and services. Both cases have the same economic impact; they raise prices, lower profits, and reduce the level of economic activity.

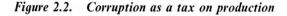

Figure 2.2. *Corruption as a tax on production*

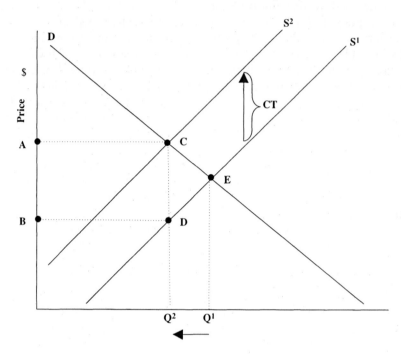

A first result of the additional cost of corruption is that it generates a transfer of resources from producers and consumers to corrupt agents equal to the total amount of bribes paid, represented by the rectangular area ABCD (where AB reflects the bribe per unit and CD represents the number of units of public services). The World Bank (2004a) estimates the total amount of bribes paid worldwide each year at around US $1 trillion. Although area ABCD could simplistically be considered simply as a transfer of resources in favor of corrupt agents, the indirect economic impact of the (partial) outflow of these resources on economic growth is not particularly clear or straightforward.

Additionally, the increase in the de facto price of public services causes a reduction in the equilibrium quantity of public service from Q_1 to Q_2, and in turn, in an overall reduction in economic activity. This reduction in economic output – both directly within the public sector, and indirectly in the public sector – reflects the real economic cost of corruption. In terms of the economic analysis in Figure 2.2, corruption generates an efficiency loss (also known as deadweight loss) represented by the triangular area CDE. This deadweight loss can be interpreted as a direct economic loss to society as a result of corruption. There is a close parallel between the cost of corruption and the excess burden costs related to distortions introduced by taxes; for the latter, we know that excess burden losses grow exponentially with the tax rate (Harberger, 1962).

As noted previously, part of both the efficiency loss and the aforementioned transfer of resources (bribes) are directly borne by producers. As such, corruption increases the per-unit cost of production, and thus decreases productivity of the private sector. To the extent that developing countries are disproportionately affected by corruption, the impact of corruption can lead developing nations to a downward spiral that undermines their ability to compete in international trade markets. Batra *et al.* (2003), explore some of the relations between investment climate constraints including governance and corruption. Based on their results, they highlight the importance of taking into account country and firm specific characteristics in this analysis, as well as unbundling different types of corruption (i.e., bribery and political capture).

How is this burden of corruption distributed between households and firms among countries? Although it is unlikely that businessmen would reveal information concerning their own involvement in corrupt acts, they may feel motivated to reveal corruption of their competitors and estimate the monetary loss suffered as a consequence. Table 2.4 illustrates

Table 2.4.   Costs of corruption to the private sector

Low costs of corruption (score ≤ 2.3)		High costs of corruption (score ≥ 4.4)	
Iceland	1.1	Bolivia	4.4
Finland	1.4	Honduras	4.4
Denmark	1.6	Romania	4.4
Sweden	1.6	Russia	4.4
Singapore	1.7	Venezuela	4.4
Austria	1.8	Panama	4.5
France	1.8	Philippines	4.5
Israel	1.9	Zimbabwe	4.5
New Zealand	1.9	Argentina	4.7
United Kingdom	2.0	Ecuador	4.7
Hong Kong SAR	2.1	Ukraine	4.8
Norway	2.1	Guatemala	4.9
Italy	2.3	Nicaragua	4.9
Japan	2.3	Nigeria	4.9
Switzerland	2.3	Paraguay	4.9
		Bangladesh	5.1

Note: Respondents were asked to indicate the extent that unfair or corrupt activities of other firms impose costs on their firms on a scale from 1 to 7. Responses were recoded to 7 = impose large costs, 1 = impose no costs/not relevant. The mean score (which happens to be also the median) = 3.3. High (low) costs defined as those with scores that lie one standard deviation (1.0) higher (lower) than the mean.
Source: Computed using data from Global Competitiveness Report (2003–2004).

the estimated costs that corruption imposes on businesses from different countries divided in three categories based on responses to *Global
Competitiveness Report* survey. While respondents of this survey do
not report an estimate of the monetary value of the loss incurred, the
scaled information obtained is nevertheless useful for comparison and
analysis.

In addition to its direct economic impact, corruption can represent
significant non-monetary costs to the overall well-being of society.[33] In this
sense, corruption has the potential to significantly weaken the rule of law,
which is the backbone of a stable and effective market economy. In turn,
assuring a stable economic environment is one of Musgrave's (1959) three
economic roles of government. Moreover, high levels of corruption can
severely undermine a government's legitimacy, and have a wide array of
political costs (Rose-Ackerman, 1999). The effects of corruption on political stability can be quite drastic as witnessed by the recent history of
Haiti. The political impacts of corruption are discussed in greater detail by
Johnston (1986), Bohn (2003), and Anderson and Tverdova (2003). For
instance, Anderson and Tverdova (2003) finds that corruption has a negative effect on citizen attitudes toward government, generating distrust and
weakening democracy.

The empirical corruption literature presents a large number of empirical
studies measuring the impact of corruption in a wide range of economic
variables. In particular, econometric research suggests that corruption has
a negative impact on per capita gross domestic product, efficiency, investment, tax revenues, productivity, health and education spending, and ultimately economic growth. A summary of results from some empirical
studies is shown in Table 2.5).

A detailed discussion of each one of the studies in Table 2.5 is beyond
the scope of this chapter. Yet a brief observation of corruption's wide
variety of negative effects helps to illustrate the broad impact of corruption
on economic growth, inequality, and public service delivery.

2.6. Concluding remarks

This chapter discussed some basic characteristics of corruption as an economic phenomenon. Corruption is not just the result of an intrinsic lack of
ethics and morals in the public sector or in society. Instead, corruption
very often arises from conscious decisions by economically rational public
officials that face a system of incentives and opportunities for corruption.

---

[33] See Abed and Gupta (2002) for an extensive review of studies reflecting the consequences of
corruption in a broad range of economic and non-economic issues including public service
provision, poverty, and income distribution.

Table 2.5. Economic impacts of increasing corruption by one unit[a]

Authors	Impact on	Finding
Mauro (1996)	Real per capita GDP growth	−0.3 to −1.8 percentage points
Leite and Weidmann (1999)	Real per capita GDP growth	−0.7 to −1.2 percentage points
Tanzi and Davoodi (2000)	Real per capita GDP growth	−0.6 percentage points
Tanzi and Davoodi (2001)	Real per capita GDP	−1 to −1.3 percentage points
Mauro (1996)	Ratio of investment to GDP	−1 to −2.8 percentage points
Mauro (1998)[b]	Ratio of public education spending to GDP	−0.7 to −0.9 percentage points
Mauro (1998)[c]	Ratio of public health spending to GDP	−0.6 to −1.7 percentage points
Gupta et al. (2001)	Income inequality (Gini coefficient)	+0.9 to +2.1 Gini points
Gupta et al. (2001)	Income growth of the poor	−2 to −10 percentage points
Ghura (1998)	Ratio of tax revenues to GDP	−1 to −2.9 percentage points
Tanzi and Davoodi (2000)[d]	Measures of government revenues to GDP ratio	−0.1 to −4.5 percentage points
Gupta, de Mello, and Sharan (2001)[e]	Ratio of military spending to GDP	+1 percentage point
Gupta, de Mello, and Sharan (2001)[f]	Child mortality rate	+1.1 to 2.7 deaths per 1,000 live births
Gupta, Davoodi, and Tiongson (2000)[g]	Primary student dropout rate	+1.4 to 4.8 percentage points
Tanzi and Davoodi (1997)[h]	Ratio of public investment to GDP	+0.5 percentage points
Tanzi and Davoodi (1997)[i]	Percent of paved roads in good condition	−2.2 to −3.9 percentage points

Source: Extracted from Transparency International (2001).
[a]Corruption is measured on a scale of 0 (highly clean) to 10 (highly corrupt).
[b]Three other measures of education spending are also reported in this study.
[c]Three other measures of health spending are also reported in this study.
[d]This study covers 15 types of government revenues.
[e]Three additional measures of military spending are also reported in this study.
[f]Four additional indicators of health are reported in this study.
[g]Four additional indicators of education are reported in this study.
[h]Two additional measures of public spending are also reported in this study.
[i]Four additional indicators of infrastructure are used in this study.

Several factors affect this decision, many of which can be influenced by policymakers to foster an environment in which less corruption occurs.

Economics also provides a rational guide for corruption control policies. Governments should spend increasing resources on corruption control as long as the marginal costs of controlling corruption is less than the marginal cost imposed on society by corruption. As a result, a sound governance strategy would seldom require corruption to be completely eliminated.

Finally, corruption imposes direct and indirect costs to society, including the distortion of several dimensions of the public and private sector performance. Recent efforts to quantify these effects in empirical studies have also begun to shed light on the multiple effects of corruption. Economics research is increasingly exploring the nature of the corruption phenomenon. Understanding this nature constitutes a pivotal step in the search for the effective design of anticorruption policy.

CHAPTER 3

Regional Patterns of Corruption Around the World

The introductory part of this book stresses corruption as a global phenomenon. The main implication is that corruption has an impact, not only in the place of origin, but also in other countries and regions in the world. Hence a comprehensive and sustained effort to reduce corruption in any particular country is also justified for the externalities it represents for other countries in the region and beyond. These efforts should aim to target, without exception, those countries and regions in which corruption is deeply entrenched.

For some time, economic studies and technical reports on corruption have noted that curbing corruption requires a comprehensive approach that recognizes the existence of characteristics that are particular to each country.[34] While the experience of each country is unique to some extent, several countries within each region share common exogenous factors such as culture, ethnicity, religion, colonial past, and many other unobserved characteristics. These factors are likely to have an influence on the forms of corruption that regions face. From a policy standpoint, identifying regional differences is important for two reasons. On one side of the spectrum, focusing on regions of the world facilitates the quantitative analysis of corruption indicators. This analysis can help to reveal not only the different extents of corruption in different geographic regions, but also the specific patterns corruption follows in those regions. Of course, this is crucial for reexamining and targeting anticorruption efforts where they are most needed as well as tailoring policy to address the forms of corruption most prevalent in each region. On the other side of the spectrum, qualitative analysis and discussion of corruption by geographic region leads to a better understanding of regional idiosyncrasies, which is vital to finding effective remedies. If countries in a region suffer from the same types of corruption, effective strategies in one country may be successfully exported or imitated in other countries in the region. Furthermore, the identification of those successful anticorruption efforts may inspire political will and civil society activism among countries within the region with similar characteristics and at the same time help unveil widely spread myths on corruption.

---

[34] See, for example, World Bank (2000d), Shah and Mathew (2003).

When we adopt a regional focus, a number of questions immediately arise. Which regions are more severely affected by corruption? Which forms of corruption are most prevalent within each region? Which factors determine these differences? What kind of specific problems are more common in each region? This chapter seeks to answer these questions through the analysis of corruption indicators and by dissecting particular regional corruption issues.

3.1. *Regional differences in the extent and nature of corruption*

As discussed in Chapter 2 of this book, quantifying corruption levels and making cross-country/cross-regional comparisons based on corruption indicators is subject to many limitations. However, with the necessary caveats, the data available on corruption may be employed in several useful ways to arrive at some fundamental insights on the extent of corruption among regions of the world.

Let us start with some aggregate descriptors. Figure 3.1 shows regional average levels for two previously discussed composite indicators of corruption: the TI's CPI and Kaufmann's Corruption Control (CC)

Figure 3.1.   *Corruption average scores by geographic region*

Geographical Distribution of Observations							
	CPI 2005				Corruption Control 2005		
Region	No. Obs.	Mean	Std. Dev.	Coef. of Var.	No. Obs.	Mean	Std. Dev.	Coef. of Var.
North America	2	8.00	0.57	0.07	3	1.6	0.34	0.08
West Europe	19	7.86	1.57	0.20	21	1.6	0.61	0.15
East Europe and Central Asia	28	3.29	1.19	0.36	27	-0.3	0.65	0.30
East Asia and Pacific	18	4.81	2.73	0.57	31	0.0	1.04	0.42
Middle East and North Africa	19	4.32	1.56	0.36	20	0.0	0.71	0.28
Latina American and Caribbean	25	3.48	1.39	0.40	37	0.1	0.82	0.32
Sub-Saharan Africa	39	2.79	0.86	0.31	45	-0.7	0.58	0.32
South Asia	6	2.48	0.54	0.22	8	-0.5	0.70	0.36
Total	156	4.08	2.20	0.54	294	-0.00	1	0.40

Source: Computed by authors based on data from Corruption Perception Index (2005) reported by Transparency International and Corruption Control by Kaufmann *et al.* (2006). Transparency International Corruption Perception Index is used to measure Corruption redefined as (10-CPI). A value of 0 represents a non-corrupt country whereas a value of 10 indicates a highly corrupt country. The coefficient of variation of Corruption Control is computed as the ratio of standard deviation to the result of corruption control mean plus 2.5.

(Kaufmann *et al.*, 2006). While these indexes differ in the methodologies used to construct them, it is interesting that the rankings on the extent of corruption across regions, from these two indexes, are fairly similar.

The regions of South Asia (SA), sub-Saharan Africa (SSA), and East Europe and Central Asia (ECA) present the highest levels of corruption (see Figure 3.1). According to these indexes, the Middle Eastern and North African (MENA), East Asian and Pacific (EAP), and Latin American and Caribbean (LAC) regions experience relatively lower average levels of corruption. Finally, North America (NA) and West Europe (WE) are the regions with the lowest levels of corruption.

Note that the groupings of countries by region tend to hide significant variations in corruption levels within regions. The CPI standard deviation and coefficient of variation are larger for East Asian and Pacific and Latin American and Caribbean regions, whereas the largest variations in the CC variable are in the East Asian and Pacific and South Asia regions. At any rate, both aggregate indicators strongly suggest, and probably to no one's surprise, that the worst cases of pervasive corruption take place in three regions of the world, sub-Saharan Africa, South Asia, and East Europe and Central Asia. Obviously, these are the areas where international anticorruption efforts should be concentrated.[35]

In the remainder of this chapter we broadly identify the main manifestations of corruption in each geographic region of the world. An important fact is that each region has its own well-defined idiosyncrasies in relation to corruption; hence, these qualitative differences need to be taken into account while designing practical strategies and solutions to fight corruption. However, caution must be exercised in not extrapolating too much from the general or common traits identified herein, given the existence of sometimes considerable differences that exist among countries within each region. Furthermore, experience shows that, even when some particular traits appear to be entrenched in a given region, those obstacles are not undefeatable as there are always at least several countries in each region that have proven to reach corruption and governance standards considerably higher than the rest of the countries in their geographic area.[36] Undoubtedly, the study of specific country cases may produce more accurate diagnostics, country tailored anticorruption design, and overpass the limitations of regional generalizations. This is a main reason for presenting in Chapter 6 a detailed discussion of a country case: Tanzania. Nevertheless, the identification of common regional traits remains a useful

---

[35] A more in-depth discussion of the specific features of corruption in these regions is presented below.
[36] These are, for example, the cases of Chile in Latin America, Slovenia in East Europe, Botswana and Mauritius in Sub-Sahara Africa, Singapore in East Asia, and Israel in the Middle East and North Africa.

step in understanding the roots of corruption and designing appropriate policy responses.

Our discussion below considers the forms of corruption most common in each geographic region but places particular emphasis on those issues that differentiate each region from the others. In addition, for each region we include a list of changes in corruption in order to identify progress on different fronts. These changes are measured using Kaufmann's CC aggregate measures. It is important to highlight the caveat that year-to-year comparisons using Kaufmann's indicators are subject to potential biases due to the weighting methodology used to generate this indicator.[37] This methodology aims to increase the precision of the aggregate index for each given year, but in doing so it also creates a cross-country dependence on changes in the group of sources used during any given year. That is, the weight assigned to each source of data is estimated using information from all sources of data available that year. This implies that if a new source of data is introduced, or if any of the existent indicators experience considerable changes, the weights estimated for all other sources will also vary. Hence, year-to-year changes for any given country score may result from this reweighting rather than from a true change in the score vis-a-vis the score in the previous year.[38] Despite these caveats, this corruption indicator is the best aggregate measurement available of corruption change, and, therefore, it will be used here.[39] For each region, the following sections report country quintiles and the change between this relative categorization in 1998 and 2005. Note again that, given the methodological limitations in measuring corruption changes over time, these remarks should only be interpreted as suggesting a trend in corruption levels relative to that in other countries in the region. Transparency International's Global Corruption Report (2001, 2003, 2004), in particular the country report sections, were particularly helpful in the identification of country-specific issues discussed below.

3.1.1. Sub-Saharan Africa

Sub-Saharan countries' deep levels of poverty and underdevelopment are in great contrast with their immense endowment of natural resources. In many countries in the region, military dictatorships and armed conflicts

---

[37] The methodology weighs the data from alternative sources on the basis of their correlation.

[38] However Kaufmann *et al.* (1999, p. 15) state that the effects of weight changes accounts only for a small fraction of the variance of the aggregate indicators. More recently, Kaufmann *et al.* (2006) have adjusted the world-wide average score for years previous to 2005.

[39] TI uses surveys from previous years to generate the CPI of any given year, for which reason it is not suited for analyzing year-to-year changes.

have undermined the role and engagement of civil society in state matters. This environment has led to pervasive corruption at the political and bureaucratic levels and to a systematic deviation of already scarce resources from the needs of the people. Furthermore, not only has corruption deprived citizenry of their own resources, but in many cases it also has deprived them of international aid resources, further perpetuating the cycle of poverty. Administrative corruption in sub-Sahara Africa manifests itself mainly in procurement processes and as graft in public service delivery, while political corruption has most often taken the form of misappropriation of revenues from natural resources and from oil and mining.

Sub-Saharan indicators of corruption rank highest among geographical regions (see Figure 3.1). The severity and changes in Kaufmann CC indicators for each country in the region is reported in Table 3.1, where positive scores mean less corruption (i.e., the country has moved to a higher quintile) and negative scores mean more corruption (i.e., the country has moved to a lower quintile). Somalia, Liberia, Cameroon, Angola, and Nigeria are the countries with most corruption (the lowest scores) in 1998. The largest increments in CC from 1998 to 2005 took place in Zimbabwe and Swaziland (moving four quintiles down) followed by Central African Republic, Ethiopia, Guinea-Bissau, and Sudan (moving two quintiles down), whereas the largest decrease in corruption took place in Gabon and Madagascar (both moving three quintiles up).

One of the main sources of misappropriation of public resources is generated by the lack of accountability of funds generated from natural resource exploitation. Countries such as Nigeria, Angola, Equatorial Guinea, and Congo are rich in oil resources. However, oil revenues in those countries are not properly accounted for and often managed through opaque off-budget accounts. Multilateral institutions have been unsuccessful in their attempts to persuade multinational extractive companies to reveal how much they pay state governments. This information could serve to hold governments accountable for the use of those resources. Oil resources in these countries have been commonly used to finance extravagant spending by political leaders or simply embezzled and transferred to foreign accounts. No systematic reporting or accounting exists in this regard, but it is not at all difficult to find sporadic reports of this type of corruption. For example, as much as US $1 billion dollars in oil resources were reported embezzled in Angola in 2000.[40] Allegations in Angola also involve the embezzlement of as much as US $3 billion from loans against mortgages of future oil cargoes, resources for which public officials are not held accountable.[41] Recent reports on Equatorial Guinea reveal

---

[40] See Global Witness (2004).
[41] See Reuters (2002).

Table 3.1.   Corruption control: sub-Saharan countries (1998 and 2005)

	1998	Quintile in 1998 (a)	2005	Quintile in 2005 (b)	Quintile change (2005 (b))–(1998 (a))
Gabon	−0.96	1	−0.61	4	3
Madagascar	−0.86	2	0	5	3
Mozambique	−0.87	2	−0.68	4	2
Tanzania	−1.04	1	−0.73	3	2
Burkina Faso	−0.54	4	0.06	5	1
Cape Verde	−0.36	4	0.21	5	1
Congo	−1.06	1	−1.01	2	1
Guinea	−0.88	2	−0.84	3	1
Kenya	−1.03	1	−1.01	2	1
Mali	−0.64	3	−0.29	4	1
Niger	−0.94	2	−0.83	3	1
Sao Tome and Principe	−0.86	2	−0.77	3	1
Seychelles	−0.36	4	0.01	5	1
Angola	−1.16	1	−1.09	1	0
Botswana	0.67	5	1.1	5	0
Burundi	−0.86	2	−0.86	2	0
Cameroon	−1.27	1	−1.15	1	0
Comoros	−0.86	2	−0.93	2	0
Ghana	−0.48	4	−0.38	4	0
Lesotho	0.14	5	−0.15	5	0
Liberia	−1.5	1	−1.08	1	0
Mauritania	−0.36	4	−0.26	4	0
Mauritius	0.24	5	0.32	5	0
Namibia	0.33	5	0.06	5	0
Nigeria	−1.13	1	−1.22	1	0
Rwanda	−0.61	3	−0.81	3	0
Senegal	−0.51	4	−0.23	4	0
Somalia	−1.5	1	−1.74	1	0
South Africa	0.49	5	0.54	5	0
Zambia	−0.61	3	−0.82	3	0
Benin	−0.82	3	−1	2	−1
Chad	−0.9	2	−1.22	1	−1
Equatorial Guinea	−0.86	2	−1.79	1	−1
Eritrea	0.4	5	−0.37	4	−1
Gambia	−0.56	4	−0.7	3	−1
Malawi	−0.55	4	−0.85	3	−1
Sierra Leone	−0.79	3	−0.99	2	−1
Swaziland	−0.13	5	−0.6	4	−1
Togo	−0.51	4	−0.7	3	−1
Uganda	−0.69	3	−0.87	2	−1
Central African Republic	−0.61	3	−1.08	1	−2
Ethiopia	−0.25	5	−0.79	3	−2
Guinea-Bissau	−0.64	3	−1.08	1	−2
Sudan	−0.81	3	−1.4	1	−2
Zimbabwe	−0.22	5	−1.24	1	−4

Note: Computed based on data from Kaufmann *et al.* (2006).

that US oil companies are making direct payments into President Obiang Nguema's account at Riggs Bank in Washington, DC.[42]

Evidence that corruption in any country may produce negative externalities in other countries is provided by reports on how corruption in African countries has served to fund terrorism globally. For a long time, the international community has been aware that resources from illicit trade in diamonds have fueled armed conflict in African countries. The illicit traffic of diamonds by terrorist groups in Africa is documented in a recent report by Global Witness (2004). This document provides evidence of several Al Qaeda operations in black markets in Kenya, Tanzania, Burkina Faso, Sierra Leone, and Liberia. For instance, Al Qaeda set up a system of diamonds-for-arms operations, which involved former President Charles Taylor and several ministers after the United Nations placed an embargo on arms and diamond trade in Liberia in 1993. Similar trade took place between Al Qaeda members and the RUF, a rebel group, which for many years captured the main diamond-mining district of Sierra Leone. In legal trade arrangements, funds generated by buying and selling of diamonds, for example, need to be transparently reported and the respective records made available to citizens of countries of origin as with any other natural resource. In this matter, an International Convention (the Kimberley Process Certification Scheme), limits legal diamond trade to those that have a certification to ensure proper accounting of funds received by exporting governments. However, due to poor monitoring, this convention has made little headway against strong elites of autocratic leaders, who find in diamonds an easy way to get arms or unreported hard cash.

Besides the high levels of political corruption in the exploitation of natural resources, there is also in Sub-Saharan Africa pervasive administrative corruption that manifests itself in several particular areas. In fact, administrative corruption is actually perceived as more prevalent in most countries of the region (Annex Figure 3.A.3). One of the most prevalent nests of corruption is in the tendering and procurement processes. Recent widely publicized examples are the Malawi Telecommunications tendering, allegedly to a group consisting of several government officials (including the minister of communications), and the scandal regarding bribes received by government members from companies participating in an arms procurement in South Africa in late 2001.[43] Similarly, corruption in the construction tendering of the Katse Dam, part of Lesotho Highlands Water Project, led to the conviction and 18-year sentence to Masupha Sole for taking more than US $6 million in bribes from British, Canadian, French, German, and American contractors.[44]

---

[42] See Global Witness (2004).
[43] See BBC (2001b) and Malawi Anti-corruption Bureau (2001).
[44] See Ryan Hoover (2002).

A second area of concentration of administrative corruption in the region is in service delivery, often in the form of bribery and extortion in exchange for public services. Administrative corruption also takes the form of diversion or embezzlement of public resources en route to service provision centers. These leakages from spending, in particular in education and health sectors, have been identified and widely exposed by studies employing Public Expenditure Tracking Surveys (PETS) in Ghana, Uganda, and Tanzania (Ablo and Reinikka, 1999; Reinikka, 2001; Reinikka and Svensson, 2002, 2004).

As mentioned above, the compound tragedy of the high levels of political and administrative corruption in sub-Saharan Africa is that they have wasted already scarce national resources and they have also significantly lowered levels of international aid. Traditionally, high levels of poverty, weak market development, food shortages, and the rapid spread of contagious diseases, more recently HIV/AIDS, in the region have made sub-Saharan countries highly dependent on international aid. However, corruption has also infiltrated the reception and use of those resources, as the multiple reported cases of misappropriation of foreign aid have witnessed. This situation has lead several foreign donors to condition their development assistance on specific anticorruption efforts and suspend aid to countries that do not reach their expected goals. For instance, in February 2002 the European Union froze, from a period of 3 years, aid funds to Cote d'Ivoire due the embezzlement of US $25 million in aid resources.[45] Denmark and Britain withdrew aid assistance to Malawi in 2002, on the bases of corruption and intolerance to political accountability of the government led by President Bakili Muluzi.[46] Similar conditioning of aid resources on CC were also imposed by Denmark on Burkina Faso, and from Britain on Sierra Leone, due to allegations of government involvement in illicit diamond trade and weak will for anticorruption efforts.[47] Similarly, the IMF and World Bank have exerted pressure on countries that did not show a credible commitment to fighting corruption by withholding aid resources and investment projects; for example, this was the policy applied to Kenya in 1997 (Wittig, 2000; Kpundeh, 2001).

3.1.2. Latin America and the Caribbean

Latin American and the Caribbean countries are also characterized by high levels of corruption relative to other regions (see Figure 3.1). However, some countries such as Chile, Puerto Rico, and Costa Rica have considerably lower levels of corruption than the average country in this region

---

[45] See Transparency International (2003).
[46] See BBC (2002).
[47] See Transparency International (2003).

(Table 3.2). A deep crisis of democratic legitimacy and dwindling civil society's confidence in political leadership have been making political corruption ever more prevalent in the region. This is also reflected by the fact that most countries in the region have higher scores on the political corruption index (Annex Figure 3.A.4). The costs of political corruption in the regions have been political instability and a weakened democratic process. The protests after evidence of embezzlement and misuse of public funds by political leaders came to light have led to the downfall of several governments in recent years. Some examples include: Alberto Fujimori,

Table 3.2. **Corruption control: Latin America and Caribbean (1998 and 2005)**

	1998	Quintile in 1998 (a)	2005	Quintile in 2005 (b)	Quintile change (2005 (b))–(1998 (a))
Dominica	−0.36	2	0.68	4	2
Belize	−0.36	2	−0.22	3	1
Colombia	−0.67	2	−0.22	3	1
Mexico	−0.46	2	−0.41	3	1
Nicaragua	−0.83	1	−0.62	2	1
St. Kitts and Nevis	−0.1	4	1	5	1
St. Lucia	−0.1	4	1.15	5	1
St. Vincent and the Grenadines	−0.1	4	1	5	1
Bahamas	0.6	5	1.32	5	0
Chile	1.13	5	1.34	5	0
Cuba	−0.35	3	−0.26	3	0
Dominican Republic	−0.59	2	−0.66	2	0
Ecuador	−0.81	1	−0.81	1	0
El Salvador	−0.34	3	−0.39	3	0
Grenada	−0.1	4	0.68	4	0
Guatemala	−0.71	1	−0.98	1	0
Haiti	−0.91	1	−1.45	1	0
Honduras	−0.82	1	−0.67	1	0
Panama	−0.34	3	−0.27	3	0
Paraguay	−1.03	1	−1.19	1	0
Puerto Rico	1.41	5	1.1	5	0
Suriname	0	4	0.05	4	0
Venezuela	−0.84	1	−1	1	0
Argentina	−0.29	3	−0.44	2	−1
Bolivia	−0.48	2	−0.81	1	−1
Brazil	0.03	4	−0.28	3	−1
Costa Rica	0.63	5	0.38	4	−1
Guyana	−0.33	3	−0.58	2	−1
Jamaica	−0.33	3	−0.5	2	−1
Peru	−0.24	3	−0.49	2	−1
Trinidad and Tobago	0.06	5	0.01	4	−1
Uruguay	0.36	5	0.78	4	−1

Note: Computed based on data from Kaufmann *et al.* (2006).

former President of Peru (who allegedly embezzled US $600 million); Arnoldo Aleman, former President of Nicaragua (allegedly US $100 million); Juan Carlos Wasmosy, former President of Paraguay (now in prison for allegedly US $6 million); Brazil's Paulo Maluf, governor of Sao Paulo (allegedly US $200 million), and currently under investigation, former President of Bolivia Hugo Banzer, and former President of Argentina Carlos Menem.[48] Other allegations of corruption involve political leaders still in office, such as Hugo Chavez president of Venezuela and Alejandro Toledo of Peru.

Other manifestations of political corruption in Latin America include, first, illegal financing of electoral campaigns. Recent examples include Roseana Sarney's withdrawal from the presidential race in Brazil, after a police investigation uncovered US $536,000 of illegal campaign financing,[49] and the allegations against Arnoldo Aleman in Nicaragua and Jamil Mahad of having illegally used state funds to run their campaigns. Second are the allegations of lack of transparency and corruption in the privatization of state-owned companies. This issue has generated social unrest and violent demonstrations involving thousands of citizens, which often forced governments to suspend the privatization of state assets. Some examples include Paraguay's retraction of the privatization of the state telecom company *Copaco*, Peru's suspension of the privatization of two state electricity companies to *Tractebel*, a company from Belgium, and Bolivia's termination of a 40-year lease of water provision to California-based *Bechtel* through its subsidiary *Aguas del Tunari*.[50] Mexico has also gone through high profile allegations of political corruption,[51] while graft and bribery in public administration and service delivery have been considered endemic. Corruption in the Mexican judicial system is seen as a main cause of the prevailing administrative corruption. A United Nations report in 2002 estimated that the share of judges involved in corruption in Mexico may be between 50 percent and 70 percent.[52]

The experience of Peru illustrates the importance of instilling ethics in the media to fight political corruption. With hindsight, Alberto Fujimori's high levels of popular support arose due to the control and manipulation of mass media. Fujimori's dismissal started with the revelation of evidence of large payments in exchange for favorable coverage and political

---

[48] These and other cases are cited in Probidad (2002), CBS (2004), and Transparency International (2004).

[49] See AAA (2002).

[50] See Transparency International (2003).

[51] For example, the investigation regarding the funneling of revenues from Petroleos Mexicanos (PEMEX), for funding the year 2000 electoral campaign of the then-ruling Institutional Revolutionary Party (PRI).

[52] See Transparency International (2003).

Table 3.3. **Corruption control: Western European Countries (1998 and 2005)**

	1998	Quintile in 1998 (a)	2005	Quintile in 2005 (b)	Quintile change (2005 (b))–(1998 (a))
Iceland	2.25	3	2.49	5	2
Austria	1.96	2	1.99	3	1
Belgium	1.17	1	1.45	2	1
Cyprus	1.32	1	0.69	1	0
Denmark	2.51	5	2.23	5	0
Finland	2.49	5	2.39	5	0
France	1.69	2	1.4	2	0
Germany	2.15	3	1.92	3	0
Greece	0.78	1	0.4	1	0
Italy	0.93	1	0.41	1	0
Luxembourg	2.1	3	1.84	3	0
Norway	2.29	4	2.04	4	0
Spain	1.52	2	1.34	2	0
Sweden	2.48	4	2.1	4	0
Ireland	2.09	3	1.7	2	−1
Netherlands	2.42	4	1.99	3	−1
Portugal	1.49	2	1.13	1	−1
Switzerland	2.52	5	2.12	4	−1
United Kingdom	2.26	4	1.94	3	−1

Note: Computed based on data from Kaufmann *et al.* (2006).

support. An alleged contract between Fujimori's government and America Television purportedly included the denial of coverage to opposition candidates and free editorial control by Fujimori's intelligence chief Vladimiro Montesinos.[53] In other countries of Latin America there has been more of a tradition of vigorous and independent media and a population with low tolerance for corruption. For instance, faced with a bureaucratic and often corrupt judicial system, citizens of several Andean communities have dealt with corruption cases by taking justice into their own hands. A recent extreme case is in Peru, where hundreds of residents from Ilave town dragged through the streets and later beat to death their Mayor Cirilo Fernando Robles who was accused of corruption.[54]

3.1.3. *Western Europe*

Countries from Western Europe are, for the most part, mature democratic systems with developed market economies. The Nordic countries (Finland, Denmark, Norway, and Sweden) plus Switzerland are among those with the lowest levels of corruption in the world (Table 3.3). But not everything

---

[53] See Bilello (2001).
[54] See CNN (2004).

is positive in the region. The most significant feature of the region is a tendency toward political corruption (see Annex Figure 3.A.5).[55] During recent years corruption scandals have involved political elites throughout the region. These events have been, characteristically, related to issues of illegal party financing, misappropriation of foreign aid funds, and, to a lesser extent, allegations of electoral fraud. Political corruption in the region has also involved cases of illegal censorship of the mass media and resistance by a number of governments to adopting higher standards of disclosure.

It must be noted that many of the possible cases of political corruption in Western European countries have not gone beyond the stage of allegations that are still unresolved. This situation is sometimes thought to be due to the convenient manipulation of the bureaucratic process and to the manipulation, harassment, or elimination of those raising allegations or conducting investigations. Some prominent examples follow. In France, recent allegations were raised concerning irregularities during the period when Jacques Chirac was mayor of Paris (1977–1995) and as president of the Gaullist RPR Party. These claims involved bribes in public printing contracts, use of municipal public funds for political party financing, and manipulation of the electoral lists.[56] However, none of these allegations was further investigated or prosecuted due to Chirac's Presidential immunity. Furthermore, concerns were raised that voters may still have a high tolerance for corruption as Chirac was reelected President of France in April 2002. In January 2004, Chirac's ally and former Prime Minister, Alain Juppe, was sentenced to 18 months in jail for illegal party financing charges.[57]

Political corruption may be sometimes related to organized crime, whose illegal gains require different forms of money laundering. This type of political corruption may not be easy to curb, as witnessed by the political scandals in Italy during the last decades over links between prominent politicians and the mafia.[58] In some instances it appears that anticorruption policy that has taken steps backward. An example is provided by the sudden changes in the Italian legislation in 2002, by which the declaration of false accounts ceased to be considered a criminal offense.[59] Similarly in 2001, legislation changes considerably undermined the ability of the Italian parliament to effectively conclude investigations of false accounting by Prime Minister Silvio Berlusconi and other members of his party, while other reforms directly undermined the independence of the

---

[55] See Mendieta (2001) for a discussion of the corruption framework in the European Union and political corruption in Spain.
[56] See BBC (2001).
[57] See New York Times (2004a, b).
[58] Della Porta (2001) and Paoli (2003).
[59] See CNN (2002).

judiciary. In other cases, the target of political corruption was not legislation itself, but rather those in charge of the investigation and prosecution of corrupt practices. This may have been allegedly the case of the suspicious number of resignations and judge case reallocations during the process of investigation of several French politicians during 2001 and 2002.[60] Journalists also turned from watchdogs to corruption victims in 2001, when a dozen French journalists were prosecuted while investigating irregularities and political corruption allegations.[61] The importance of the media as watchdogs for political corruption cannot be overstated. Where the role of the media is suppressed and censored, political corruption thrives.

3.1.4. East Europe and Central Asia

Eastern Europe and Central Asia are, for the most part, countries in transition from planned socialism to market economies, in many cases with struggling democracies and in some cases still under totalitarian regimes which tend to suffer from high levels of corruption (Table 3.4). Although countries in Western Europe suffer noticeably lower levels of administrative corruption, this form of corruption is deeply entrenched in most countries of Eastern Europe, the Baltic States, and other countries from the former Soviet Union (FSU). Many of these countries have a lasting permissive attitude toward petty administrative corruption. Under the Soviet Union, bribery was ingrained even in the most ordinary bureaucratic processes. In particular, survey data reveal that both administrative and political corruption is deeply entrenched in the region (Annex Figure 3.A.6). This is also supported by data from BEEPS (Hellman *et al.*, 2000).[62] Petty corruption appears to be quite common in basic social services, such as health and education (Lewis, 2000).

The combination of permissive societal morals regarding corruption and the complex process of transition from communism to market economies, involving (among other issues) massive privatization policies, created particularly favorable dynamics for political corruption in all Central and Eastern Europe (CEE) plus the FSU countries. During this transition period of reform, enormous gains could be easily obtained by the manipulation of public decision-making at high levels of government. These transition countries had to create sometimes from nothing an entire system of laws and regulations, including anticorruption measures. Despite considerable efforts, in many of these countries corruption flourished because of the lack of monitoring, oversight, or enforcement of the laws. During

---

[60] See Transparency International (2003).
[61] Ibid.
[62] This information is based on a composite index of responses from the BEEPS for 1999.

Table 3.4. Corruption control: East Europe and Central Asia (1998 and 2005)

	1998	Quintile in 1998 (a)	2005	Quintile in 2005 (b)	Quintile change (2005 (b))–(1998 (a))
Ukraine	−0.97	1	−0.63	3	2
Albania	−0.99	1	−0.76	2	1
Croatia	−0.39	3	0.07	4	1
Georgia	−0.71	2	−0.57	3	1
Slovak Republic	−0.15	4	0.43	5	1
Armenia	−0.78	2	−0.64	2	0
Azerbaijan	−1.08	1	−1.01	1	0
Bosnia-Herzegovina	−0.41	3	−0.32	3	0
Bulgaria	−0.56	3	−0.05	3	0
Czech Republic	0.29	5	0.42	5	0
Estonia	0.43	5	0.88	5	0
Hungary	0.63	5	0.63	5	0
Latvia	−0.17	4	0.33	4	0
Lithuania	0.01	4	0.26	4	0
Romania	−0.44	3	−0.23	3	0
Russia	−0.76	2	−0.74	2	0
Slovenia	0.77	5	0.88	5	0
Tajikistan	−1.18	1	−1.08	1	0
Turkey	−0.07	4	0.08	4	0
Turkmenistan	−1.19	1	−1.3	1	0
Uzbekistan	−1.04	1	−1.07	1	0
Belarus	−0.66	3	−0.9	2	−1
Kazakhstan	−0.93	2	−0.94	1	−1
Kyrgyz Republic	−0.76	2	−1.06	1	−1
Macedonia	−0.36	4	−0.5	3	−1
Moldova	−0.57	3	−0.76	2	−1
Poland	0.43	5	0.19	4	−1

Note: Computed based on data from Kaufmann *et al.* (2006).

the transition, private individuals had powerful incentives to try to influence political decision-making in ways that favor their vested interests by bribing policymakers or buying parliamentarian votes. Survey data used in this book show that the countries with the highest levels of political corruption are Romania, Ukraine, Slovak Republic, the Russian Federation, and Serbia. Based on survey data from BEEPS, Hellman *et al.* (2000) report that the countries with the highest levels of state capture include Azerbaijan, Moldova, Ukraine, the Russian Federation, Kyrgyztan, Bulgaria, and Croatia.

The process of privatization of state assets, of unprecedented scale in most of these countries, was characterized by an extended number of financial scandals and allegations of corruption. What makes the case of corruption in the privatization of state assets in transitional economies unique is the fact that it took place despite the recent design of new legal frameworks, which were to prevent corruption in the first place. What seems to have failed, where there was adequate legislation, was a still unprepared judicial system, with lawyers and courts unable to settle cases, and many corrupt themselves, favoring the interest of organized crime through bribery and extortion. The most prominent example may have been the privatization process in the Russian Federation, where a public official estimated that as much as 30 percent of the public assets privatized from 1992 until the summer 1993 were in control of the Russian mafia.[63] The privatization of state assets in the Russian Federation also led to the concentration of immense fortunes in the hands of few individuals, who became known during the 1990s as the Russian oligarchs. There have been multiple allegations of political corruption whereby Russian federal government officials favored some of these oligarchs in the further privatization of state assets either in a hidden way or sometimes in rather open ways, as was the case in the "loans-for-shares" deals that some oligarchs were able to close with President Yeltsin from 1995 to 1996 (Salacuse, 1998). Allegedly, the Yeltsin administration, in need of cash to prop up the troublesome presidential campaign, sold at bargain basement prices highly profitable companies and assets to the oligarchs (Glinkina, 1999).[64] This episode may be one of those cases where it is difficult to draw the line between dubious political behavior and political corruption.

In some countries the effectiveness of independent journalism and news media to monitor corruption was decimated over the last decade. One recent example is provided by Ukraine, where 11 assassinations of investigative journalists took place during the period 1997–2003; this sent a clear message to the media in Ukraine that those who engage in the surveillance of potentially corrupt activities might pay with their lives. Furthermore, investigative journalism in Ukraine has been greatly undermined by passing legislation that prohibits the collection of personal information without previous consent of those being investigated, no matter whether those investigated have a public life or not. Multiple cases involving harassment of opposition parties and the independent media have been reported in several of the Asian Central Republics.

3.1.5. South Asia

South Asia is one of the poorest and most highly populated regions of the world. The region also confronts high levels of political instability due to a war in Afghanistan, tensions between Pakistan and India, and separatist movements in Nepal and Sri Lanka. Some observers have seen in these political problems, to some extent, a cause and a consequence of the high

---

[63] See Celarier (1997).
[64] Allegedly cash received from small cooperatives in exchange for state company assets exchanged at a 1:3 ratio, that is, 3 rubles worth of assets for 1 ruble of cash.

Table 3.5.   Corruption control: South Asia (1998 and 2005)

	1998	Quintile in 1998 (a)	2005	Quintile in 2005 (b)	Quintile change (2005 (b))–(1998 (a))
Maldives	−0.61	2	−0.28	4	2
Nepal	−0.66	1	−0.71	2	1
Bhutan	0.4	5	0.84	5	0
Pakistan	−0.82	1	−1.01	1	0
Sri Lanka	−0.3	3	−0.31	3	0
India	−0.24	4	−0.31	3	−1
Bangladesh	−0.47	3	−1.18	1	−2

Note: Computed based on data from Kaufmann *et al.* (2006).

levels of corruption that exist in the region (Table 3.5). Relative to other regions in the world, the average score of the Corruption Perception Index of South Asia is the highest.

High levels of administrative corruption are a trademark of the region, often involving the public procurement systems (Annex Figure 3.A.7). In particular, corruption allegations in defense procurement (a form of grand administrative corruption) are familiar in many of the countries in the region. Most recently, Transparency International (2003) raised concerns regarding the defense procurement systems in India and Pakistan and the need to reform the procurement procedures in general in those two countries. Several recent accounts of corruption illustrate well the nature of the problem. For example, in 2001, Indian Defense Minister George Fernandes resigned after journalists revealed video-taped evidence of military personnel, politicians, and bureaucrats of that ministry involved in bribery and arms trafficking. In 2000, bribery resulting from a military equipment deal involving US $2.7 billion led to the extradition to the US of former Pakistani naval chief Admiral Mansur ul-Haq. Similarly, Sri Lanka also suffered from corruption allegations in year 2000, regarding irregularities in defense procurement of armament for a value of US $800 million.[65]

These countries are also characterized by the presence of petty administrative corruption in the form of bribes and extortion of citizenry in the delivery of public services. In India, cases of bribes in exchange for public health services are commonly reported, as in Bangalore, where the staff of a maternity hospital extorted low-income women in exchange for maternal health care services. Illegal payments required by hospital staff in this case included one payment after giving birth in order for a mother to receive her own baby, under the threat of swapping babies among those who do not pay the bribe.[66]

---

[65] See Transparency International (2003).
[66] Ibid.

Political corruption scandals have also reached the highest levels of government in several countries of this region. Prominent examples include the case of Indian Prime Minister Narsimha Rao's conviction and sentencing to 3 years of imprisonment in 2000. In Bangladesh, Hussein Mohammed Ershad, former Prime Minister, was sentenced to 5 years in prison in 2000.[67] Similarly, in Pakistan five successive governments in all have been dismissed over corruption charges since 1970, including former Primer Minister Nawaz Sharif now exiled in Saudi Arabia.[68]

In some of these countries political corruption is often alleged in the electoral processes, which undermines the legitimacy of governments and the overall policy stand and practical enforcement toward corruption. Most recently, in both Bangladesh and Sri Lanka there were accusations of electoral fraud during the 2001 parliamentary elections. Furthermore, the charges of electoral fraud in Sri Lanka led to the assassination of a leading investigative journalist, raising further concern in relation to the role of the independent media serving as watchdogs against political corruption.

The high presence of all types of corruption has led to the creation of national anticorruption or investigative agencies in most countries in South Asia. However, quite symptomatically, these anticorruption bodies are not independent of the administrations. This has generated country scenarios in which corrupt institutions are the ones in charge of anticorruption efforts. The lack of independence of these institutions is such that the Commission for Investigation of Abuse of Authority (CIAA) in Nepal and the Bureau of Anticorruption (BAC) in Bangladesh require approval of the Prime Minister in order to start investigations of corruption cases. In many cases, these anticorruption bodies have become too politicized and rather than performing the appropriate surveillance of incumbent administrations, they have been used as political instruments dedicated to the continuous investigations of previous administrations, usually of opposition political parties. As a result, anticorruption platforms and accusations of corruption against opposition parties have become the common denominator of electoral campaigns in the region, devaluing whatever effectiveness anticorruption campaigns and institutions could have achieved.

Fortunately, there has been increasing awareness and growing concern in the region regarding the use of investigative bureaus and anticorruption campaigns of governing parties as instruments against opposition leaders. Such types of concerns have been raised in relation to the Central Bureau of Investigation (CBI) in India, BAC in Bangladesh, and the National Accountability Bureau in Pakistan. The CBI in India, for example, found

---

[67] Ibid.
[68] See Kronstadt (2003).

Jayaram Jayalalitha guilty of corruption charges and sentenced her to 5 years in prison only immediately after she separated from the governing party (Bharatiya Janata Party). Similarly, new intelligence evidence in Pakistan revealed that former Prime Minister Nawaz Sharif manipulated the trial of former Prime Minister Benazir Bhutto for political reasons. This new evidence led to the dismissal of Bhutto's conviction and a retrial.

The manipulation and control of the BAC by the ruling party, the Awami League (AL), in Bangladesh has raised serious concerns. An example of this type of manipulation is illustrated by the case of former President Ershad from the opposition party Bangladesh National Party (BNP), who was convicted of corruption charges but released after he joined the AL party. Probably not surprisingly, he was convicted again of corruption charges immediately after he decided to return to the opposition BNP. This type of opportunistic use of anticorruption laws at the highest level of government, of course, tends to weaken national morale toward corruption and any ongoing enforcement strategies.

3.1.6. East Asia and Pacific

The East Asia and Pacific region is perceived to have low levels of corruption relative to other regions (Figure 3.1). However, as in other regions, but here perhaps more than elsewhere, there is great diversity in the severity and patterns of corruption within the region. This may be seen by contrasting the exceptionally high CC score of Singapore (2.24) in 2005, or even those for New Zealand (2.24) and Australia (1.95), with the low scores for Myanmar (−1.37), North Korea (−1.32), Tonga (−1.28), and Cambodia (−1.12) (Table 3.6). Furthermore, there are no particular patterns revealing the prevalence of political or administrative corruption in the region (Annex Figs. 3.A.2 and 3.A.8).

While the exceptionally high number of convictions of high level officials is a signal of the commitment to achieve greater political accountability and the fight against corruption, the conviction of political leaders in several consecutive government terms may also be interpreted as an indication of the deep roots of corruption in the region. Singapore, Hong Kong, and Japan are seen as models for the region. These countries have strong anticorruption agencies and the legal and judicial support required to successfully curb corruption.

However, corruption appears to be carved into the cultural and institutional structure of other countries in the region. Part of the problem in these other countries is the absence of an independent judicial system and a free media. Some nations are compelled to compensate for these institutional weaknesses by adopting maximum punishments for corruption charges. For example, in China, where economic transition reform has also opened new opportunities for corruption, the trials of public officials

Table 3.6.   Corruption control: East Asia and Pacific (1998 and 2005)

	1998	Quintile in 1998 (a)	2005	Quintile in 2005 (b)	Quintile change (2005 (b))–(1998 (a))
Kiribati	−0.61	2	0.22	4	2
Vanuatu	−0.36	2	0.26	4	2
Indonesia	−1.03	1	−0.86	2	1
Marshall Islands	−0.61	2	−0.43	3	1
Micronesia	−0.36	2	−0.28	3	1
Samoa	−0.36	2	0.17	3	1
Solomon Islands	−0.61	2	0.02	3	1
Vietnam	−0.67	1	−0.76	2	1
Australia	2.14	5	1.95	5	0
Brunei	0	4	0.25	4	0
Cambodia	−1.34	1	−1.12	1	0
Hong Kong	1.67	5	1.68	5	0
Japan	1.1	5	1.24	5	0
Korea, South	0.04	4	0.47	4	0
Laos	−0.77	1	−1.1	1	0
Malaysia	0.67	4	0.27	4	0
Myanmar	−1.37	1	−1.44	1	0
New Zealand	2.48	5	2.24	5	0
Papua New Guinea	−0.77	1	−1.08	1	0
Singapore	2.43	5	2.24	5	0
Taiwan	0.8	4	0.63	4	0
Thailand	−0.32	3	−0.24	3	0
North Korea	−0.61	2	−1.32	1	−1
Mongolia	−0.34	3	−0.55	2	−1
Philippines	−0.34	3	−0.58	2	−1
Tonga	−0.36	2	−1.28	1	−1
China	−0.2	4	−0.69	2	−2

Note: Computed based on data from Kaufmann *et al.* (2006).

accused of corruption led to several executions in recent years. A few highly publicized executions on corruption charges have also been conducted in Vietnam. However, it is not at all certain that the severity of these punishments will be effective as anticorruption strategy compensating for the lack of independent institutions (the judiciary and the media).

The recent experiences in Thailand, Malaysia, Philippines, and Indonesia reveal the importance of a comprehensive anticorruption strategy. These experiences demonstrate the value of the appropriate functioning of three components in the fight against corruption: adequate legislation, active watchdog agencies, and an independent judiciary system. Only when all of these factors are in place, can the fight against corruption become effective. Malaysia and the Philippines are examples of countries with strong watchdog agencies, as indicated by the high number of corruption cases reported by these agencies. However, the relative efficiency of these agencies is neutralized by a non-independent judiciary system, which at least in these countries, leads to lower criminal prosecution rates.[69] Likewise, a broad range of reform efforts in the judiciary and in the legal framework for anticorruption have been taken in Indonesia since 2000, including the creation of new anticorruption institutions.[70] While some institutions such as the Supreme Audit Commission, the Financial Transactions and Analysis Centre, and the Attorney General's Office have begun to deliver tangible results, these reforms appear not to have been strong enough to reduce endemic levels of corruption in the judiciary system, other levels of government, and among some State-Owned Enterprises (World Bank, 2001c, 2006).[71]

The impact of the lack of independence of the judiciary can be compounded by the existence of corruption among its ranks. For example, survey data in Philippines and Thailand reveal the commonly held perceptions that court decisions can be settled by bribing judges. In Thailand as many as 30 percent of the respondents involved in court cases were actually asked for a bribe during this process.[72] Low rates of conviction in Philippines and Indonesia are, in addition, a result of closed bureaucratic systems imposed by the current legislation. The legislation framework in some of these countries places very high standards of proof for the prosecution, which may result in impassible hurdles for anticorruption efforts, given that most corrupt acts are hardly documented. In the Philippines this type of legislation has been coupled with legislation that protects the secrecy of bank transactions, making prosecutions for corruption cases nearly impossible. A diametrically opposed approach is presented in Singapore and Hong Kong, where only intent of corruption (requesting or accepting a promise of illegal gratification) is enough to ensure conviction.[73] These different legal approaches have been considered by some observers to be important factors in the success of Singapore and Hong Kong in curbing corruption.

Despite the lower scores of political corruption in the overall rankings worldwide, the East Asia-Pacific region has not been free of political corruption scandals. For example, in 2001 Japan's Minister of Economic and Fiscal Policy and Minister of Labor were forced to resign after allegations

---

[69] See Transparency International (2001).

[70] New anticorruption Institutions in Indonesia include the Anticorruption Commission (KPK), Anticorruption Court, The Interagency Task Force (TimTasTipikor), the Hunting Team (Tim Pemburuan), the Judicial Commission, the Police Commission, and the Prosecutorial Commission.

[71] Cases of petty corruption, such as bribes and illegal payments requested from truck drivers for the use of the road system, were reported as having a substantial negative impact the Tsunami reconstruction in province of Aceh.

[72] See Phongpaichit *et al.* (2000) and Warsta (2004).

[73] See Singapore's Prevention of Corruption Act (article 241), Ofosu-Amaah *et al.* (1999), and Transparency International (2003).

of bribery. In Indonesia there were recently investigations for corruption by President Abdurahman Wahid, widespread allegations of corruption against former President Suharto, and the conviction of Suharto's son for the murder of a judge that had previously found him guilty of corruption. On the other hand, in February 2004 the Supreme Court of Indonesia unexpectedly overturned the corruption conviction of a high ranked politician, who had been previously found guilty of embezzling US \$4.8 million in public funds. Similarly, in recent years there were allegations of corruption against Thailand's Prime Minister Thaksin Shinawatra and the Philippines' former President Joseph Estrada. The deeply rooted culture of high-level corruption in the region is illustrated by the case of South Korea where the indictment of two sons of President Kim Dae Jung for corruption charges, led to his resignation in May 2002. Former South Korean President General Roh Tae-Woo was also convicted after evidence of receiving US \$650 million from top business groups to be administered through a secret fund. In addition, the courts had found illicit funding of the electoral campaign of former President KimYoung-Sam during the 1992 presidential run.[74] Political corruption has also hit democratic processes in the region, as in the case of electoral fraud problems in Thailand, Philippines, and Cambodia.

Corruption in service delivery appears to be widespread in several East Asian and Pacific countries. Public servants in some countries seem to seize opportunities for extortion and bribery in almost every function of public services. In Indonesia, for instance, it has been reported that school teachers ask parents for bribes in order to get school report cards for their children.[75] In our own fieldwork in Indonesia, we were confronted with widespread allegations that high-level administrative posts were bought through bribes at high prices.

In all, the anticorruption performance of the East Asia and Pacific region is one of extremes, with very lows levels of all types of corruption in countries like Singapore, New Zealand, and Australia and high levels and entrenched corruption in countries like Indonesia, Thailand, Philippines, South Korea, and Cambodia.

3.1.7. Middle East and North Africa

The Middle East and North Africa region is characterized by the prevalence of administrative corruption (Annex Figs. 3.A.2 and 3.A.9). Networks exist

---

[74] Allegedly, political corruption in South Korea has also been characterized by a strong circle of influences by which powerful economic elites and corporate groups have captured the state. Family-owned industrial conglomerates and regional clans have often been linked to illegal activities. In some views, corporate bribing of government officials has been practically institutionalized as a way to conduct business. See, for example, Blechinger (2000).

[75] See Transparency International (2003).

Table 3.7.   Corruption control: Middle East and North Africa (1998 and 2005)

	1998	Quintile in 1998 (a)	2005	Quintile in 2005 (b)	Quintile change (2005 (b))–(1998 (a))
Algeria	−0.77	1	−0.43	2	1
Jordan	0.15	3	0.33	4	1
Lebanon	−0.39	2	−0.39	3	1
Malta	0.6	4	1.04	5	1
United Arab Emirates	0.72	4	1.13	5	1
Bahrain	0.34	4	0.64	4	0
Djibouti	−0.86	1	−0.64	1	0
Iran	−0.7	2	−0.47	2	0
Iraq	−1.43	1	−1.27	1	0
Kuwait	1.01	5	0.84	5	0
Libya	−0.97	1	−0.89	1	0
Morocco	−0.11	3	−0.09	3	0
Qatar	0.75	5	0.82	5	0
Syria	−0.64	2	−0.59	2	0
Tunisia	0.15	3	0.13	3	0
Egypt	−0.23	3	−0.42	2	−1
Israel	1.34	5	0.76	4	−1
Oman	0.83	5	0.69	4	−1
Saudi Arabia	0.28	4	0.23	3	−1
Yemen	−0.64	2	−0.63	1	−1

Note: Computed based on data from Kaufmann *et al.* (2006).

between entrepreneurs and government officials, and bureaucracies where personals connections and bribery are widespread, which leads to relatively high levels of corruption (Table 3.7).

Another significant feature of the region is "captured" judicial systems. The lack of independence and, in fact, the infiltration of corruption in the judicial systems is revealed by the number of high-ranked officials who have been brought to trail on conspicuous corruption charges and who have been subsequently released for trumped-up reasons. This was the case, for example, of the release on bail and order for retrial in 2000, of four members of the Egyptian parliament who had been sentenced previously to 15 years in prison.[76] Another example is the case of the unexpected release by an Appeals Court in Jordan of former consul Tawfiq Abu Khajil, who had been prosecuted on 86 charges including corruption and fraud.[77]

[76] See Transparency International (2001).
[77] See National Integrity Systems (2001).

The score on political corruption is mixed. On the one hand, in some countries in the region there appears to be a commitment to fight political corruption. For example, former Israeli Prime Minister Benjamin Netanyahu was tried for corruption charges including fraud, bribery, and obstruction of justice, although the case was later dismissed for lack of evidence. In Syria, corruption investigations during 2001 revealed the embezzlement of US $52 million from public funds since the beginning of year 2000, leading to the indictment of several high ranking officials including former prime mister Mahmoud el-Zoubi, who later committed suicide. On the other hand, there appear to have been cases of unpunished political corruption in countries such as Egypt, Morocco, and Tunisia. These countries were engaged in economic reforms and liberalization programs in the late 1980s, including significant privatization of state assets. These privatization processes allegedly benefited elite groups by selling public assets at prices below their market value.[78] Of course, much higher levels of political corruption, but with little transparency, have existed in Libya and the Iraq of Saddam Hussein.

A final feature of the region is that many countries have experienced attacks on local academics, media, and citizens who have tried to denounce and fight corruption. This reveals the absence of security guarantees for whistle-blowers, witnesses, or media in these countries. In Morocco, for example, Captain Mustapha Adib was sentenced to 5 years in prison by a military court after denouncing corruption in the army in 1999. A similar fate met publishing manager of Algeria's *Al Rai*, Ahmed Benaoum, who landed in prison for 2 months after publishing an article implicating a senator in a corruption case in 2001. Similarly, the owner and editor of the daily *Al Shoumou* in Yemen spent 6 months in prison for charges of defamation after the publication of corruption allegations against a government minister. In Algeria, civil demonstrators against corrupt authorities were fired on by security forces on several occasions in 2001, and many restrictions to freedom of expression, human rights violations, and electoral fraud were alleged in the country.[79] Similar obstacles to press freedom continue in Iran and Syria.

3.1.8. North America

Corruption issues in the United States and Canada tend to have similar characteristics and show considerably lower scores relative to other regions in the world (Figure 3.1). Nevertheless these two countries have experienced some cases of alleged political corruption related to corporate governance (e.g., the recent Enron bankruptcy scandal). The prevalence of

---

[78] See Dillman (2001) as cited in Transparency International (2003).
[79] See Yacoubian (2001).

Table 3.8.   *Corruption control: North America (1998 and 2005)*

	1998	2005	Change
Canada	2.44	1.92	−0.52
United States	1.89	1.56	−0.33

Note: Computed based on data from Kaufmann *et al.* (2006).

some forms of political corruption in North America is also supported by survey data (Annex Figs. 3.A.2 and 3.A.10). Some cases of administrative corruption can be found in the United States in the procurement and tendering processes. Petty corruption, such as bribery in the delivery of services is much less common in the two countries, though some concerns have been raised recently regarding corruption in public school management in the United States (Segal, 2004).[80] Overall, corruption in North America tends to be low (Table 3.8)

3.2. Concluding remarks

This chapter studies corruption from a regional perspective. We find that not only are some regions more severely affected by corruption than others, but also that corruption takes quite different forms across regions of the world. While administrative corruption is more prevalent in some regions, in others, this type of corruption seems to be controlled relative to certain forms of political corruption. This is an indication of the importance of assessing the nature of corruption before designing anticorruption policies so that policymakers will be able to prioritize objectives and use available resources more efficiently. To some extent, understanding the differences in the natures and "structures" of corruption across regions and countries can help explain the puzzle of why we observe the failure of some responses in some places, which have proven quite successful under other circumstances. Naturally, other explanations exist for the ineffectiveness of certain anticorruption responses in some countries. For example, it is more common than most policymakers would like to admit that the very institutions in charge of fighting corruption have themselves been "captured" and behave in corrupt ways. In some other cases, anticorruption efforts cannot be sustained due to the insufficient resources or the lack of political will required to guarantee their effectiveness. All these considerations again point to the importance of conducting careful country case studies in order to understand the nature of corruption and to design effective anticorruption strategies.

---

[80] See Glaeser and Goldin (2006) for a review of the trends in corruption levels in the US during the period 1870–1920.

Figure 3.A.1.   **Scatter plot political vs. administrative corruption around the world**

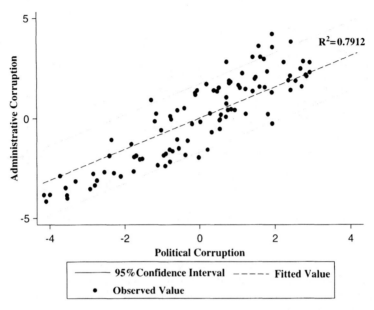

Note: Computed based on survey data from Global Competitiveness Report (2003–2004).

Annex 3.A. A quantitative analysis of patterns for administrative and political corruption

This annex provides a preliminary quantitative analysis of regional patterns of corruption. Four survey questions from the Global Competitiveness Report (2003–2004) are relevant for political corruption, while five others better characterize administrative corruption.[81] Two composite measures of corruption, administrative and political corruption are constructed from these data (see details in Annex 4.B). The scatterplot of the composites for administrative corruption versus political corruption for the entire sample of available countries shows a positive correlation between these forms of corruption (Figure 3.A.1). Thus, in general, those countries that have higher levels of one form of corruption also have higher

---

[81] We should note that the use of a unique source of data for the derivation of these indicators imposes significant limitations, such as potential institutional biases of different sorts. Because of this caveat, our results should only be considered as suggestive. Improving this procedure would require pooling data from different sources (poll of pools) in the calculation of the indexes. Yet, as discussed in Chapter 2 pooling various sources of data together has its own drawbacks and limitations.

**Figure   3.A.2.   Average   administrative   and   political   corruption   by
geographic region**

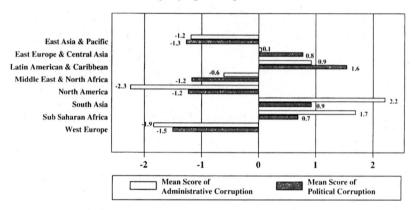

Note: Computed based on survey data from Global Competitiveness Report (2003–2004).

levels of the other. A study conducted by the World Bank (2000a) for
transitional countries equally supports the existence of this relationship
based on data from BEEPS. For the whole sample of countries, these
indicators do not reveal patterns indicating a tendency toward political or
administrative corruption.

However, some patterns arise when we aggregate countries by geographic regions (see Figure 3.A.2). An average of the political and administrative indicators by region reveals the existence of regional
tendencies toward specific forms of corruption. This can be seen by the
differences between the average values of administrative and political indicators within each region. Figure 3.A.2 shows, on the one hand, the
prevalence of political corruption in West Europe, East Europe and Central Asia, Latin America and Caribbean, and North America, and on the
other hand, a prevalence of administrative corruption in East Asia and
Pacific, Middle East and North Africa, South Asia, and the sub-Saharan
countries.

Figures 3.A.3–3.A.10 present country-specific indicators of political
and administrative corruption gathered by geographical region. These indicators are useful to depict a broad picture of the severity of these forms
of corruption in each of the countries available.

Figure 3.A.3. Administrative and political corruption: sub-Saharan Africa

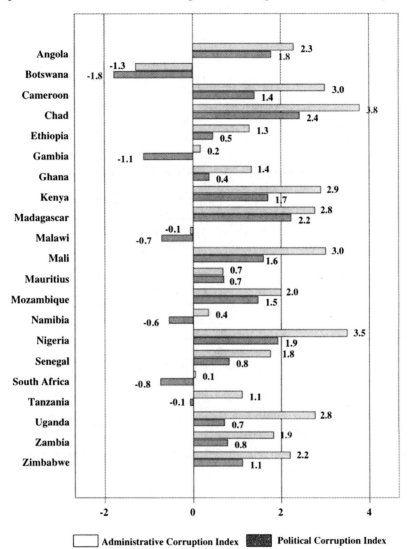

Administrative Corruption Index   Political Corruption Index

Note: Computed based on survey data from Global Competitiveness Report (2003–2004).

Figure 3.A.4.   Political and administrative corruption: Latin America and Caribbean

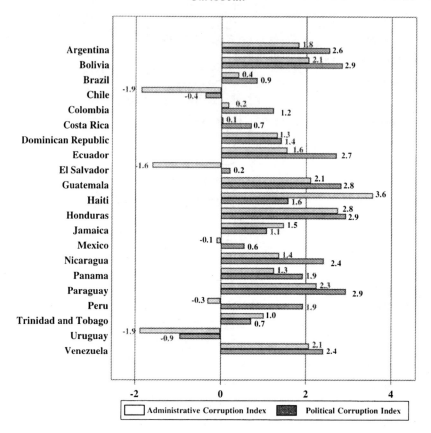

Note: Computed based on survey data from Global Competitiveness Report (2003–2004).

Figure 3.A.5. Political and administrative corruption: West Europe

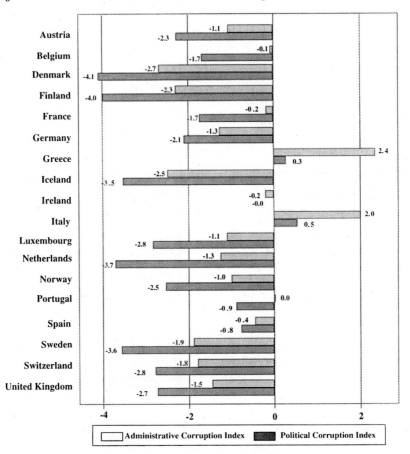

Note: Computed based on survey data from Global Competitiveness Report (2003–2004).

Figure 3.A.6.   *Political and administrative corruption: East Europe and Central Asia*

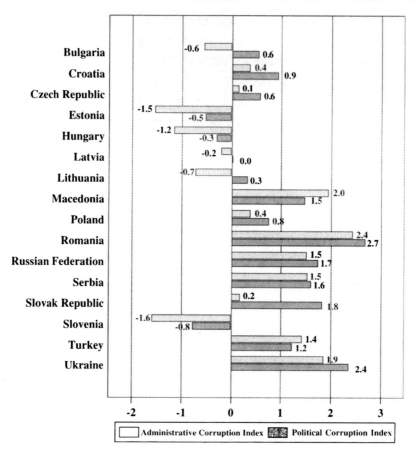

Note: Computed based on survey data from Global Competitiveness Report (2003–2004).

Figure 3.A.7. *Political and administrative corruption: South Asia*

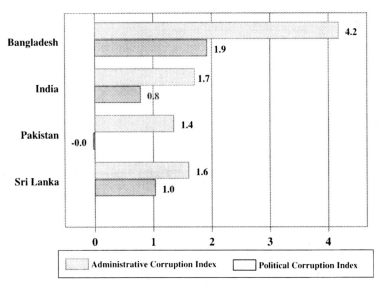

Note: Computed based on survey data from Global Competitiveness Report (2003–2004).

Figure 3.A.8. *Political and administrative corruption: East Asia and Pacific*

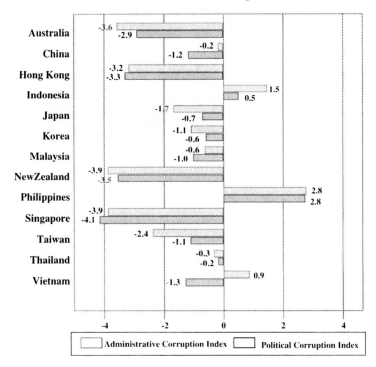

Note: Computed based on survey data from Global Competitiveness Report (2003–2004).

Figure 3.A.9. Political and administrative corruption: Middle East and North Africa

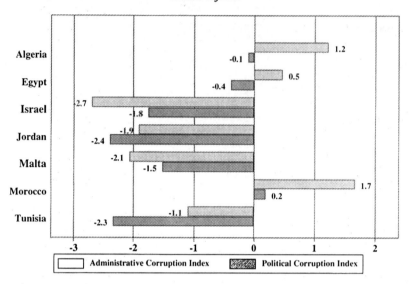

Note: Computed based on survey data from Global Competitiveness Report (2003–2004).

Figure 3.A.10. Political and administrative corruption: North America

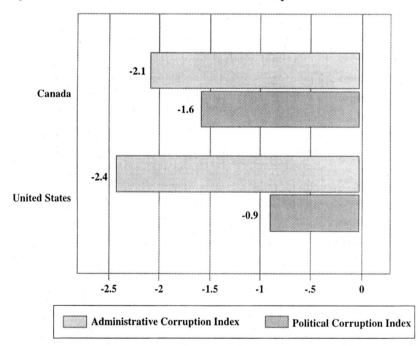

Note: Computed based on survey data from Global Competitiveness Report (2003–2004).

CHAPTER 4

Fiscal Dimensions of Corruption

The introductory discussions of fiscal corruption in Chapters 1–3 of this book leave us with several fundamental thoughts about corruption. First, corruption is widespread. Although corruption is notoriously hard to measure in a precise way, as Chapter 1 indicates, corruption is widely prevalent not only in developing and transition economies but also in developed countries, as shown in Chapter 3. Nevertheless, corruption tends to be more of a poor country disease. Second, corrupt behavior is likely to be rational and self-interested. In Chapter 2 we considered how economic theory can explain the corrupt behavior of government officials as the result of a rational economic calculus. This means that an effective fight against corruption needs to go beyond political speeches and calls for more ethical behavior; rather, anticorruption strategies should focus on the economic incentives and opportunities that induce government officials to engage in this type of behavior.

However, we know that not only the level of corruption varies across countries, but also that the types of corruption activities vary from country to country. When corruption is considered in the context of fiscal policy and fiscal administration, corruption can take three different forms:

- First, corruption can take place on the revenue side of the budget as public resources are collected.
- Second, corruption can occur on the expenditure side of the budget as these resources are spent in the delivery of services and the building of infrastructure.
- Third, corruption can occur outside the budget in quasi-fiscal transactions, such as the imposition of economic regulations or the financial operations of parastatal enterprises.

In order to combat corrupt practices in each of these three areas, it is fundamental that we understand the basic nature of the corrupt practices that public officials engage in, as well as the motivations (incentives) and risks faced by the corrupt officials. An effective anticorruption strategy should also consider the detrimental impact of different types of corruption on the economy. Although the potential for corruption is inherent to any country, we should realize that the types and extent of fiscal corruption are heavily influenced by the overall fiscal structure of a country, as well as by the fiscal management systems that the country uses. For instance, a poorly formulated tax system with lots of complexity, such as large variations in multiple tax rates, may make taxpayers more prone to try to bribe tax collectors. Similarly, poor expenditure management controls and oversight may lower the risk for government officials of getting caught, and thereby stimulate corrupt practices.

This chapter aims to provide an overview of the real-world types and modalities of corruption that are observed in fiscal systems, and the fiscal policy factors or fiscal management practices that may stimulate or aggravate them. For this purpose, this chapter is broken into three subsections, each providing an overview of corrupt practices in the three different segments of the public sector (revenues, expenditures, and quasi-fiscal activities). The next chapter, (Chapter 5) follows essentially the same structure, but seeks to come up with policy responses to each of the different dimensions of corruption, which could be pursued by governments and perhaps supported by international donor agencies.

4.1. Corruption in public revenue collections

Among the many effects of corruption on the economic conditions of a country, one theme that consistently receives significant attention from policy analysts and researchers is the relationship between corruption and public revenues. The relationship between these two variables can be quite complex.

Public revenues and corruption. As a starting point to analyzing this relationship, Figure 4.1 plots corruption against tax revenues (specified as a percent of Gross Domestic Product (GDP)) across countries. The figure shows a negative relationship between these two variables. This negative relationship is quantified by the negative correlation coefficient between corruption and tax revenues as a percent of GDP: the correlation coefficients are $r = -0.51$ for FY 1998 ($n = 61$) and $r = -0.35$ ($n = 40$) for FY 2001. The negative relation between corruption and the tax ratio is obtained without controlling for a host of exogenous factors, which can also affect the administration efforts to collect revenues. These factors include changes in tax rates and bases, external trade liberalization, efficacy of the judicial system, and so on. Yet, the existence of a basic negative relation between corruption and revenue collections is also supported by the findings in several cross-country and case studies of transitional and developing countries, which were able to control to different extents for the effects of some of those exogenous factors (World Bank, 2000a).

What may explain the basic negative relationship between corruption and revenue collections? A first possible explanation for the inverse relationship is direct causality: if tax collectors or tax administration officials engage in corrupt practices (either by directly stealing from the treasury, or by allowing taxpayers to evade taxes in return for a bribe), then corruption on the revenue side will result in direct decreases in overall revenue

Figure 4.1. Relationship between tax revenue collection and corruption level

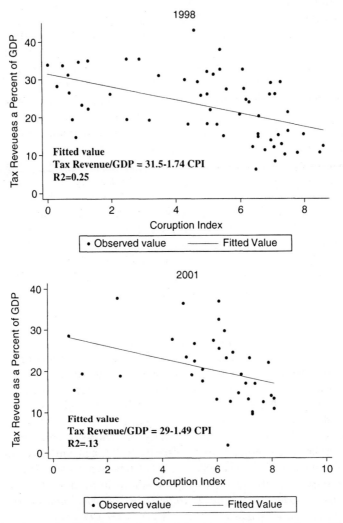

Notes: TI's Corruption Perception Index is redefined to measure corruption as (10-CPI); a value of 0 represents not corrupt whereas a value of 10 indicates a highly corrupt country. Source: Computed by the authors based on Transparency International (1997, 2001) and tax revenue data from World Bank (2003b).

collections. Clearly, in the case when tax officials directly steal public funds (for instance, by failing to deposit taxes paid by a taxpayer in the government accounts), there is a one-to-one relationship in the amount of corruption and the loss in revenue collections to the public sector. In those cases where tax officials facilitate or condone tax evasion there is no direct appropriation of funds but the immediate impact on overall collections is clear and direct.

A second possible explanation for the inverse relationship between corruption and collections is that corruption may work indirectly to reduce the tax bases or even the overall level of economic activity (as discussed in Section 4.2.2.5) with the end result of reduced revenue collections. Box 4.1 explores some of the possible indirect links between corruption and government revenue collections. However, the remaining discussion in this section largely focuses on the direct effects of corruption on government revenue collection since its causes are directly observable and therefore may be directly addressed from a policy point of view.

Even though the inverse relationship between collection and revenues is intuitive and appealing we must be aware that a negative correlation coefficient does not necessarily imply a causal relationship between the two variables. It could, for instance, be the case that both corruption and low revenue collections could be caused by an external common factor, such as low levels of development and high levels of poverty. What this simultaneity of effects would mean is that one could not simply increase revenues by reducing corruption or that the latter may not be possible without addressing more fundamental problems.[82]

In practical terms, corruption in the collection of public revenues can manifest itself in a number of ways.[83] In its most elementary form, a corrupt act can be perpetrated by a single individual: unilateral corruption typically involves theft of revenue collections by a single tax collector, often even before the money reaches the treasury. On the other hand, multiparty corruption usually involves forms of coalitions, either between several tax administration officials or between tax collectors and taxpayers. Tanzi (1998a) discusses several forms of corruption in tax and customs administrations which can arise from a variety of processes, some of them including policy decisions such as the provision of tax incentives or the use of foreign trade taxes. Tanzi (1998a, p. 114) also presents a very useful catalog of multiparty corruption forms in tax administration: "*(1) provision of certificates of exemption from tax to persons who would not otherwise qualify; (2) deletion or removal of a tax payer's records from the tax administration's registration, filling and accounting systems; (3) provision of confidential tax return information to a taxpayer's business competitors; (4) creation of multiple false taxpayers identifications to facilitate tax fraud; (5)*

---

[82] See Bird *et al.* (2004) for a discussion of the economic, institutional, and political factors that may be behind the relative level of revenue effort exercised across countries.

[83] We make a clear distinction between corruption and tax evasion. Although tax evasion can include a bribe to tax officials, tax evasion in itself is an act of private sector agents, which does not have to involve complicit public sector officials. For a review of tax evasion issues see Alm (1998) and Andreoni *et al.* (1998).

Box 4.1. Indirect effects of corruption on revenue collections

Several indirect effects of corruption on revenue collections are easily identifiable. First, corruption decreases the tax base by reducing the size of the formal sector, something that is widely observed in transition and developing countries (World Bank, 1997; Giles and Caragata, 1999; Johnson *et al.*, 2000; Friedman *et al.*, 2000; Schneider, 2003). Of course, the larger the shadow economy the smaller the tax base (formal sector), and, thus, the lower the revenue collection. The existence of a positive relationship between corruption and the size of the shadow economy is supported by data from 89 developing and industrialized countries; the value of the correlation coefficient between the size of the underground economy (Schneider, 2003) and corruption (Transparency International, 2003) for FY 2001 is $r = 0.70$.

Second, by reducing the amount of resources used to finance public spending, corruption, in effect, hinders social expenditures on education and health and possibly on investment in infrastructure, which leads eventually to lower rates of economic growth. Third, corruption may also reduce the amount of revenues formally reported through the budgetary system, while increasing the share of the real total revenues actually collected that are funneled through extra-budgetary accounts. These funds are usually spent less efficiently on non-priority items and they can also be more easily embezzled.

Furthermore, corruption can reduce the level of formal private sector activity through several mechanisms: (i) corruption increases the cost of doing business and general transaction costs, similar to a tax, and therefore it reduces employment and output; (ii) corruption leads to the under provision of public infrastructure, hence decreasing the return to investment; (iii) corruption lowers productivity as firms compete in terms of bribes rather than in quality of their product; (iv) companies that are successful in smuggling profitable activities into the informal sector do not pay taxes on those activities. As a result, firms in the shadow economy have a comparative cost advantage over the firms remaining in the formal economy, some of which are forced to leave the formal market economy (Giles and Caragata, 1999; Johnson *et al.*, 2000).

---

write-off of a tax debt without justifications; (6) closure of a tax audit without any adjustment being made or penalties being imposed for an evaded liability; (7) and manipulation of audit selection."

The key question for policy makers is which factors determine the existence or the degree of severity of these forms of corruption? Regardless of whether revenue loss is caused by unilateral or multiparty corruption, the occurrence and the extent of corruption are determined by two broad categories of factors, notably *motivating factors (or incentives)* and *windows of opportunity*. First, we will discuss motivations for corruption: what influences the decision by a public official to engage in corruption once an opportunity arises? Second, given the propensity of tax officials to be more or less corrupt, what contextual factors influence the degree to which windows of opportunities for corruption exist?

4.1.1. Revenue collections and corruption: motivations for corruption

As discussed in greater detail in Chapter 2, the most basic motivation for government officials to engage in corruption is often personal financial gain. However, one should consider that the decision by individual tax officials whether or not to engage in corrupt practices is influenced by a number of (fiscal as well as non-fiscal) motivating factors, including:

(i) Lack of moral and ethical behavior by tax officials.
(ii) Low probabilities of detection.
(iii) Weak penalization and prosecution.
(iv) Inadequate wages and incentive-compatible compensation.
(v) The size of the window of opportunity (for instance, through pressure from taxpayers seeking to evade taxes).

4.1.1.1. Moral and ethical persuasion. Increasing moral and ethical standards among tax officials is the first line of defense against corruption. If tax officials – as a matter of cultural, religious, professional, or personal conviction – are strongly committed to the difference between "mine" and "thine", then they will be less likely to engage in corrupt practices. Corruption is likely to flourish when standards of moral and ethical behavior, regarding issues such as conflict of interests or acceptance of gifts, are not made specific to civil servants. Moral and ethical orientation of tax officials is also determined by a number of factors, including education, religious beliefs (Paldam, 2001), and even gender (Swamy *et al.*, 2001; Gokcekus and Mookherjee, 2002).

The overall degree of corruption in society is also likely to affect public moral values through a contagion effect, or due to negative externalities within government structures (Caselli and Morelli, 2004).[84] Similarly, some

---

[84] Caselli and Morelli (2004) go further to observe that the negative externalities of incumbent corrupt governments not only affect current administrations, but also act as a bad seed for corruption in future administrations.

studies argue that cultural practices might have an impact on the overall ethics and morals of society (see Box 4.2). It has been hypothesized that own values of citizens and public officials depend to a considerable extent on their views and trust in others (Andvig and Moene, 1990; Chand and Moene, 1997). Thus, fostering trust in the legitimacy of the government, and trust in fellow tax officers is important to curb corruption. In addition, it appears that corruption in governmental higher levels has a contagion effect on lower levels. High levels of corruption may affect otherwise honest officials by simply making it pointless to behave in the legitimate way (World Bank, 1997).

4.1.1.2. Probabilities of detection. Once an opportunity for corruption arises, and the tax official lacks the moral fortitude to resist the opportunity, a second motivating factor in the decision to engage in corrupt behavior is the probability of detection. Although internal audits of tax collection records may reveal certain instances of corruption, in other cases, official records are modified by tax officials (possibly in collusion with evasive taxpayers) in order to avoid detection. In these cases internal tax auditing alone would fail to detect both evasion and corruption. Hence, the probability of detecting corrupt activities in the realm of revenue collections is determined by the ability that senior-level tax administrators to oversee tax collectors, for instance through direct monitoring and internal and external audits (Acconcia *et al.*, 2003).

There is little empirical evidence on the (otherwise intuitive) relationship between lower probabilities of detection and corruption. One of the available studies, by Goel and Rich (1989), finds that higher probabilities of detection are negatively correlated with corruption cases (number of convictions in bribery charges) in the United States. But if we extrapolate from the evidence available in the field of tax evasion, the probability of detection is very likely to be a deterrent for engaging in corruption. In the case of tax evasion, there is ample statistical, experimental, and survey evidence that taxpayers are significantly less likely to evade taxes if they perceive that the probability of getting caught is significantly increased (Alm, 1998; Andreoni *et al.*, 1998).

A different but related issue is how to increase the perceived probability or, in fact, the actual probability of detection of revenue corruption. Again, strategies to combat tax evasion can provide valuable lessons for successful programs aimed at detecting corruption. Tax administration authorities may be motivated to improve monitoring and tax auditing procedures if the agency and/or the tax inspectors themselves are rewarded in proportion to the additional tax revenues collected from fines and penalties. These are programs that are not free of controversy, since they may lead to abuses from "too eager" tax officials. Thus, the possibility of directly compensating internal auditors and other monitoring officials for the detection of internal corrupt practices needs to be carefully weighed, and

Box 4.2. The impact of culture on corrupt practices

Curbing corruption is made more difficult if corruption is perceived by corrupt agents as acceptable and even expected by ties within large families. It is argued, for example, that gift giving in African nations is a cultural practice and a reflection of good manners (de Sardan, 1999). However, the gift-giving argument may over-justify its cultural incidence on corruption as significant differences between bribes and culturally accepted presents might make bribers aware of their wrongdoing. As Alatas (1986) points out, cultural gift giving does not need to be practiced in secret. In other cases, corruption by bureaucrats is not necessarily a function of financial self-enrichment, but it is driven by the cultural need to help its direct community circle. In a study of Revenue Authorities of Tanzania and Uganda, Fjeldstad *et al.* (2003), posit two alternative cultural catalysts of corruption namely *solidarity networks* and *redistributive accumulation*. The former entails "obligations of mutual assistance" among members of the family group, ethnic groups, and friends, while the latter represents an obligation to share wealth with others.

Carney (1998) calls for caution not to confuse genuine cultural practices with a high tolerance for corruption in societies where its widespread practice is justified. While the distinction may seem semantic it serves to stress the point that this, so-called, cultural motivation for corruption does not result from cultural identity, but rather from socially justified bad habits, that can and should be modified. Widespread corrupt practices are often so socially accepted that culprits feel little shame if exposed or fired for corruption acts. There is also some theoretical research on the relation between culture and corruption. Hauk and Sáez-Mart (2002) develop a model on the cultural transmission of corruption, which stresses the value of educating the young to prevent corruption, instead of relying on fines and costly monitoring programs. These authors find their results consistent with the success of campaigns of the Independent Commission Against Corruption in Hong Kong, which aimed to instill ethical values in the society. Empirically, cultural determinants of corruption have been analyzed under the assumption that cultural factors can be reflected by geographic areas or by religion (Treisman, 2000; Paldam, 2001).

perhaps first tried on an experimental basis. However, there are some other means of increasing the probability of detection for corrupt tax officials. These are discussed in more detail in the next section. Suffice it to say here that this can be achieved, among other ways, by increasing the number of supervisory personnel and their training, increasing the quality and frequency of internal audits and probes, and implementing the use of computerized information systems.

4.1.1.3. Weak penalization and prosecution. Penalties, like the probability of detection, are an intrinsic part of the rational decision by tax officials to engage in a corrupt act. Individuals compare the benefits of the illegal behavior (the size of the theft or bribe for the tax successfully evaded) against the costs of possible penalties. The anticipated costs and benefits are weighed against the probabilities of being detected. But unlike the case of increasing the probabilities of detection where substantial resource costs may be involved, the cost to a government of imposing high penalties is small (if any). Thus, at least in appearance, the imposition of high levels of penalties constitutes a cost-effective tool to deter corruption. A priori, it would also seem like penalties should be an effective anticorruption tool. Basic analysis of the costs and benefits that tax officials face when deciding whether or not to engage in corruption suggests that the effect of penalties can be substantial.

It is logical to anticipate that the deterrent effect of the penalty should increase proportionally with its size and nature. However, the role and effectiveness of penalties and sanctions in preventing corrupt behavior, although widely referred to in the literature, have not been systematically researched.[85] While the impact of sanctions in deterring corruption is difficult to identify, anecdotal evidence reveals that the absence of appropriate sanctions can lead to high levels of corruption. For example, Fjeldstad *et al.* (2003) reports that a deep restructuring of the tax revenue authorities in Tanzania and Uganda resulted in a round of dismissals on misconduct charges of 35 percent of staff members in Tanzania and 14 percent in Uganda, respectively. While this can be a result of several factors besides weak sanctioning under the previous administration, the lack of effective monitoring and sanctioning undoubtedly led the number of corrupt officials to grow until reaching such high level.

4.1.1.4. The compensation of tax officials. The importance of ensuring a fair level of wages for public officials has been widely recognized as a

---

[85] Again, there has been more systematic research of the impact of penalties in the related literature in tax evasion. This information is useful because the rational calculus to evade taxes is quite similar to that involving the decision to engage in corrupt practices. Many statistical studies of tax evasion find responsiveness of taxpayers to higher penalty rates (Alm, 1998; Andreoni *et al.* 1998).

requirement to reduce corruption. Klitgaard (1989) notes that many countries suffer from what can be called *"incentive myopia"*, a failure to connect financial rewards and performance to each other, resulting often in a crisis in public sector incentives. High differentials between public and private sector wages lead skilled and qualified labor to abandon the public sector. Where this is true, it is reasonable to expect that the management of the state is in the hands of the least capable staff (those that will not be hired by the private sector). Alternatively, it may be assumed that if skilled labor remains in the public sector it is because they are able to make up the wage differential by resources obtained from illicit means.

Poorly paid tax officials may have a relatively bigger financial incentive to engage in corrupt practices, whether through the unilateral theft of public funds or through multiparty bribes and kickbacks for allowing tax evasion. Wage levels that are inadequate to cover basic needs would motivate tax officials to explore alternative opportunities to "earn" additional income. Tanzi (1998b) finds a negative relationship between corruption and wage levels. According to Tanzi, levels of corruption that correspond to wage levels below the minimum required for the family of a public worker to subsist can be categorized as "corruption due to need" while corruption above that minimum level may be better assumed as "corruption due to greed". Officials may justify corruption in terms of affordability (i.e., arguing that they cannot afford not to accept bribes in order to survive) or in terms of fairness of compensation (arguing that bribes are needed to get even for not getting what they deserve for their work).[86] On the other hand, if official compensation levels were higher, public officials would consider the possibility of losing a job that provides high wages as an "opportunity cost" of engaging in corruption. Therefore, higher official wages could be a motivating factor for tax officials to engage in less corruption.[87] This line of thinking is also dependent on the probability of being detected and fired and also on the possibilities of employment alternatives (i.e., for how long can the individual expect not to be paid until he/she finds a new employment).

The existence of a correlation between payment levels and corruption is supported by only a few empirical studies. Goel and Rich (1989) find a negative correlation between salaries and corruption in the United States using data from the U.S. Department of Justice. Based on a cross-country dataset of developing and lower-income OECD countries, Van Rijckeghem and Weder (2001) also find a negative relationship between civil service

---

[86] The latter justification is in line with the fair wage hypothesis posited by Akerlof and Yellen (1990).
[87] This is in line with the *shirking model* of wages and work performance (Van Rijckeghem and Weder, 2001).

wages and corruption.[88] Experimental evidence also supports the existence of this relation, as reported by Frank and Schulze (1998).

On the other hand, Treisman (2000) fails to find evidence of a relation between wages and corruption, while Giedion *et al.* (2001) and Jaen and Paravisini (2001) find a positive relation between wages and corruption. These authors explain these findings on the grounds of endogeneity due to public officials' wage capture. That is, corrupt agents might have the ability to manipulate their own wage levels.[89] However, this is not necessarily a complete explanation of this riddle and further research will be needed.

At any rate, increasing tax administrators' wages to competitive levels in order to reduce corruption can be seen as a costly response.[90] Several economic studies have pointed out the cost effectiveness of increasing penalties in contrast to increasing wages in order to deter corruption (Becker, 1968; Polinski and Shavel, 1991; Flatters and Macleod, 1995). This is not surprising given that once corruption is detected, increasing the severity of the punishment is frequently less costly.

4.1.1.5. Pressure from tax evaders. The decision of tax officials to engage in multiparty corruption and accept a bribe can to some extent be driven by a desire by some taxpayers to evade their obligation to pay taxes. As such, we should expect a direct relationship between the degree of tax evasion in an economy and the degree of corruption in the collection of public revenues.[91]

Taxpayers may evade taxes by distorting their self-reported tax liabilities or by failing to report their income liability altogether. Yet, as already noted earlier, despite being an illegal form of non-compliance, tax evasion does not directly fit the definition of corruption used in this study – "misuse of public power for private benefit." As a result, issues related uniquely to delinquency by private agents or among private firms, are outside the main scope of this study. However, there are likely strong links between tax evasion and corruption. In particular, there would seem to be a relationship of double causation (endogenous relationship) between tax evasion and corruption. That is, the presence of tax evasion certainly would

---

[88] Fisman and Gatti (2002a) also find evidence of a negative relation between public wages and corruption. They use wage measurements as a control variable in a study of the effects of fiscal decentralization on corruption.

[89] Others, such as Fjeldstad *et al.* (2003, p.69), argue *"since corruption to some extent is more a question of lack of social stigma than low wages, high wages will not in themselves keep people away from corrupt practices."*

[90] This may not be the case in reality at all if the actual increase in tax revenues that could accompany higher wages is taken into account. A different matter is whether it is at all feasible to raise wages for tax officials and not for the other public servants. Chapter 5 discusses several solutions to this dilemma.

[91] See Alm *et al.* (2004) for a similar argument for tax evasion and the underground economy.

generate incentives for corruption as it increases the compensation or bribes taxpayers are willing to provide to potentially corrupt tax officials. At the same time, corruption decreases the effectiveness of penalties and auditing probabilities as tools for evasion deterrence, motivating private agents to evade more. This is because evasive taxpayers believe that, even if discovered, it is possible to avoid penalties or other legal sanctions by bribing tax auditors to overlook tax evasion.[92] The overall reduction in the risk associated with corruption should lead to increases in overall tax evasion. This is an area that still lacks direct empirical evidence.

Several fiscal factors determine the degree of tax evasion in an economy, one of them being the overall level of taxation. High tax burdens, especially when accompanied by public services of poor quality, have long been shown to lead to higher levels of tax evasion. Excessively high tax burdens also are breeding grounds for corruption in the fiscal arena. For example, the anticorruption guidelines for tax reform suggested by the World Bank, emphasize that "tax rates that exceed what taxpayers view as legitimate or what tax offices can administer encourage the informalization of the economy and induce tax evasion and the corruption of tax officials" (World Bank, 1997, p. 37).

Excessive tax rates also have an impact on other manifestations of fiscal corruption. According to Tanzi (1997), the imposition of high rates of excise and import duty on tobacco and alcohol products have frequently initiated or worsened smuggling problems, leading to increased bribery of public officials and the involvement of criminal organizations in smuggling activities.

4.1.2. Revenue collections and corruption: opportunities for corruption

A popular cliche says "I would if I could, but I can't so I won't." The statement helps illustrate the distinction we are making in this section between, on one hand, the factors or incentives motivating corruption and the "windows of opportunity" for corruption, on the other hand. Regardless of whether a tax official is inclined to engage in corruption, he or she will not be able to engage in corrupt practices unless the opportunity to do so materializes. As such, we should expect corruption to grow in proportion to the opportunities offered by the institutional structures in place.

Structural deficiencies in the tax structure and tax administration can create opportunities for systemic corruption. This is true both for cases of

---

[92] An important non-fiscal factor identified as a determinant of taxpayers' motivation to evade taxes is the of risk aversion (Martinez-Vazquez and Rider, 2005). Other non-fiscal factors determining evasion include individuals' wealth (Polinski and Shavel, 1991), and tax morale (Torgler, 2003).

unilateral corruption, as well as for cases of multiparty corruption. While the opportunity for unilateral corruption can generally be reduced by instituting oversight and control mechanisms, multiparty corruption can prove harder to prevent, because in this latter case, other tax official or taxpayers are accomplices in the corruption. Tax evading taxpayers strategize the avoidance of detection by engaging in bribery the tax collectors in charge of revenue collection (or subsequently, tax assessors or tax auditors). Similarly, corrupt importers can utilize the discretionary powers of classification or assessment of customs officials to alter the reported values of imported goods or to reclassify goods under types with lower import rates (Flatters and Macleod, 1995).

Some of the main factors that create "windows of opportunity" for corruption in public revenue administration include:

(i) Absence of basic oversight and control of tax administration.
(ii) Complexity of the tax and custom systems.
(iii) Discretionary power of tax and customs officials.
(iv) Politicization of civil servants.

Again, we explore each of these windows of opportunity in greater detail below.

4.1.2.1. Absence of basic oversight and control on tax administration. There is a need for basic controls to prevent opportunities for unilateral corruption. While pointing out the critical importance of simple and logical procedures for checks and controls may seem trivial, ignoring them would suggest that there is no scope for learning and improvement in the fundamental processes of tax administration. For instance, leaving someone alone in a room with cash, or a cashier window without a paper trail or a control process to follow the paper trail is a recipe for corruption. Most tax administrations around the world have learned effective lessons like this for many years. But in some developing economies, particularly in the collection of local revenues, some of these basic procedures are lacking. Obviously, it is harder to create a paper trail in a cash economy, but it is still possible to separate the assessment of the tax from the actual payment to a cashier.

4.1.2.2. Complexity of the tax and custom systems. Tax systems with unclear and complex tax laws, which are subject to many interpretations, multiple tax rates and exemptions, or tax codes that are subject to continuous changes, are potentially rife with corruption. Complex tax systems tend to increase compliance costs, encourage evasion by taxpayers, and facilitate corrupt practices of tax officials. Complexity of the tax system is usually accompanied by a lack of transparency of the tax administration process.

The unshakable complexity of many tax systems has been explained by some economists as the result of a political process in which politicians need to gain the vote of a variety of groups and interests in society.[93] Other economists have argued that the existence of widespread bureaucratic regulations and complicated tax systems are part of deliberate strategies in order to facilitate corruption in many developing countries (Myrdal, 1968; Flatters and Macleod, 1995; Tanzi and Davoodi, 2000; Fjeldstad and Tungodden, 2002). At the most basic level, simplified tax systems diminish the number of transactions in which public officials are involved, and, as a result, decrease the opportunities for corruption (Huther and Shah, 2003).

4.1.2.3. Discretionary power of revenue officials.   The opportunity for undetected corruption practices increases with the lack of accountability and higher degrees of discretion of public officials. For example, if tax officials are given considerable discretion to set penalty rates, this will clearly open greater opportunities for bribes and corrupt deals. In general, probabilities of undetected corruption increase when the degree of discretion allowed public officials is high. For instance, tax administration systems in which taxpayers are bound to specific tax collectors (or inspectors) are more prone to corruption, because of the "monopoly power" provided to the tax collector and the familiarity created by the continued contact between tax officials and taxpayers. In order for the taxpayer to be deemed compliant with the tax laws, he or she will have to "please" the tax collector.

Often, the discretionary powers of public officials are not legally sanctioned but are more the implicit result of the lack of detailed regulations in tax administration systems. For instance, corruption may arise due to the lack of a regulatory framework for taxpayer audit selection. In other cases, even when regulations are in place, public officials may effectively have discretionary power due to the absence of appropriate monitoring systems of lower levels of the tax administration. Long holdings and encroachment in specific functions of the tax administration may also increase the effective discretionary power of civil servants. The secrecy of illegal actions is better kept when an official does not require cooperation of others.

The absence (or poor quality) of taxpayer services, through which taxpayers are able to gather information, get second opinions on compliance issues and lodge informal complaints, also tend to favor corrupt practices. Similarly, absence of proper appeals procedures can leave taxpayers at the mercy of corrupt tax officials.

4.1.2.4. Politicization of civil servants.   Politically driven personnel changes, especially in tax departments, are not uncommon in developing

---

[93] See, for example, Hettich and Winer (1988, 1999).

countries with weak or absent civil service law. In some cases the turnover rates are so high that institutional stability is jeopardized. For instance, Taliercio (2004) reports that in 1997 a government change in Bolivia led to the replacement of as much as three quarters of their internal revenue agency. A similar case is the high turnover in the Albanian customs administration. After the 2001 elections even the director general position was changed five times during a period of 15 months (Tisne and Smilov, 2004). Where turnover rates are high, public officials often see their temporary positions as opportunities for enrichment. Weak civil service systems tend to provide more opportunities for corrupt behavior. Not surprisingly, it is often the case that public officials that are politically appointed serve the interests of their political masters rather than serving the interests of the community.

Corruption among tax officials and the rest of the civil service arises due to the absence of merit-based recruitment practices, lack of regulated career prospects, and lack of mechanisms that protect civil servants from abuse of authority. Even when some regulations against the abuse of authority are in place, civil servants are often ignorant of their labor rights and duties when exposed to corrupt pressures or bullied by politicians.

4.2. Corruption on the expenditure side of the budget

In the first section of this chapter we presented the motivations and modus operandi of tax and customs official to engage in corruption, and how revenue corruption affects the ability of governments to collect public revenues. This section provides a similar overview how corruption can arise in the process of spending these resources on the expenditure side of the budget.

Compared to the relatively limited number of tax and customs officials in a country, there are many more public officials involved in determining how public resources are spent, as well as in the process of executing these spending decisions. Potentially every public servant with the power to influence public spending or with control over resources has the opportunity to engage in corruption. As such, there are many more possible scenarios of corruption on the expenditure side of the budget than on the revenue side. Although the list below is by no means intended to be complete, let us consider the following examples:

- A government accountant disburses public funds into his own bank account, or for the benefit of a senior public official, instead of for the intended public purpose.
- A headmaster sells school books to students, even though the books are distributed to the school free of charge.
- Government officials in charge of hiring and firing can demand a bribe before hiring someone as a public servant.

- Government officials in charge of hiring and firing can hire a relative (or even a non-existent "ghost worker") and collect the wages for this position.
- A public service provider may simply not show up for work (or purposely provide substandard services) while accepting public salary.
- A public service provider (teacher or doctor) may demand a "copayment" (bribe) before providing good services.
- An agriculture extension officer may be bribed to provide non-qualifying farmers access to subsidized seed and fertilizer, or accept a bribe from seed/fertilizer producers to give preferential treatment to certain brands.
- An influential politician (e.g., a member of parliament or a government minister) may support the funding of a certain project not as a result of the merit of the activity, but rather as a result of a bribe received by potential beneficiaries, or due to the private gain to himself or herself.
- A government official or tender board may select a contractor for an infrastructure project as a result of a bribe.

As in the discussion of corruption on the revenue side of the budget, we think it is helpful to distinguish on the expenditure side of the budget between *motivation* or incentives for corruption and the *windows of opportunity* for corruption. Here we will distinguish between two different types of opportunities to engage in corrupt behavior. In the first, we have opportunities for administrative corruption, which includes direct or indirect embezzlement of funds in the process of budget execution, and so on. In the second set of opportunities, politicians and high-level bureaucrats abuse their political powers over the resource allocation process for personal gain.

4.2.1. *Motivations for corruption on the expenditure side of the budget*

As in the revenue side of the budget, we ought to expect unscrupulous bureaucrats to act rationally in the embezzlement or misuse of funds. Given the opportunity, a government official would be motivated to accept a bribe or engage in theft if he or she "could get away with it" based purely on an economic calculus of potential costs and benefits.

Most of the motivating factors that play a role in the decision of individual government officials on whether or not to engage in corrupt acts on the expenditure side of the government budget are similar to those on the revenue side of the budget (see Section 4.2.1). These include lack of moral and ethical standards, low probabilities of detection, weak penalization and prosecution, or inadequate wages and incentive-compatible compensation. Incentives for corruption in the expenditure side of the budget include the following factors:

(i) Absence of a culture of honesty, ethics, and political will.
(ii) Weak mechanisms for monitoring and expenditure tracking.

(iii) Weak penalization and prosecution.
(iv) Inadequate wages and incentive-compatible compensation.

4.2.1.1. A weak ethics culture and lack of political will. Because of the larger number of public servants involved in the spending of government resources, the impact of motivating factors may be felt differently on the expenditure side of the budget than on the revenue side. While it may be possible to select a relatively limited number of tax officials with good ethical record for the collection and the handling of public funds, it would be much harder to hold every school headmaster, every hospital administrator, and every head of a government expenditure programs in a country to the same high standard. Because there are many more public officials commanding the use of public resources on the expenditure side of the budget it is also more likely that there will be contagion effects, with the notion that it is fine to engage in some types of corrupt practices since "everybody is doing it." Furthermore, corruption on the expenditure side – as we discuss in greater detail below – also more clearly entails issues of political corruption, which involves different determinants from those generally considered on the revenue side of the budget.

Stamping out incentives for corruption has often been interpreted as a matter of political will. The validity of this notion has been questioned in the case of anticorruption policy as it is relatively easy to find examples of countries that have actively pursued corruption controls but have been unable to even reduce it significantly. At the same time, it does seem to follow that while political will is not sufficient to inspire high ethical standards in public service and eliminate corruption, the presence of political will certainly may be a necessary condition.

The truth of the matter is that mustering the political will to fight corruption is not at all a common occurrence, especially among developing and transitional countries. Tanzi (1998b) describes cases in Latin America, Africa, and Asia in which actions of the countries leadership have openly revealed their unwillingness to curtail corruption. For example, Presidents refused to fire ministers widely known as corrupt, redressed corruption charges by changing a minister to head a different ministry, and even attempted to place the allegedly corrupt official as head of an anticorruption commission. There are several factors that inhibit a country's ability to develop the political will to fight corruption. The most important of these is that corruption itself weakens society's institutions and mechanisms that would otherwise help strengthen the development of political will. As such, the political will to keep probity in government is lower where democracy is weak. This is because civil society may be unable to vote out of office their corrupt leaders, while corruption may be also entrenched in the electoral system. Corrupt electoral processes also undermine citizens' perception of government legitimacy and therefore their own attitude toward corruption.

Corruption also leads to political instability, characterized by constant changes of regulations and policies. This type of scenario helps increase the perception that little will be done in revising and following up decisions made shortly before. This scenario is also a breeding ground for corruption. An apt intuition for these processes is that corruption acts like a virus by attacking and weakening the very system needed to exterminate it.

4.2.1.2. Weak mechanisms of monitoring and expenditure tracking. Monitoring and detecting corruption on the expenditure side of the budget can be harder, especially in larger developing countries where public accounting practices are weak and telecommunication and transportation are poor. As far as acts of petty corruption, vertical accountability is substantially weakened when citizens who would like to lodge a complaint against a public servant would have to walk two days to district headquarters to raise the matter with the district supervisor or the local ombudsman.

Detecting grand corruption (corruption at the policymaking level) is clearly more difficult and less common than detecting petty corruption. Given the nature of state capture, the mechanisms for monitoring political corruption should be placed outside the sphere of political influence in order to be effective. As such, the fight against grand corruption should thus rely on institutions such as supreme audit agencies, civil society organizations, and investigative media.

4.2.1.3. Weak penalization and prosecution at high and low levels of government. Given the greater dispersion of responsibilities for spending public resources, it is not only that the probability of detection may be lower for any type of corruption on the expenditure side, but it is also likely that prosecution and penalization are also weaker than on the revenue side of the budget. Cases in which corrupt acts are not penalized even after discovered by control agencies are not uncommon. Adverse Comptroller and Auditor General (CAG) reports about misuse and misappropriation of funds in many countries are habitually overlooked or ignored. Some governments find it difficult to take remedial action as CAG's reports raise transparency questions about most governmental activities. For instance, this was the case in Ecuador, where 95 percent of reports approved by the Comptroller General for FY 2001 showed signs of severe irregularities in the handling of public funds (Global Corruption Report (Transparency International, 2001, p. 171)). Likewise, active watchdog agencies often report cases of corruption, which are never prosecuted or end up dismissed due to inaction or corruption in the judicial system or due to legislation that complicates conviction in corruption cases by imposing extremely high standards of proof on the prosecution.[94] In situations where the rates of

---

[94] Cases of Thailand and Philippines are discussed in Chapter 3.

corruption investigations that result in criminal prosecution are low, the effectiveness of statutory penalties to deter corruption is also greatly undermined.[95] The effectiveness of penalties in deterring corruption among public officials requires strong detection mechanisms, legislation suited for corruption conviction, and an independent and efficient judicial system.

4.2.1.4. Inadequate wages and incentive-compatible compensation. The effects of public sector wages on the motivation of public officials to engage in corruption on the expenditure side of the budget are basically identical to those reviewed above on the revenue side of the budget (Section 4.2.1). However, the number of public servants involved on the expenditure side is considerably larger than the number of employees of tax administrations. Increasing wages to all civil servants is often simply not feasible without a significant rationalization ("down-sizing" or "right-sizing") of the public service. Hence, the impact of low wages on expenditure corruption is an issue of much larger scope and severity. Incentive-compatible compensation schemes also face challenges of a different nature than those on the revenue side. For example, the provision of social services relies on front-line civil servants (e.g., teachers and doctors), whose productivity outcomes are not easy to measure and whose relation to corruption may be quite indirect.

4.2.2. Opportunities for corruption: administrative (bureaucratic) corruption in government expenditures

Perhaps one of the widest opportunities for corruption in the public sector arise in the exercise of administrative functions in the disbursement and allocation of public expenditures. This is known as administrative or bureaucratic corruption. These opportunities for corruption take several forms:

  (i) Inadequate systems of public service spending control.
 (ii) Poorly designed public procurement mechanisms.
(iii) Insufficient Control of Civil Service Structure and Payroll.
 (iv) Weak control of social security resources and government subsidies.
  (v) Limited oversight by parliament and civil society.

4.2.2.1. Inadequate systems of public spending control. Inadequate tracking and accounting of public funds have a substantial potential to affect the availability and quality of public goods and services. Absent

---

[95] Furthermore, corruption weakens the effectiveness of the legal system. Herzfeld and Weiss (2003) present empirical evidence of an interrelationship between legal effectiveness and corruption whereby they reinforce each other.

appropriate financial management mechanisms, public resources can be siphoned off while they are channeled to the front-line service providers responsible for providing government services. In many developing countries, public resources are commonly embezzled or used for private benefit instead of financing the delivery of public services. To cite one well-known example, surveys on a sample of schools in Uganda show that more than 85 percent of non-wage resources assigned for primary school education were embezzled or misused on their route from the Ministry of Finance to school facilities (Ablo and Reinikka, 1999; Reinikka and Svensson, 2004).

Two main factors affect the ability to deviate funds while en route to fund public services:

(a) *Public sector structure and the system of intergovernmental fiscal relations.* Opportunities for corruption commonly arise through inconsistencies in expenditure assignments, lack of coordination among levels of government, and lack of financial monitoring of the system of intergovernmental revenue flows. Fiscal decentralization reforms are generally believed to be effective instruments to increase transparency and accountability when accompanied by an increasing ability of local communities and citizens to monitor local governments. However, it is also widely acknowledged that to accomplish decentralization well, reforms should be applied in a comprehensive manner. Piecemeal reforms are more likely to result in counterproductive outcomes, such as higher levels of corruption. For example, government controls are weakened if devolution reforms are applied to economies in which the legal or monitoring institutions are not yet well-developed. Similarly, the central government monitoring abilities are impaired when financial management systems are not able to integrate local government accounts. Weak financial management of local government accounts constitutes an ideal breeding ground for corruption, especially if accompanied by soft budget constraints and unclear subnational debt regulations.

Well-structured fiscal decentralization may have additional benefits vis-a-vis corruption. It is argued that decentralized systems can reduce corruption through the control of unnecessary spending. This hypothesis is based on the ability of fiscal decentralization to increase government (interjurisdictional) competition (Brennan and Buchanan, 1980).

(b) *Citizens access to public information.* Corruption usually thrives under the cover of secrecy. Public accounts and other official information should be available to individual citizens' scrutiny as a way to guarantee accountability of the government to the people. Making public finance information public has power in itself to deter corruption. If nothing else, the availability and openness of government information can improve society's perception of the government, neutralizing the contagion effects of corruption. To make governments accountable, the financial information available to the public needs to be relevant and contain enough detail so it is useful for monitoring by ordinary citizens. Relevant fiscal information includes:

- the total amount of public funds available,
- the mechanisms of distribution among regions,
- the entities responsible for distributing and routing funds in each tier of government,
- the specific amounts of resources received by local providers of public services, and
- the budgets of these providers.

When this information is made public each agent responsible for the routing of resources and the provision of services is more likely to be accountable to the ordinary citizen.

When spending control mechanisms are absent, public officials may misappropriate funds while accounting them as fictitious items in the budget. Hence the absence of effective expenditure tracking procedures allows corruption levels to grow to enormous proportions in many developing countries.[96] A clear illustration of these proportions is the detection of 20,000 ghost schools in Pakistan (Azfar, 1999).

Overspending on public service inputs is also another common manifestation of corruption in public spending. Public officials may favor the acquisition of inputs from particular sellers, usually at considerably higher prices, in exchange for a bribe. This type of corruption may be seen in the purchase of medical supplies in the health sector and school material contracts. The experience of Argentina illustrates that the monitoring of purchasing procedures can lead to significant reduction in input prices (see Bliss and Di Tella, 1997). Similarly in Colombia *"the overpayments for seven specific medications and supplies were estimated to total more than US $2 million per year – enough to cover medical services for an additional 24,000 people"* (Di Tella and Savedoff, 2001, p. 85). Likewise, in 1999, an investigative journalist in Philippines reported that 20–65 percent of textbook contracts were commonly distributed by publishers as bribes to a long chain of public officials who contributed to secure the award, including supply officers, accounting clerks, and the Director of the Department of Education (Chua, 1999). Azfar (1999) presents many other common types of administrative corruption arising in the provision of health and education services (Table 4.1).

---

[96] However, accountability and expenditure tracking issues are not exclusive to developing countries by any means. For instance, a recent book by Segal (2004), notes several cases regarding lack of accountability and corruption in public schools in the United States.

Table 4.1. The nature of corruption in the health sector and education sector

Health sector

Patient–doctor	Payer–hospital	Hospital–supplier	Within hospital/Ministry
Bribes for treatment	Fraudulent billing for fictional treatment	Kickbacks for purchase orders for drugs, equipment, supplies, meals and cleaning services	Sale of jobs and promotions and transfers
Induced demand for: Unnecessary procedures, e.g., Caesarian deliveries	Patients with coverage get prescriptions for those without	Bribes for approval of drugs	Theft of funds
Diluted vaccines		Doctors bribed by drug companies for prescribing their drugs	Theft of supplies
Absenteeism		Non-profits and other organizations accept donations for recommending drugs	Fraudulent billing for expenses
Negligence		Kickbacks for construction	
Bribes for illegal procedures like abortions			

Education sector

Student–teacher	Payer–school	School–supplier	Within school/ministry
Bribes for admission	Ghost schools for processing vouchers	Kickbacks for purchase orders for textbooks, equipment, supplies, meals and cleaning services	Sale of jobs and promotions and transfers
Bribes for grades and promotions	Inflating number of students to get reimbursements	Bribes for approval of textbooks	Theft of funds
Induced demand for: Private Institutions	Loan officers bribed to give loans to rich students or non-students	Board members bribed by publishing houses for selecting their textbooks	Theft of supplies
Absenteeism	Students who stay in university for decades to collect stipends	Bribes for turning blind eye to photocopying textbooks and violating intellectual property	Fraudulent billing for expenses
Teaching badly		Kickbacks for construction	Under-allocation to education
Sale of exams and bribes for letting professional exam takers take exams for students			

Sources: Extracted from Azfar (1999), p. 9.

4.2.2.2. Poorly designed public procurement mechanisms. While the government has the responsibility to provide public goods and services it may find it beneficial to buy those from the private sector. In particular, the private sector has proven to have a comparative advantage in the provision of capital projects. In addition, the production of recurrent government services can be done by private companies. In some countries, for example, private schools are paid to provide education services (such as in Netherlands and Chile), while private clinics can receive public funds to provide health services (such as in Brazil). The contracting and delegation of production of public goods and services to the private sector has the potential to improve the quality of goods provided and to reduce government administrative costs. This is because competition among firms for awards drives them to improve quality of services and to lower costs.

However, transparent procedures and monitoring are needed at each stage of the tendering process and in the control of quality standards. Poorly designed or implemented procurement procedures can easily lead to corruption and thus undermine the expected benefits of private provision of public goods and services.

The typical entry point for corruption in the tendering process is to nullify or restrict the market competition process and assign contract awards to those firms that are ready to pay the highest bribes (see Box 4.3). Thus bribing companies are not required to offer a higher quality product or do the work at a lower cost in order to be awarded a contract. When corrupt practices are well-established, companies have an incentive, and get away with recovering the amount bribed by either inflating the cost or by reducing quality. Thus, corruption translates into a lower quantity and quality of public services. From the viewpoint of the whole economy, these corrupt practices lead to waste of economic resources as firms compete for corrupt politicians, and spend funds as they partake in rent-seeking behavior. In short, corruption absorbs resources that could otherwise be put to productive uses elsewhere in the economy, contributing to undermine overall economic growth.

Some other types of corruption in the procurement process arise from preferential treatment policies, which are typically the result of the manipulation of the procurement process in more subtle ways than bribery. For example, a common practice across countries is that of limiting the competition in the procurement process to just domestic companies. Regardless of the legality or legitimacy of the arguments leading policymakers to introduce preferential procurement regulations, the resulting framework is likely more suitable for corruption. The exclusion of foreign firms limits the competition to a smaller local group of firms. The local firms have a better chance to collude with local agents responsible of the procurement implementation, which in turn can lead to higher levels of corruption. Ades and Di Tella (1997) present empirical evidence supporting this conjecture based on cross-country survey data from the World Competitiveness Report.

Box 4.3. Corruption in public procurement

Although public procurement processes tend to be quite complex and with significant peculiarities across countries, all public procurement processes consist of three main phases: first, procurement planning and budgeting; second, procurement solicitation; and third, contract award and performance verification.

Corruption can arise in various forms in each of these separate phases of the procurement process. In the planning and budgeting phase, the government entity determines what good or service to buy (the requirement) and how much to spend (the budget). In both of these cases there are opportunities for corruption. In determining the requirements, reports could falsely inflate actual needs in order to create an excess supply that could be used for corrupt purposes. The procurement requirements could also be written to favor or disfavor particular suppliers. Budgets could be set artificially high so that excess allocations can be stolen or diverted. In addition, programmatic budgets could be devised in such a way that there are overlapping budgetary allocations among separate organizations or departments that could likewise be applied in a corrupt manner.

In the procurement solicitation phase, the main tasks are compiling the tender documents and conducting the evaluation. Again, the evaluation criteria in the tender documents could be drafted to favor a particular supplier or service provider or likewise could be drafted to emphasize weaknesses of a particular competitor. Later during the evaluation of the proposals or tenders, the evaluation criteria could be misapplied or otherwise further defined or amended after receipt of the tender. During this phase it is also possible that advance information could be provided to a particular favored supplier. Corruption opportunities also abound at the contract award and performance phase of the procurement process. For example, an offer could propose an unrealistically low cost in the hopes that after the contract is awarded procurement officials will allow amendments to increase costs. Likewise, a firm could offer exceptionally high caliber products or more qualified personnel to meet a particular requirement and then upon contract award substitute inferior products or personnel. Finally, after the evaluation is complete, it is possible to award a contract that materially differs from the terms of the solicitation in terms of specifications, quantity, or delivery schedule.

Source: Matechak (2002).

4.2.2.3. Insufficient control of civil service structure and payroll. As mentioned earlier in this study, politically driven personnel changes have strong effects in the likeliness of patronage and inefficiency in the public sector. The absence of civil service regulations (or their inconsistent application) is also a main source of corruption in public spending. Corrupt government officials may have the opportunity to increase civil service expenditures by enlarging the public sector with political appointees or by placing "ghost workers" on the public sector payrolls.

The problem of ghost workers takes enormous proportions in some African and Latin American countries. In Nigeria, for example, physical count audits of the number of federal public employees verified that the total payroll number contained 40,000 workers less than officially reported. Officials of the Nigerian state of Lagos reported also the discovery of 4,000 non-existent workers in their state official list of public employees (Aluko, 2003a). Another example of corruption in civil service, in this case in Latin America, is presented by Dehn *et al.* (2002, 2003) using the World Bank's Public Expenditure Tracking Survey (PETS). The study aimed to test the hypothesis that, given the current abilities of central government to monitor the payroll in Honduras, it was impossible to detect the existence of ghost workers in education and health sectors. The study found that ghost workers in Honduras represented 8.3 percent of general practitioners and 5.1 percent of staff in the health sector, whereas in the education sector the figures for ghost workers were 5 percent of teachers and 3 percent of education staff. High levels of civil service corruption are usually accompanied by high payroll expenditures and, therefore, a larger size of the public sector.

4.2.2.4. Weak control of social security resources and government subsidies. Pension funds constitute an enormous temptation for corrupt activities, given the large amounts of resources that they represent. The means for corrupt practices in the use of social security resources is in many ways similar to that with civil service corruption. One type of corruption in social security is due to the lack of audits of actual pensioners. In Nigeria pensioner audits discovered as many as 24,000 ghost pensioners (Aluko, 2003b). Similarly, an audit of the Pakistani Railway company found 25,000 ghost pensioners.

Another form of administrative corruption takes form through subsidies granted by governments to certain industrial or agricultural activities. Corruption arises when these subsidies are captured by firms (or even entire industries) for which the subsidies are not designed. The frequency with which subsidies are used and the appearance of corrupt administrations are likely simultaneously reinforcing processes. Mauro (1997) reports a positive correlation across countries between the level of subsidies available to companies and the perceived corruption index in the country.

4.2.2.5. Limited oversight by parliament and civil society. Opportunity for corrupt practices diminishes with greater oversight and auditing practices by parliament, greater involvement by civil society organizations, and interest by the media in fiscal and budgetary practices. One of the most important roles for parliament is to control the discretionary power of executive authorities, denounce abuses to the courts, and audit all public accounts for fraud. Where legislative oversight of the executive is strong, especially with democratic participation of the political opposition, there is less room for corrupt practices.

Civil society participation in public affairs not only improves governance but also increases the willingness of those communities to comply with rules. Similarly, mass media has the ability to engage in awareness campaigns that inform citizens how to fight and denounce corruption and bribery, and make populations aware of the costs of corruption to society. Moreover, media can expose individual complaints and press higher levels of government for responses to corruption in lower levels. Corruption is more likely to succeed in societies where civil society and mass media scrutiny is absent.[97]

4.2.3. Opportunities for corruption: political "capture" of government expenditures

Political corruption arises when politicians or senior-level bureaucrats are able to capture the state apparatus for their own private benefit or for the benefit of those close to them. Political corruption does not regularly involve the direct execution of openly illegal or fraudulent activities, but rather the use of political power to influence the resource allocation process or the regulatory framework so that private gains are obtained as a result of public power under the veil of "legal" means.

Some detractors might even argue that political corruption or "state capture" is not a form of corruption since no outright or open violation of the law is involved. It could also be argued that it is impossible to draw a consistent and definite line between corrupt practices and legitimate (albeit possibly morally questionable) use of executive power. However, these arguments are generally disingenuous. It is quite correct that one cannot classify as corruption the benefits provided to a specific group of people or a single individual by laws approved by a democratically elected parliament, which nevertheless has been intensively lobbied by those directly benefiting from that legislation. But, one would be hard pressed not to classify as political corruption a decree or regulation that grants, for example, exclusive monopoly rights (for imports, production, or sale) to the family or associates of a despot. In summary, it may be difficult to

---

[97] See, for example, the case of Fujimori's media manipulation in Peru discussed in Chapter 3.

distinguish exactly where political corruption ends and where questionable yet legitimate use of state power starts. However, there are too many clear cases of political corruption and state capture to dismiss this type of corruption in the fiscal arena (or elsewhere in the exercise of government power) from the purview of this book.

Political corruption can take many shapes and forms, from subtle ways, such as the unnecessary recruitment of political appointees as payoffs for political support to outright buyoffs of potential political opponents through payments and bribes. Several institutional factors help provide windows of opportunity for state capture or political corruption:

(i) Discretionary systems of decision-making and lack of participatory planning mechanisms.
(ii) Lack of completeness in budget formulation.
(iii) Absence of rent-seeking regulations.

4.2.3.1. Discretionary systems of decision-making and lack of participatory planning mechanisms. Opportunities for political corruption are more likely to arise in institutional arrangements that allow for high levels of discretion in the distribution of public resources. Even assuming that governments effectively avoid fraud and deviation of public resources for private use, and that the totality of resources are indeed used to finance public services, high levels of discretion in the decision-making process can lead to highly biased distributions of public resources for political gain. For example, discretionary (ad hoc) transfers may be used for political reasons as remunerations for local government's loyalty to the central government interests. Eliminating the use of political favoritisms requires the introduction of more objective mechanisms and predictable institutions, such as the use of formula-based transfer systems.

Participatory processes can be one of the most effective tools to curb political corruption by allowing citizens to participate in public affairs by giving them a voice in development decisions and institutional reforms. Whenever citizens have a voice in deciding public issues, allocative efficiency tends to be enhanced. Participation may also enhance equity by empowering minorities and marginalized groups of society. However, achieving real participation of those groups is a challenge even when the political and legal instruments are in place, at least in theory (Cornwall, 2003; Eversole, 2003).

Some compositions of public expenditure provide more opportunities for corruption and graft than others. Based on cross-country data, Mauro (1998) finds evidence that corruption is correlated to composition of public expenditures, in particular to lower spending on education. In a similar vein, Gupta *et al.* (2001) find that corruption increases the share of military spending. This is a sector in which obscure procurement procedures have led often to corruption allegations. While the composition of public expenditures is the result of many different factors, participatory planning mechanisms can help ensure responsiveness to priority needs and avoidance of opportunism and favorable conditions for graft by policymakers.

The lack of proper political representation and democratic institutions opens up many opportunities for political corruption. As put by Camerer (1997, p. 6): "*The corrupt act is inherently undemocratic. It involves the exercise of a pubic duty contrary to the wishes of the electorate which has determined that duty and employs the relevant official to perform it properly.*" Corrupt officials have incentives to alter democratic outcomes or even avoid them completely if their involvement with corrupt activities has been exposed to the electorate. Corrupt political leaders may undermine the ability of the electorate to vote them out of office by means of electoral fraud and vote buying. This type of corruption is still common in a number of developing countries. For example, in 2001, Thailand's Commission for election to the Senate received 1,000 allegations of fraud, disqualified eight candidates, and had to call for five rounds of voting before accepting the electoral results as valid (Transparency International, 2001) Similarly, dominant parties might reduce political contestability by harassing members of opposition parties or the opposition parties themselves. Ironically, in some countries the very anticorruption agencies are the ones being manipulated by incumbent governments in order to imprison opposition leaders over allegations of corruption, which were proven not to be true.[98]

Democratic institutions are not always effective in controlling political corruption, and in some cases they, themselves, may be used for corrupt activities. While political competition is identified with enhanced corruption controls, political fragmentation (participation of a large number of political parties in the democratic process) has both advantages and disadvantages. On one hand, the participation of multiple parties in the democratic process may give a strong voice to opposition points of view and thus a closer oversight of the executive branch. On the other hand, "*excessive political competition can undermine state capacity and thus create conditions especially conductive to administrative corruption and sate capture*" (World Bank, 2000a, p. 40). Under proportional electoral systems, it is often the case that political parties wanting to govern must bargain with other parties in order to form coalitions. Multiparty government structures often are characterized by the placement of the dominant party members in key governmental positions, while secondary spheres of the government apparatus are left to members of other parties of the coalition. In some cases ministries and top agencies are divided among the coalition parties

---

[98] For instance, this type of situation has been reported in Pakistan, India, and Bangladesh. This issue is further discussed in Chapter 3.

creating a lack of consistency and requiring lots of attention to conflict management. This type of political segmentation of the public apparatus tends to undermine centralized control and contributes to the deterioration of political accountability. In the case of multiparty coalitions, constituencies have fewer options to vote out parties involved in corruption. Furthermore, coalition parties that attempt to prosecute corruption of other members of the coalition bear the risk of losing political support in the parliament.

4.2.3.2. Lack of completeness in budget formulation. The application of clear and comprehensive budgetary practices is required in order to achieve accountability, efficiency, and tightness in expenditure policy formulation. Extra-budgetary funds, funds that are not included in the standard budget, and earmarked funds – resources conditioned to a specific use – are usually managed through special off-budget bank accounts. Off-budgetary accounts may be composed of investment resources, project loans, and grants from external sources. In many countries fees and charge revenues from education and heath services are also managed out of the budget and spent at the discretion of ministries and special spending units.

Discretionary off-budget accounts enable government officials to underreport budget revenues and thus subvert budget disciplinary controls and sectoral lobbying over those resources. While there are no reasons to assume that these transactions are exempt from the budget scope for illegal purposes, the existence of extra-budgetary funds fosters not only uncertainty and lack of transparency, but also a generally increased risk of political corruption.

Governments like to justify the existence of off-budget expenditures on grounds of fiscal flexibility, national security, or the inadequacy of the budget procedures to manage certain categories of expenditures. However, in practice, but for a few instances where there is adequate public monitoring, such as in the case of social security funds, extra-budgetary funds not only increase the opportunities for bureaucrats to divert public funds, but also obstruct the ability of democratically elected institutions to prioritize the use of public resources, exercise appropriate control of national indebtedness, and monitor actual expenditures.

4.2.3.3. Absence of rent-seeking regulations. The political manipulation of government decisions by private agents and corporations in order to capture extra profits (rents) is known in the economics literature as "rent seeking" (see Box 4.4). However, not all forms of rent seeking are corrupt; rather, corruption is only one of many forms of rent seeking (Lambsdorff, 2003). Legal rent-seeking activities entail private agents' requests for preferential treatment from the government by exposing their strategic contribution to public welfare or the economy as whole. These cases may be assessed by policy makers in a transparent way by weighing the

---

Box 4.4.   Rent and rent seeking

For economists the term "rent" or "economic rent" is the amount of resources generated from market power privileges (i.e., monopoly power) in the production or trade of commodities, which in some occasions entails restrictions to alternative suppliers (Tullock, 1967). The term "rent seeking" refers to activities aimed at attaining these market privileges. Sometimes rents result from factors determined by nature, such as innate characteristics. For example, the talents of famous actors, singers, and sports players are not common to the ordinary citizen. Few candidates would attempt to compete against the looks, singing, and dancing capabilities of Ms. Brittney Spears or the scoring of basketball player Saquille O'Neal. Due to limited substitutes in supply these privileged individuals gain millions in economic rents. Likewise nature confers market power to countries rich in natural resources limited in supply to other countries, such as oil and mineral resources.

In other cases, monopolies arise from the restrictions to market entry. Common market barriers are quotas or tariffs, which generate enormous rents to domestic producers. For instance, import-licensing rents in a sample of African countries during the period 1975–1987 were estimated to range between 6 percent and 37 percent of GDP (Gallagher, 1991). Hence, private firms and corporations have strong incentives to gain preferential treatment from policymakers by means of competitive lobbying but also by corruption.

---

costs (including the effects on competing industries or companies) and the benefits of adopting the preferential treatment, object of the lobby.

In contrast, political corruption entails rent-seeking activities whereby politicians or legislators receive favors in exchange for policies that enable private agents to capture economic rents. Unfortunately, there are no clear lines defining when rent-seeking behavior becomes corruption. Two points have been raised in this regard: first, focus might be placed on the legality of private rent-seeking activities. Defining political corruption in this way stresses one important issue: political corruption is endogenous to the country's legal framework. Thus, legislation standards of a country may rule as unlawful what in others is perfectly legal (Bull and Newell, 2003). Second, emphasis can be placed on the nature of the infringement (i.e., the mechanism that allows the capture of rents). This may be gauged in terms of whether it is detrimental to public interests (Rogow and Laswell, 1970), or whether it involves unlawful payoffs, such as the violation of public contracts or tendering process, emission of licenses to firms that do not fulfill legal requirements, etc. (Della Porta and Vannucci, 2005).

How do private agents buy political favors? Probably the most universal way of illicit lobbying is through the payment of bribes to high ranked public officials. One of countless illustrations world-wide is the case of top business donations to the off-budget "governing fund" of former South Korean President Roh Tae-Woo. Some of the contributors included the Hyundai and Samsung group (US $32.7 million each), the Daewoo Group (US $31.4 million), and the Lucky Goldstar Group (US $27.5 million) (Blechinger, 2000).[99]

A common mechanism for rent seeking is private funding of political parties. In many democracies of the world, electoral campaigns are mainly financed from private sector contributions. These contributions can often be traced to later payoffs and favors by government officials exploiting their incumbency. The line of what is illicit and what is not depends on the existent regulations on political financing. For example, some countries have regulated political party funding by introducing regulations regarding political contribution limits, campaign spending ceilings, campaign finances register, and so on. Campaign financing violations are often behind corruption accusations. A select sample of recent allegations includes those against Canadian Prime Minister Chretien regarding untendered contracts awarded to corporations that donated funds to the Liberal Party and allegations raised in 2003 accusing French President Jacques Chirac of illicit party financing in early 1990s (BBC, 2003).

4.3. Quasi-fiscal corruption

No review of the motivations and opportunities for corruption in fiscal systems would be complete without paying some attention to several closely related areas of public financial management, which we can refer to as quasi-fiscal policy. Quasi-fiscal corruption is not directly related to the collection or disbursement of public resources as part of the regular fiscal processes. Instead, quasi-fiscal decisions cover the range of public financial transactions that typically fall beyond the range of the regular fiscal discourse, such as the privatization of state assets; the regulation of markets, exchange rates, and price levels; as well as other quasi-fiscal decisions that fall within the realm of the public sector, such as the management of natural resources. This section reviews how corruption practices may arise in these quasi-fiscal sectors.

---

[99] Mixon *et al.* (1994) argue that legislators in the United States may be bribed by significantly smaller amounts, such as entertainment at high priced restaurants.

4.3.1. Privatization

Particularly during the 1990s, market liberalization reforms – not only in the transition economies of the former Soviet bloc but in many developing and industrialized countries around the world – were accompanied by the privatization of hundreds of thousands of public enterprises. The main motivation behind these market reforms and privatization is the notion that private ownership of productive resources and the competitive pressures of private markets result in a more efficient allocation of resources than is possible under state-controlled economic systems. Besides greater efficiency, a list of alternative reasons for privatization includes ideological objectives (such as making regular citizens shareholders), taking public enterprises out of the bankruptcy left by poor central authority management, and simply acquiescence to pressure from IFIs like the International Monetary Fund (IMF) and the World Bank (Meseguer, 2002).

Corruption itself is often part of the privatization rhetoric, as privatization is assumed to be able to reduce corruption in the public sector by the depolitization of public enterprises and the control of the discretionary power of public managers.[100] However, the process of transfer from the public to the private sector is highly sensitive and complex and many times can itself lead to corruption. In some cases, the decision to privatize itself may even be driven by corrupt motivations (Shleifer, 1998). The example of the Russian Federation – where an overwhelming share of public wealth ended up in the hands of handful of "oligarchs" – demonstrates that unless the privatization process is properly regulated, the push for privatization can be perverted by high levels of corruption (Manzetti and Blake, 1996; Celarier, 1997; Kaufmann and Seigelbaum, 1997; Salacuse 1998).

Similar to the problems encountered with corruption in public procurement, corruption in the pursuit of privatization reforms often occurs as part of the tendering process. The relationship between privatization and corruption has been studied by Kaufmann and Siegelbaum (1997) for the case of the transition economies of the FSU and CEE. These authors find that, while certain methods of privatization are less prone to corruption (such as voucher-based mass privatization, liquidation, or initial public offerings), other methods such as spontaneous privatization, or management and employee buyouts are much more prone to corruption. Besides faulty tender procedures, corruption in privatization is aggravated when performed within inadequate or incomplete legal and regulatory structures, and in the presence of high levels of corruptibility in the courts system.

---

[100] When a public company is privatized, private owners have a strong incentive to reduce corruption, to increase their own private benefits.

4.3.2. Excessive regulation of markets

In addition to taxation and public spending, government regulations are one of the main policy levers that governments have in order to ensure the proper functioning of the economy. Government regulations – in one kind or another – form an important element across virtually all sectors of the economy, from the issuance of business licenses to the regulations defining labor conditions, regulations on prices and exchange rates, regulations assuring the solvency of the banking system, to regulations that prevent the degradation of the environment due to industrial pollution.

Unfortunately, those economic agents that are constrained by regulations have an inherent incentive to seek to relax or even circumvent such regulations, and in the process may seek to bribe public officials (either the politicians who determine the regulatory framework or the bureaucrats who monitor compliance) in order to achieve that goal. For instance, environmental regulations are often against the interests of business corporations, and corruption helps circumvent or modify these regulations (Fredriksson *et al.*, 2004).

Thus, the larger the number and stringency of these regulations, the greater the window of opportunity for corruption. Additionally, market structure may also affect corruption; for instance, Ades and Di Tella (1997) and Clarke and Xu (2004) find that markets with fewer firms and low levels of competition lead to higher levels of corruption. Likewise, market interventions through industrial policy aiming to promote investment in strategic sectors of an economy are often correlated with higher levels of corruption. This is likely to be the case when there are no clear mechanisms to choose the sectors or firms that will be favored or there is discretionary power in the design of those criteria.[101]

Although the prescription to reduce potential corruption in regulatory institutions and customs administrations is clear – deregulation of market controls, price controls, and international trade liberalization – the deregulation would have to be carried out by the same public official that benefit the most from their regulatory powers (Huther and Shah, 2003).

4.3.3. Corruption in pricing of public utilities

Since many public utilities (including water, sewer, electricity, and telephone) are subject to extensive scale economies, their provision often takes on the form of a "natural monopoly". As a result, in many countries these public utilities are directly provided by the public sector financed by user

---

[101] Ades and Di Tella (1997) present empirical evidence supporting the contention that active industrial policies are positively corrleated with higher levels of corruption.

charges, or the private provision of public utilities is closely regulated by the public sector. Corruption in the provision of public utilities typically takes two forms. First, employees of the public utility can illicitly demand payment for services or supplies that should be provided at a lower price or freely. This practice not only raises the cost of public services, but often also results in denying access to services for marginalized segments of the population, while specific elites are well-served. Second, bureaucrats or politicians might extract gains from the manipulation of public utilities' pricing mechanisms.

As previously discussed, the existence of rents creates opportunities for rent-seeking behavior, which in turn, provides a window of opportunity for corruption.

4.3.4. Corruption in natural resource exploitation

Countries rich in natural resources offer special opportunities for corruption. This type of development is commonly used in the literature to explain the phenomenon of nations that, despite abundant natural resources, exhibit low levels of economic growth. In this matter, Leite and Weidmann (1999) find that internationally, large natural endowments lead to corruption through higher rent-seeking behavior. In a similar vein, Ades and Di Tella (1999) present evidence that higher rents from natural resources are correlated to higher levels of corruption.

In many countries rich in natural resources, corruption arises due to the absence of mechanisms to hold governments accountable for revenues generated from natural resource exploitation. As a result, corruption in the management of natural resources is deeply entrenched in several sub-Saharan countries (further discussed in Chapter 5). Several other cases can be cited in this regard. For instance, Khan (1994) explains Nigeria's high levels of corruption on the basis of the abundance of oil resources. It has also been reported that as much as US $1 billion dollars of oil resources were embezzled during year 2000 in Angola (Global Witness, 2004). Likewise, recent evidence in Equatorial Guinea revealed that US oil companies were making direct payments into President Obiang Nguema's personal account at Riggs Bank in Washington, DC (Global Witness, 2004).

Finally, a long list of cases could also be cited in relation to corrupt agreements between governments and the logging industry leading to unsustainable exploitation of forests, such as the widely cited cases of Cambodia and Indonesia. In Indonesia alone, it is estimated that the total amount of liabilities from timber exploitation, such as export taxes, reforestation payments, and royalties, that are evaded is close to US $600 million per year (Transparency International, 2002, p. 3). In order to acquire the right to exploit these high rents, it is likely that some of the amount will be kicked back as bribes to public officials.

Table 4.2. *Fiscal dimension of corruption: a summary*

	4.1 Corruption in public revenue collections	4.2 Corruption on the expenditure side of the budget		4.3 Quasi-fiscal corruption
		4.2.1 On the expenditure side of the budget	4.2.2 Administrative (Bureaucratic) Corruption	
Motivations for corruption	(i) Lack of moral and ethical behavior by tax officials (ii) Low probabilities of detection (iii) Weak penalization and prosecution (iv) Inadequate wages and incentive-compatible compensation (v) Pressure from taxpayers seeking to evade taxes		(i) Absence of a culture of honesty, ethics, and political will (ii) Weak mechanisms of monitoring and expenditure tracking (iii) Weak penalization and prosecution at high and low levels of government (iv) Inadequate wages and incentive-compatible compensation	4.3.1 Corruption and Privatization 4.3.2 Corruption and Excessive regulation of the market
Opportunities for corruption	(i) Absence of basic oversight and control on tax administration (ii) Complexity of the tax and custom systems (iii) Discretionary power of tax and customs officials (iv) Politicization of civil servants		(i) Inadequate systems of public service spending control (ii) Poorly designed public procurement mechanisms (iii) Excessive control by bureaucrats over civil service decisions (iv) Weak control of social security resources and government subsidies (v) Limited oversight by parliament and civil society	(i) Discretionary systems of decision-making and lack of or weak enforcement of participatory planning mechanisms (ii) Lack of completeness in budget formulation (iii) Absence of rent-seeking regulations 4.3.3 and 4.3.4 Corruption in pricing of public utilities and natural resource exploitation

4.4. Concluding remarks

Understanding the basic nature of corrupt practices and their determinants is a necessary step to find anticorruption remedies. This section provided an overview of the main types of corruption observed in fiscal systems by broadly considering revenue corruption, expenditure corruption, and quasi-fiscal corruption (Table 4.2). For each of these three building blocks of public finances, we identified the main motivations for corruption, the opportunities for corruption, as well as the main fiscal policy factors or fiscal management practices that stimulate or facilitate corrupt activities.

In considering how corruption manifests itself, it is important to recognize that corruption is perpetrated by two different types of public officials. On one hand, bureaucrats and public servants may engage in a variety of (generally petty) acts of corruption, broadly referred to as administrative or bureaucratic corruption. On the other hand, politicians may use their political power and influence for their own personal gain, typically through acts of grand corruption.

The distinction between administrative corruption and political corruption is very important, because the nature of these two types of corruption is very different, and therefore the responses also need to be different. Nevertheless, tackling simultaneously both types of corruption is important, as an interdependence exists in fighting these two types of corruption. It would be extremely hard to establish a corruption-free ethic among civil servants unless political corruption is visibly addressed, whereas it would be hard to maintain a campaign against political corruption in a public sector where corruption is pervasive at the administrative level. Chapter 5 will present in some detail the various policy responses that governments have pursued in their fight against corruption, and discuss their relative success.

Fiscal Response to Reduce Corruption

In the previous chapter we identified the main motivations and windows of opportunity for corruption. In this chapter we aim to present remedies and policy interventions for the different forms of corruption based on best practices in the international arena. To the extent possible, the discussion in this chapter also assesses the degree of success that each policy response is likely to achieve. For completeness, the discussion in this chapter is organized along the same lines as in Chapter 4. In particular, here we review mechanisms designed to address each specific issue described in Chapter 4. In addition, we will also review programmatic policy interventions that can address several of these issues simultaneously.

It needs to be acknowledged that this form of organizing the discussion of possible policy responses to different forms of corruption should not be understood as suggesting a mechanistic or formula-based approach to fighting corruption. From our previous discussion it should be clear that corruption is a multifaceted phenomenon and that corruption in each country is likely to adopt different forms and nuances and that, therefore, needs to be studied in the context of that country's particular circumstances. The contribution of this chapter is to present some options aimed at showing that there are practical instruments to be used in fighting different manifestations of corruption. This can-do attitude is vital in convincing politicians that corruption is not invincible. Furthermore, it is possible and worthwhile to fight it.

The organization of the current chapter is as follows. Fiscal policy responses to corruption are classified into groups according to whether they are aimed to address corruption in revenues (Section 5.1), expenditures (Section 5.2), and quasi-fiscal issues (Section 5.3). In addition, Section 5.4 reviews broad-based governance reform that may have a significant impact on corruption, notably fiscal decentralization reform. Other programmatic responses to corruption are discussed in Section 5.5. Although there may be some ambiguity in the short run on how effective the implementation of such programmatic reforms are in fighting corruption, it is much clearer that structural reforms are required for the long-term comprehensive control of corruption.

5.1. Reducing corruption in the collection of revenues

Following the structure of our discussion in Section 4.1 in the previous chapter, this section discusses measures in tax policy and tax administration and customs aimed at reducing the motivations and opportunities for corruption in revenue collections. We also provide an overview of several program responses that can be used to curb corruption on the revenue side of the budget.

5.1.1. Reducing motivations for corruption on the revenue side of the budget

Recall that in Chapter 2 of this book we developed a conceptual model of corruption, which suggested that the core motivating factor for corruption is the financial gain received by the corrupt official. However, this does not mean that governments are completely helpless in shaping the factors that motivate tax collectors and revenue officials to engage in corrupt practices. Possible avenues open to governments to reduce the motivation for corruption include:

 (i) Instilling ethics in tax officials.
 (ii) Increases in the probability of detection.
(iii) Increases in and stricter enforcement of penalties for corruption.
(iv) Increases in wages in the public sector and the establishment of incentive-compatible compensation mechanisms.
 (v) Decreases in the overall tax burden on taxpayers.

5.1.1.1. Instilling ethics and trust in tax collectors and revenue administrators. A first response to the presence of corruption within the tax administration apparatus is to strengthen the moral and ethical behavior of tax administrators and other revenue officials. A variety of forums, conferences, and internal training programs may be used in order to sensitize employees that deal with revenue collections, with the aim of increasing ethical and moral behavior within the tax administration.

In addition to directly instilling ethical behaviors in tax administrators, there is a strong link between the prevalence of corruption in tax collection agencies and the overall level of corruption in society. Ethical behavior by tax officials is difficult to achieve within a wider "culture of corruption" so that anticorruption campaigns within the tax administration should also aim to decrease citizens' tolerance to corruption. Similarly, the level of ethics, moral, and social norms in a country may be increased by changing the norms in society and fomenting information campaigns that encourage tax compliance by increasing taxpayers' awareness of their social commitments and the specific government services supported by their taxes (Blumenthal *et al.*, 2001). In the words of the former Prime Minister of Singapore, Lee Kuan Yew "*the strongest deterrent {against corruption} is in a public opinion which censures and condemns corrupt persons; in other words in attitudes which make corruption so unacceptable that the stigma of corruption cannot be washed away by serving a prison sentence."* (Statement to Parliament, January 1987 in Yak, 1995).

Legal reforms introducing preventive measures against corruption can also be effective tools for building ethics among civil servants. Such is the case with the establishment of a *Code of Conduct*, which clarifies expectations for ethical behavior and puts emphasis on high ethical standards among civil servants. A number of countries have had a Code of Conduct for many years, such as Japan (1948), United States (1977), Australia (1987), Ghana (1992), Singapore (1960, revised 1993), and Hong Kong (1971). The General Assembly of the United Nations adopted the International Code of Conduct for Public Officials in 1996. This document stresses that "the ultimate loyalty of public officials shall be to the public interests of their country."[102] The code treats many relevant issues including conflict of interest and disqualification, disclosure of assets, acceptance of gifts or other favors, confidential information, and political activity.

The effectiveness of a Code of Conduct depends on how well governments publicize it and expose and educate public officials on their contents, and then follow up to enforce those ethical standards. Besides its educational value, a Code of Conduct can be enforced with the same rigor of other general laws. Enforcement can be based on the same general system to enforce other laws or may rely on a specialized system. The latter may rely on several special enforcement institutions including a bureau of investigation and prosecution and specialized courts. A good example of the latter approach is provided by Singapore's Corrupt Practices Investigation Bureau (CPIB), which reflects the strong commitment to fight corruption in that country. The CPIB counts on a Corruption Review Committee, an intelligence unit, and broad investigative powers including the rights to use polygraph testing in their investigations.[103] In contrast, other countries, such as Nigeria, that have established a Code of Conduct (Bureau) have not managed to enforce it. In these latter cases, the Code of Conduct remains some sort of moral guideline without much impact on the behavior of civil servants.[104]

The adoption of a Code of Conduct and the integration of ethics sensitization in the training, evaluation, and promotion of tax officials must be considered a minimum starting point for a successful anticorruption strategy in revenue collections. However, ethics and moral-building campaigns are usually not enough to modify the behavior of the majority of tax

---

[102] See United Nations (1997).
[103] Related legislation and further information of the CPIB is available at http://www.cpib.gov.sg\
[104] See Ofosu-Amaah *et al.* (1999).

administrators (see Box 5.1). In fact, as we have seen, corrupt practices in many countries are often not linked to shame, due to the cultural legitimization of corruption. In order to prevent corruption contagion effects, moral-building campaigns must be accompanied by strategies that aim to identify and weed out officials that are perceived as "highly" corrupt. This generally requires effective monitoring mechanisms to identify officials suspected of wrongdoing and consequently to purge them out of the civil service. Corrupt officials may be difficult to identify and even when identified it may be difficult to get rid of them. In particular, it is likely that public employees recruited due to their political loyalties are more likely to engage in corruption but also the more difficult to fire.[105] More drastic purging strategies can be employed on the basis of merit-based recruitment. Such systems reduce opportunities for patronage and complicate the existence of corruption networks, which in turn also reduce corruption contagion effects.[106] Several country experiences are considered quite successful in this matter. For example, during Peru's tax agency reform in 1991, all staff members were given the choice to resign or reapply for their positions. Only less than one third of the applicants passed the three-phase exam required for rehiring, which included, among other things, an evaluation of moral judgment (World Bank, 2001a). Likewise, the Tanzanian government dealt with extensive corruption within the tax administration agency by firing all employees and rehiring back only those that were not suspected to have been engaged in corrupt practices.[107]

Preventive measures and the effects of campaigns aimed at building morals and ethics in the population are hard to quantify. For corruption, similar to crime, measuring the effectiveness of preventive measures is complex because objective analysis would require knowing what would happen in a counterfactual world where the preventive measures are not in place. But at any rate, a society with high ethical and moral standards is likely to be very effective in preventing corruption. Therefore, different kinds of efforts to instill higher ethical standards should not be underestimated as important tools in the fight against corruption.

5.1.1.2. Increasing the probability of detection. The most powerful disincentive for public officials to engage in corrupt activities is the punishment received in case they are caught. As such, the probability of detection is an important factor in motivating public officials not to engage in corruption.

---

[105] Their propensity to get involved in corrupt activities is enhanced by the knowledge that their positions may only last until the next change in government.

[106] Further issues regarding rehiring practices are discussed in subsection 5.2.1. Depolitization of public servants.

[107] For further detail on this topic see Chapter 6.

Box 5.1. *Political will without an institutional framework: the case of Georgia*

Without doubt, one of the most important ingredients needed to build ethics in a society is to reflect a strong and sustained political will against corruption. Yet, political campaigns against corruption are often short lived if they do not count with the institutional support needed for a systemic approach against corruption. One example of this is provided by the anticorruption efforts being led by Georgia's President Mikheil Saakashvili in 2004.

Saakashvili's anticorruption campaign has been characterized by reflecting a strong drive to fight corruption even at the highest levels. A list of higher officials and political figures being prosecuted for corruption or tax evasion include the former Minister of energy and transport, the head of the Georgian Railways, and the son-in-law of former President Eduard Shevardnadze (Ratiani, 2004). Anticorruption efforts have mostly focused in targeting the demand for corruption from the taxpayer's side. A strong list of investigations of prominent businessmen has also led to many arrests and trails sending a signal that even big fish will be prosecuted if found partaking in corruption acts or evasion. Typically, the accused people have been jailed and then let free after agreeing to pay certain amounts in due taxes (Schriek, 2004).

Despite the strong political will to fight corruption by the President and the new executive, the approach being applied in Georgia has substantial shortcomings. Georgia's strategy is for the most part focusing on tax evasion, which may or may not entail the collusion of taxpayers with public officials, while this effort has not been supported by a systematic reform of the tax administration. For this reason, many Georgian citizens have expressed doubts about the current anticorruption approach, raising questions of whether "businesses are being sacrificed to an old corrupt system." Furthermore, constant arrests and releases undertaken by security organs and law enforcement agencies are over passing the authority of the judiciary and existing legal procedures, while a tax amnesty promised by the President to those that declare and pay previously evaded taxes is also inconsistent with the existing legal framework. The more important question is whether President Saakashvili's political will to fight corruption is sustainable and will be effective in the longer run.

A strong political will against corruption needs to be coupled by institutional development and legal reforms that make take

years to be fully effective. Comprehensiveness in the institutional framework of the anticorruption strategy is a key point
for success, as noted by the notion of National Integrity Systems, a framework of analysis that stresses the importance of
at least eight institutional pillars for anticorruption efforts to be
effective (Dye and Stapenhurst, 1998). A strong reflection of
political will at an initial stage by purging corruption at the
highest levels of public and private sectors is by all means a
desirable starting point anytime the institutional environment
is able to ensure the consistency and fairness of this process.
Nevertheless, this is unlikely to be sustainable if anticorruption
reform in other areas, such as the legislative framework and
the judiciary, are not being undertaken with the same rigor. The
need for a strong starting push is recognized by policymakers
and students of corruption. Aidt (2003), for example, argues
that a "big push is needed to reduce corruption in societies in
which corruption is endemic" (p. 649). Yet, the same study
notes that anticorruption measures need to be sustained for a
long time, since "a reversal of the reform before crossing a
minimum threshold would bring the country back to high corruption equilibrium" (p. 649). Furthermore, an enforcement
approach that targets uniquely the demand for corruption from
the side of the taxpayers, as the approach being applied in
Georgia does, is unlike to be effective without an simultaneous
reform of: (1) the tax policy framework, and (2) the structure of
incentives and opportunities of corruption within the tax administration and the public sector in general.

Increasing the probability of detecting corrupt behaviors within the tax
administration apparatus requires the introduction or strengthening of
evaluation mechanisms designed to monitor the collection performance of
tax officials. These mechanisms need to target officials that are directly
responsible for tax collection, assessment, and audit, and thus have the
largest window of opportunity to engage in corruption. The simple analysis
of collection performance by individual tax collectors (e.g., variations in
revenue collection rates) can signal whether tax administrators are potentially receiving bribes in exchange for lowering taxes due.

Another strategy for detection is to rely on the cooperation from other
public employees by encouraging them to report corruption practices in the
workplace. While Zipparo (1999) shows that most employees believe that
reporting workplace corruption is their responsibility, this presumes that
reporting channels are indeed available. Practical strategies to increase
workers' motivation to report corruption – and thus to increase the

probability of detection – include spreading information of internal and external reporting procedures; spreading information related to whistle-blower protection programs; and introducing whistle-blower protection legislation.

Legislation regarding the possession of unexplained wealth or property, such as the mandatory declaration of assets, can be a powerful indirect mechanism to increase the probability of detection. Some countries in which the declaration of assets is enforced by the law include Tanzania, Ghana, Uganda, Hong Kong, Mozambique, Malawi, and the United States. When this legislation is in place, an independent institution is required in order to guarantee the enforcement, accuracy, and compliance with the reporting requirements; it is also important to have investigations of suspicious cases. However, the enforcement of effective investigations can be cumbersome as the assets of corrupt officials can be camouflaged by transferring them to friends or relatives. For this reason, the legislation in some countries (such as Malawi, Tanzania, and Hong Kong) support the investigation of assets of close relatives, who are suspected of having received illegal assets from the indicted party (Ofosu-Amaah *et al.*, 1999).

The probabilities of detecting evasion and corruption are also increased by the application of many of the instruments aimed at increasing transparency and accountability which are discussed in the next subsections, including training for tax administration personnel, improvements in the tax administration's information collection systems, the creation of large taxpayer units (LTUs), and so on.

Again, the existence of internal monitoring and detection mechanisms within the tax administration apparatus are elements of any minimal anticorruption strategy.

5.1.1.3. Increasing and enforcement of penalties. Another conceptually unambiguous motivating factor in limiting corruption in tax administration is the imposition of stringent penalties once corrupt activities are detected. Sanctions for tax collectors found to have engaged in theft of tax payments or found to have accepted bribes from taxpayers could not only consist of monetary sanctions and/or job dismissal, but might also be combined with prison sentences.

In practice, things are not so straightforward. A general problem with the enforcement of swift and harsh penalties on tax officials is often that – unless the revenue authority has a special status – tax administrators are somewhat shielded by red tape and protective safeguards accorded to civil servants. High penalties (e.g., significant prison sentences) are sometimes left unapplied because those in charge of applying them, including the courts and juries may find them disproportionate. Here, like in the rest of the penal system, it is likely more effective to have moderate penalties that are applied than to have harsh penalties that are seldom or only randomly applied. However, even relatively moderate penalties are not so easy to apply and maintain. For example, there is anecdotal evidence from Uganda and Tanzania that it may in fact be difficult to sustain dismissals over time. And sometimes dismissals may not be an effective penalty, despite the loss of wages, the loss in employment opportunities, and even the potential social stigma associated with dismissal. For example, in Uganda, Fjeldstad *et al.* (2003, p. 7) report a perception among some tax administration officials that a job at the agency is a place to stay for a few years only to make money. Then, if one is finally caught in corrupt activities the burden of dismissal (and its impact on motivating behavior against corruption) can be rather limited.

Countries use a variety of penalties as anticorruption tools. These penalties range from administrative discipline (including job dismissal) to criminal prosecution (including monetary penalties and jail time). It is common in many countries to observe cases in which corrupt officials are prosecuted to the full extent of the law. However, these individual cases, more often than not, seem to be chosen as examples, rather than being representative of a systematic practice. In certain countries (e.g., China and Vietnam) some types of corruption, such as misappropriation of public funds by government officials, has been punished with the death penalty (see Box 5.2). However, the effectiveness of severe penalties relative to probability of detection continues to be questioned.[108]

Lacking evidence on the appropriateness of different penalty schemes to fight corruption, we should note that several studies have concluded that low penalties for corrupt tax officials such as job dismissal, may not be effective to decrease pervasive corruption levels. For example, according to Flatters and Mcleod (1995) job dismissal is only effective if accompanied by higher sanctions such as jail terms and financial penalties. These authors and Van Rijckeghem and Weder (2001) argue that if job dismissal is the maximum penalty used to deter corruption, substantially higher levels of wages for tax officials would be required to increase the financial impact of the penalty (since lost wages would be the primary punishment). This observation brings us to the policy responses for the next motive for evasion.

5.1.1.4. Increase in wages and incentive-compatible compensation. The importance of ensuring fair and competitive compensation levels for tax

---

[108] Curiously the statistical, and even the experimental, evidence suggests that the effect of penalties in deterring tax evasion is weaker than the effect of probability of detection. This result is somewhat puzzling and it may be due to the difficulty in obtaining enough statistical variation in penalty rates (the same penalties apply equally for all individuals) and that penalties are made to vary lightly and are highly discounted in experimental settings. However, the empirical research on criminal behavior also finds that the deterrent effect of the certainty of punishment (even when light) is significantly larger than that of the severity of punishment, which in many cases is not even statistically significant (Grooger, 1991).

**Box 5.2. Death sentence upheld in state embezzlement cases
in Vietnam and China**

The death penalty is applied to cases of corruption in some
countries such as China and Vietnam. As reported by the *Viet
Nam News* journal on Tuesday, April 6, 2004, the death sentence of a former director of an Agriculture and Rural Development Ministry agency was upheld by an appeals court in
Hanoi after the public employee was convicted of embezzling
US \$4.9 million.

In China, also, some widely publicized cases of high-ranked
officials receiving death sentences include that of National
Peoples Congress Vice-Chairman Cheng Kejie executed for the
embezzlement of US \$5 million, former deputy governor of
Jaingxi province Hu Changqing for taking US \$650,000 in
bribes (executed March 2000), and the death sentence with 2-
year reprieve to former Shengyang Mayor Mu Suixin (for misuse of public funds and taking bribes). As part of a massive
campaign to curb corruption in China in the year 2000, more
than 200 trials took place and 14 public officers were sentenced
to death because of corruption charges.

Sources: BBC (2000), CNN (2000), Vietnam News (2004),
China.org.cn (2000).

---

administration officials has been widely recognized as a requirement to
reduce corruption. High differentials between wages in the public and private sectors often contribute to the fact that skilled and qualified workers
(often the more honest workers) abandon the public sector, leading to
generalized expectations that the public sector is not able to attract or
retain well-qualified staff. Although some well-qualified individuals may
still pursue a career in the civil service for other motives; in other cases it
must be assumed that skilled staff remain in the public sector because they
are able to make up the wage differential by illicit means. These realiza-
tions are not new in many developing countries, but rather are widely
known and accepted by policymakers and citizens at large.

There are some prominent international examples where wage parity has
been used successfully in curbing corruption. One such case is Singapore.
One component of Singapore's anticorruption strategy consisted of gradual wage rises and constant revisions of wage levels to guarantee that
public salaries were competitive with those of the private sector. The results
of this strategy are perceived by many as highly successful in fighting
corruption and increasing the efficiency and transparency of Singapore's
public sector (Langseth *et al.*, 1997; Leak, 1999).

However, it is important to recognize that in many instances this solution is not necessarily feasible in all developing or transition countries. Increasing salaries for tax officials to competitive levels in the private sector might either be politically unacceptable or simply be prohibitively costly. In addition, it is likely that while increased pay rates for tax officials have a long-term cost impact, the benefits may not be equally long-lasting. While a solitary (one-time) boost in pay rates for tax officials should result in increased effort and reduced corruption, a subsequent failure to maintain the new wage levels in real terms may lead to a reversal of effort and a return to corruption. The overall effect may be counterproductive if notions of fair wages among tax administrations go up with the one-time boost in pay rates.

The significant constraint to fighting corruption in tax administration imposed by low wages in the entire public sector has been addressed in a number of countries by creating a separate semi-autonomous tax administration agency (SUNAT) not subject to general civil service rules and pay scales. This has been the approach followed in more than 15 countries.[109]

Besides advocating the provision of fair salary levels for public servants, anticorruption policies should address the incentive structure that public officials face. A wide variety of incentive schemes may be applied to improve the productiveness of public officials in detecting evasion and increasing the implicit costs of engaging in corruption.[110] Performance-linked compensation, such as bonus systems may offset the benefits a public official could receive from a bribery system. This is possible if, for example, bonus payments are determined as a fraction of revenues collected above given benchmark levels. A bonus scheme with these characteristics was applied, for example, in Ghana (see Box 5.3). Alternative bonus salary systems in revenue departments are used in Albania, Brazil, Denmark, Latvia, Morocco, and Philippines (World Bank, 2001b). Performance-based bonus and salary supplement strategies are not without dangers. In the first place they require that lower levels of administration perceive that higher levels of the administration are not corrupt. That is, lower level officials will not be discouraged from accepting bribes if they perceive that the deal is being settled by a higher level of bureaucracy (Fjeldstad and Tungodden, 2003). With perceived corruption at higher levels of administration, lower level bureaucrats would give up additional income from bribes and also income from bonus possibilities as corruption in higher levels of government would impede the achievement of higher revenue targets. Another important caveat is that a tax administration entity performs multiple tasks, which makes it difficult to link enhanced

---

[109] See Taliercio (2004). See also the subsection below on SARAs for more details.

[110] See Besley and McLaren (1993) for a discussion of alternative incentive-compatible payments schemes for tax inspectors.

Box 5.3. Anticorruption efforts in Ghana: bonus schemes for tax officials

Recent tax administration reforms in Ghana help illustrate the use of compensation-based anticorruption strategies. In the 1960s and 1970s Ghana experienced an economic crisis, which was coupled by a decline in taxable capacity. Tax collection agencies were unable to retain qualified staff due to low wages, low morale, and due to the tradition through which corruption was prominent in order to compensate for erosion in salaries. Tax evasion became out of control as the tax ratio reached a low of 4.8 percent of GDP in 1984 from about 16 percent of GDP in 1976. Several extreme measures were implemented as ways to increase tax revenues, albeit without much success. Among these were the execution of corrupt officers; increases in tax rates and sanctions for non-payment; and the creation of (i) a "National Investigations Committee" (NIC) and (ii) the "Office of Revenue Commissioners" (ORC) to enforce fiscal obligations. Unfortunately, these measures had only transitory effects.

As part of the Structural Adjustment Program (SAP), in 1985 a new autonomous institution called the National Revenue Secretariat (NRS) was created which replaced the two revenue departments (Customs, Excise and Preventive Service (CEPS) and the Internal Revenue Service (IRS)). Moreover, within a year a Collective Bargaining Agreement (CBA) was signed to include a bonus rate of 15 percent of annual basic salary (normal bonus) for tax and customs officers, implemented to reward if revenue collections exceeded the annual target. Funds for bonus payments come from a set percentage of the excess of tax revenue collected over the target level. The normal bonus is paid at the end of the year to all employees depending on the employee's rating on a Performance Review Report (PRR). At times, the bonus has been paid twice a year if an early trend existed that would achieve the annual target. The tax restructuring and bonus system in 1986 had a positive impact on revenue collection as government revenue increased from 14 percent of GDP to a high of 23.6 percent of GDP in 1993. In that same year, the government implemented a policy to consolidate emoluments and allowances paid to all Public and Civil Servants.

Nevertheless, Civil Service salaries increased over the period due to constant protests. This lessened the salary advantage of NRS service over the comparable positions in other public service organizations. This led the Ministry of Finance to negotiate in 1994 an incentive bonus in addition to the normal bonus, which was again structured to encourage collections exceeding the annual set targets. Lastly, the government adopted the Ghana Universal Salary Scheme in 1996, which eventually resulted in comparable remunerations of Tax Revenue Administration employees with Civil Service. The consequences were again comparatively lower salaries and unattractive service schemes.

Although empirical analysis is yet needed to determine whether or not the increase in government revenue was solely a result of the tax administration bonus strategy, some significant effect is quite likely. Several studies have pointed out that the introduction of annual targets and bonus schemes also improved employee behavior and internal organization of the NRS.

Sources: World Bank (2000b), Burgess and Stern (1993), Terkper (1994), Chand and Moene (1997), Bejakovic (2000).

(revenue) performance to any one department and/or individual. Furthermore, performance-based compensation schemes also need supervision and control to prevent abuses from tax administrators too eager to find tax evasion where there is none or just innocent negligence by taxpayers.

5.1.1.5. Reducing the overall tax burden on taxpayers and increasing fairness. As reviewed in Chapter 4, the final motivating factor which may cause otherwise honest tax officials to engage in corruption is that they are often approached by taxpayers who want them to accept bribes in exchange for allowing them to evade taxes. Tax systems that impose excessively high burdens on taxpayers or those where there are significant horizontal inequities and, thus, are considered particularly unfair, tend to motivate taxpayers to engage in fraudulent activities and can easily lead to higher incidence of corruption.[111]

As such, to the extent that corruption among the ranks of tax officials is motivated or driven by taxpayer requests, anticorruption policies should aim to simplify and modify the tax system by reducing marginal taxes and broadening tax bases by getting rid of special treatments. Other avenues for reducing tax burdens and improving the fairness of the tax system are

---

[111] Mann and Smith (1988), for example, find a positive correlation between perceived tax inequities and compliance behavior.

further discussed in the following section, where we discuss policy interventions to reduce windows of opportunity for corruption.

5.1.2. *Reducing opportunities for corruption on the revenue side of the budget*

Given the powerful motivation provided by bribes and other "incentives," it is unlikely that policies targeting motivating factors alone will be able to eliminate corruption as long as the opportunities for corruption are numerous. This section reviews policies aimed to decrease the opportunities that arise for public officials to partake in corruption. These include the following:

(i) Introduction of basic oversight mechanisms.
(ii) Simplification of the tax system.
(iii) Reduction of discretionary power of revenue officials.
(iv) Depoliticization of civil servants.

5.1.2.1. Introduction of basic oversight mechanisms. External audit and evaluations of the tax administration agency by the Supreme Audit Institution of a country, such as is the case of the evaluations performed by the General Accounting Office and the Congressional Budget Office on the Internal Review Service in the United States, can be quite effective in keeping corrupt or abusive behavior of public officials in check.

The collection of survey opinions from taxpayers by independent units aimed at fighting corruption and extortion by public officials may serve as an additional tool in detecting corrupt officials and decreasing their power to manipulate the system.

In more developed economies, payments by check and credit cards can eliminate much of this problem. More complex tools and techniques can be used to analyze revenue collection patterns. For example, computer software can track collection levels for specific collectors to flag any suspicious activities or unusual collection patterns. More transparent tax administration systems and broader supervisory mechanisms (computerized paper trails, institutionalized routine cross-checks, internal and external audits, etc.) makes it harder for any two tax officials (say, the collector and the supervisor) to collude. The loot would have to be shared by more insiders, thereby decreasing the payoff benefit, and increasing the risk of getting caught.

Other common-sense tax administration procedures, which are not hard to devise, can help to eliminate corruption opportunities. For instance, in cash economies there can be a simple requirement that taxpayers can observe and verify that their payment is being recorded in the balance book, including a signed receipt for the taxpayer. Another common solution is to separate the functions of assessment and receipt of the tax and actual payment at a cashiers window. Tax administration reforms in South Korea, for example, restructured several tax departments in order to separate tax officials in charge of each of these two functions (see Box 5.4).

5.1.2.2. Simplification of the tax system. Corruption among tax officials and opportunities for evasion and bribes tend to be less frequent in tax systems that are relatively simple and transparent. For example, the high level of corruption in Russia and many other former Soviet republics during the 1990s has been explained by highly complex and non-transparent tax laws (Martinez-Vazquez and McNab, 2000).

The simplification of the tax system should be aimed at decreasing the number of taxes and simplifying the rate structure, to inform taxpayers on how to comply, to decrease the number of forms and unnecessary regulations that only add steps required to pay taxes, to decrease the number of exemptions and special treatments, and to avoid the constant modification of tax rules. These policies target three main objectives:

- First, making the tax system understandable to the ordinary citizen decreases the need for discretionary interpretation of regulations. This in turn minimizes contact between taxpayers and public officials.
- Second, reducing bureaucracy by decreasing the number of clearances that are required from taxpayers to complete the compliance process (i.e., the number of forms, certifications, signatures, stamps, etc.). This not only reduces the opportunities for extortion, but also decreases the taxpayer's compliance cost in terms of time or money, which in turn reduces his/her motivation to evade and bribe officials.

Some of the comprehensive tax reforms in transitional and developing countries in recent times, such as in the case of Russia's new Tax Code of 2002, have strived to simplify the tax system. However, the results of recent tax reforms have not always been greater simplicity and transparency (Martinez-Vazquez and McNab, 2000; Tanzi and Zee, 2000).

5.1.2.3. Discretionary power of tax revenue officials. One pivotal step toward corruption control in tax and customs administrations is to reduce to the minimum the discretionary power exercised by public officials. A lower number of exemptions and elimination of discretionary powers to grant them decrease the opportunities for rent seeking by firms for which the exemptions are not intended in the first place. The degree of public officials' discretion on tax preferential tax treatments, tax assessments, as well as valuation and classification of traded merchandise can be minimized by the elimination of many of those special treatments, the application of rules, the introduction of simplified classification schedules, and standardized and computerized systems of tax assessment and merchandise classification. In those cases where tax assessments are difficult to monitor, such as in the taxation of small businesses, objective presumptive tax

Box 5.4. Tax administration reform client service in South Korean tax administration

After a financial crisis of 1997, the government of South Korea embarked on a series of reforms aimed at improving government effectiveness in curbing corruption. The problem of corruption had been commonly cited among main causes of the financial crisis itself. The National Tax Administration (NTA), widely perceived as an abusive and corrupt government agency, undertook several drastic changes in its operation. The reform changed the mission of the tax administration from the imposition and collection of taxes to taxpayer protection and taxpayer service provision, and was coupled with streamlining and modernization of administrative procedures.

Under the previous administration, administrative offices were organized in units by tax type (i.e., income tax, property tax, etc.) and officers were assigned to specific jurisdictions. Under a tax-type system a unique officer could assume simultaneously the functions of taxpayer registration, tax assessment, collection, and investigation. This conferred a high degree of discretionary power upon NTA regional officers over taxpayers in their jurisdictions, and, thus, constituted a perfect setting for corrupt behavior. The administration reform separated these functions by consolidating regional officers and reorganizing them by function (i.e., service center division, collection division, investigating division, etc.).

Several measures were taken also to improve taxpayer services and to facilitate tax payments. One of the most important was the introduction of mail and phone tax filing mechanisms. These steps were highly successful in replacing personal contact, to the extent that 68 percent of returns were filed by mail in year 2000. Strengthening ombudsmen divisions and creation of the Charter of Taxpayer Rights were aimed to protect their rights to inform and educate citizens regarding tax-related issues. This strategy was coupled by other changes in administrative procedures that included: (a) the expansion of the computer network system and the establishment of an integrated computerized tax system; the replacement of manual assessment by computer-assisted assessments; the establishment of clear standardized rules in the manual of procedures for each function. (b) Mechanisms aimed at encouraging use of credit cards by offering a deduction of 10 percent of taxes on any consumption paid by credit card. This measure was particularly successful in identifying the tax base, especially of small businesses that tend to underreport all cash transactions.

The success of this policy as an anticorruption tool was un-ambiguous. According to studies developed by a private re-search institution in South Korea, the reforms reduced opportunities for corruption by 70 percent. In addition, the success of taxpayer services was reflected in an increase in the client satisfaction index from 44 percent in 1999 to 74 percent in 2000.

Sources: Sang-Yool (2000), Korean Herald (2001).

regulations can serve as a substitute for personal assessments (World Bank, 1999). Similarly, clear and automatic mechanisms of tax audit selection are likely to decrease opportunities for corruption.

Separating officials responsible for the assessment, the collection, and audit, as well as random assignments of cases to public officials limits the opportunities for planned fraud schemes. In some tax administrations this reform entails changing the entire structure of the agency from an organization based on type of tax to one based on main functions (see the discussion of South Korea's tax administration reform in Box 5.4). This approach has proven to be successful example in Singapore (Bird and Oldman, 2000).

In addition, the establishment of appeal mechanisms and taxpayer service bureaus can limit the ability of tax officials to exercise their power over taxpayers. An independent tax appeal court is necessary to resolve ambiguities and contradictions that arise within tax systems. Effective appeal mechanisms protect taxpayers from arbitrary assessments, allowing taxpayers to challenge tax officials' resolutions. An independent appeals court decreases the opportunities for corrupt tax officials to extort taxpayers. Additionally, the mere existence of tax appealing mechanisms underpins the perception of the fairness of the tax system, which in turn, decreases the incentives for corruption. Even simpler measures like the existence of an anonymous tax ombudsman can make it much more difficult for corrupt tax officials to coerce honest taxpayers into paying bribes.

Rotation of staff is also used as a tool to avoid close relationships between taxpayers and officials, which may breed corrupt practices, to reduce monopolies in the execution of specific functions, and to increase the monitoring of activities. Several tax administration agencies in developed economies include rotation of tax and customs administration personnel as a measure to avoid the formation of coalitions in specific functions of the administration.[112]

---

[112]See Hyun (2003) for a discussion of the effectiveness of job rotation to reduce tax evasion and corruption in tax administrations. His study was motivated by success of the job rotation system applied in the private and public sector in Japan since the 1950s.

5.1.2.4. Depoliticization of tax officials. The practice of arbitrary changes of tax administration personnel for political reasons tends to create an atmosphere of dependence and internal clientelism, which in turn lead to a higher incidence of corrupt practices. The introduction of professional career regulations, merit-based recruitment, and transparent compensation and promotion of public servants may greatly reduce political patronage of tax officials and the incidence of corruption in this area.

The effectiveness of recruitment reforms in reducing the politicization of public officials has been mixed, depending on the commitment to reforms demonstrated at the highest level of government. For example, in 1993 a drastic customs administration reform in Bolivia introduced the immediate replacement of the entire staff at airports and customs posts, to be followed by a merit-based hiring process. However, this measure had little effect due to strong political pressures, which led quite shortly to the gradual replacement of the newly hired officials. Later attempts to use merit-based recruitment in 1997 also failed; the already selected new officials were never able to take their posts due to a change of government (Hors, 2003).[113] On the other hand, some countries, such as Peru (see Box 5.5), appear to have been successful in the depoliticization of tax administrations by granting some degree of autonomy to their revenue authorities. The role and effectiveness of semi-autonomous agencies in curbing patronage and politicization is further discussed in the next subsection. Similarly, in Tanzania *"all former staff members were dismissed and had to re-apply for a position in the new Tanzania Revenue Authority (TRA). More than a third (35%) were rejected on evidence or suspicion of misconduct. Almost 1,200 previous staff members, of whom 500 were former Customs officers, were not re-employed. All new employees were given a one-year probation period before being accepted on a permanent basis."* (Fjeldstad et al., 2003, p. 7). However, the merit recruitment policy applied in Tanzania may have been distorted by some irregularities in the application process.[114]

5.1.3. Programmatic responses to reducing corruption on the revenue side

The previous subsections reviewed specific "piecemeal" policies designed to reduce incentives and opportunities for corruption. In some cases, anticorruption programs are designed more comprehensively, encompassing several anticorruption initiatives, in order to pursue several objectives simultaneously. These more comprehensive approaches are known as

---

[113] Likewise, Hors (2001) identifies corruption purges of customs administrations in Pakistan and Philippines as measures that 'do not work' mainly due to the absence of political will and the lack of consistency in hiring policies.

[114] For a more detailed discussion of this issue, see Chapter 6.

Box 5.5.   Curbing corruption in Peru's tax administration: the case of semi-autonomous revenue agencies

The government's response to systemic corruption in tax administration in Peru was the creation of a Semi-Autonomus Revenue Authority (SARA) in 1991: the Superintendency of National Tax Administration (SUNAT). "The reform had several key elements: granting SUNAT meaningful administrative and financial autonomy, implementing radical personnel reform, investing in infrastructure, and information technology, and generating public support." (World Bank, 2001a, p. 1).

The considerable degree of autonomy granted to SUNAT allowed flexibility and innovative management but also helped to protect the agency from political patronage, which was endemic in the previous administration. Additionally, a strong system of incentives to improve collection and reduce corruption was imposed at both the agency and at the personnel levels. At the agency level SUNAT's budget was set as an automatic sharing deposit of 2 percent of collections; supposedly this generated an institutional motivation to increase collections. Personnel incentives to fight corruption were addressed by merit-based recruitment of the entire staff, and by a drastic increment in salaries from an average of $50 to $1000. Further provisions were taken to guarantee that salaries at SUNAT would remain competitive with those in the private sector.

As discussed in Section 5.2 of this study, hard data on corruption is typically inexistent. Yet, the effectiveness of Peru's SARA in curbing corruption can be assessed by citizens' responses to a perception survey. The perceptions that SUNAT had contributed to curb corruption in the tax administration were exceptionally strong. Respondents that considered corruption was much less and substantially less than prior to the reform accounted for 85 percent of the total. Those percentages contrast with the weaker ones for the same kind of experiment in Mexico and Venezuela.

To what extent is there more corruption in the tax agency than before the reform?

	Much less (percent)	Substantially less (percent)	Slightly less (percent)	No change (percent)	Slightly more (percent)	Substantially more (percent)	Much more (percent)
Peru	52	33	10	0	0	0	4
Mexico	4	17	34	36	6	0	2
Venezuela	8	18	53	18	0	0	4
Bolivia	2	6	18	48	16	6	4

Source: Talercio (2000).

Despite the success of the SUNAT during its first years it is widely believed that around early 1997, the SUNAT lost the strong commitment and the political support that it had when it was created. The decline of political commitment against corruption was also noticed on the effectiveness of the judicial system and the police, leaving SUNAT's anticorruption efforts without the required institutional support to be fully effective. The lack of sustained political commitment purportedly reduced the efficiency of the SUNAT and generated once again internal corruption, infiltration of political interests and management manipulation. Revenues from tax collection delegated to the SUNAT (last column in Table 5.A.1) experienced a moderate increment after the establishment of the SUNAT, yet revenues decreased after year 1997.

Sources: Estela (2000), Taliercio (2002), McCarten (2004), Mann (2004).

programmatic responses. Besides the synergies and economies of scale that such programmatic responses may offer over piecemeal strategies, programmatic responses also offer international financial institutions and bilateral donors entry points and better opportunities in general to support anticorruption efforts in any particular country.

Programmatic responses in reducing corruption on the revenue side of the budget include: the reform of the tax system, which may involve tax policy reform, or tax administration reform, or both. Two types of tax administration reform deserve special mention among programmatic responses to corruption: the creation of an autonomous revenue authority and the formation of LTUs.

5.1.3.1. Tax policy reform. As noted earlier, overly complex tax systems with multiple exemptions and deductions, with special regimes granted illegally by powerful tax authorities, and with high tax rates and large tax rate differentials provide virtually insurmountable opportunities for bribery of tax officials. These windows of opportunity tend to be wider in developing and transition countries because in these countries there is a higher concentration of revenues from just a few large taxpayers, who often can hire tax prepares with superior technical skills to those of tax inspectors. The windows of opportunity tend to be wider in developing countries because of their heavier reliance on trade taxes and customs revenues where massive fraud can take place through the misclassification of goods or the wrong valuation of merchandise. As such, reforms aimed at rationalizing and simplifying the tax system by broadening the tax bases through the elimination of tax incentives and special regimes, reducing exemptions and deductions, and lowering and harmonizing tax rates (e.g., between corporate and income taxes) should be considered first strategies for reducing corruption among tax officials. Although many tax reforms in developing and transition countries over the last decade have pursued the simplification of the tax systems,[115] there have been powerful political incentives (including vote-buying and political support of special interest groups), to make simplification and transparency difficult to attain.[116] However, there have been some relative successes in some countries, advanced enough to make a difference in the overall fight against corruption. These successes have been notable in some transitional countries of Eastern Europe and the FSU, such as the case of the Tax Code adopted in 2002 in the Russian Federation.[117]

5.1.3.2. Broad tax administration reform. Tax administration (and customs) systems of many developing and transitional countries suffer from poor institutional structures, inefficient operations, and lack of resources to invest in training and computerization. These conditions lead to poor tax collections and tend to favor corrupt practices. Any country strategy to fight corruption on the revenue side of the budget needs to seriously consider the modernization and general upgrade of the tax administration apparatus. In fact, tax administration reforms have become quite common among developing countries (Bird and Casanegra de Jantscher, 1992; Bagchi *et al.*, 1995; Tanzi and Pellechio, 1995; Silvani and Baer, 1997).

One of the most successful approaches has been the application in a small number of countries of what is known as NPM theory.[118] This approach to public management shifts the public administration from a process and control approach (which targets opportunities of evasion) to a customer-oriented approach that addresses a growing demand for public administrative services, lowers taxpayer compliance costs, and promotes a favorable perception of the role of government and the use of public funds.[119]

Several other reforms used in the modernization of tax administrations can be effective in reducing corruption:

- *Changing the organizational structure from being organized around types of taxes to being organized around main* functions. In this second approach, functions such as tax assessments, audits and collections are performed by different individuals in different offices, and therefore it

---

[115] See Martinez-Vazquez and McNab (2000).

[116] See Hettich and Winer (1988, 1999).

[117] See Martinez-Vazquez, Rider, and Wallace (forthcoming).

[118] For references see CLAD (1998), Bird and Oldman (2000), and Yamamoto (2003).

[119] A prominent example is that of Singapore's tax administration reform in 1992 (World Bank, 2000c; Bird and Oldman, 2000).

makes it more difficult for tax officials to collude and engage in corrupt practices.

- *Electronic filing.* Electronic filing serves two purposes. First it limits the interaction between taxpayers and public officials. Second, electronic information facilitates data management within the tax administration and also facilitates verification cross checks with other databases.
- *Self-assessment.* As in the case of electronic filing, self-assessment (as opposed to official assessment of tax liabilities) reduces interaction between taxpayers and tax officials; it also tends to neutralize the degree of discretionary power of public officials in the assessment process.
- *Payments through the banking system.* Banks are generally efficient institutions in cash management and have practically no access to tax records. Thus, attempting evasion by bribing a bank cashier is almost never an option.

Two particular types of tax administration reform strategies have been applied in several transitional and developing countries with the objective, among others, of reducing corruption. These are the creation of Semi-Autonomous Revenue Agencies (SARAs) and/or the introduction of specialized LTUs. The next subsections discuss some of their advantages in relation to corruption.

Autonomous revenue authorities. A third programmatic response to corruption on the revenue-side of the budget is the establishment of an autonomous (or semi-autonomous) revenue authority. Semi-autonomous revenue authorities (also known as SARAs) have been somewhat of a trend, with SARAs being introduced in countries as diverse as Malaysia, New Zealand, Singapore, Ghana, Kenya, Malawi, Rwanda, South Africa, Tanzania, Uganda, Zambia, Bolivia, Guatemala, Guyana, Mexico, Peru, and Venezuela (Bird, 2003; Taliercio, 2004).

Most of the benefits of the SARAs arise from their ability to circumvent the deficiencies related to the traditional public sector and civil service rules, including low wages, inflexible operating procedures, promotions based on seniority rather than merit, and excessive job protections even in the case of malfeasance. Professionalization of the tax administration is not only aimed at curtailing corruption among the ranks of revenue officials but also at improving the quality of service received by taxpayers. Civil servants in SARAs are usually offered higher incentives and higher wages than those in other government ministries and agencies. SARAs usually operate on the basis of meritocracy (merit-based recruitment, promotion, and compensation). The SARAs can also operate outside the regular sphere of political influence, thereby limiting the potentially corrupting influence of politicians over the revenue collection process. Overall, better paid, more skilled, professional, and independent tax administrations lead to significant reductions in corruption. Some examples of SARA successes in curbing corruption are those of Peru, Kenya, and

South Africa.[120] Peru's reform was considered so successful in reducing systemic corruption, during the first years of its creation that it was used as an example for the later creation of SARAs in Venezuela, Mexico, Bolivia, Guatemala, Argentina, and Colombia (see Box 5.5). However, a more recent study of the impact of SARA's in controlling corruption by Mann (2004), concludes that SARA's in some developing countries including Peru, Guatemala, and Tanzania may have made some initial inroads into reducing corruption, but corruption has continued to ebb and flow without (perhaps) trending decidedly downward.

However, the creation of SARAs should not be considered a panacea for solving the problems faced by tax administration authorities in developing countries. For example, the creation of a SARA may produce the perverse effects of high political instability and lack of intergovernmental coordination (World Bank, 2000b). Detractors have also argued that by applying an "enclave" reform approach, the introduction of a SARA may simply avoid addressing larger problems faced by the entire administration in the public sector.

From the perspective of this study, the most important question is whether SARAs are effective in curbing corruption in tax administrations. The effectiveness of SARAs in combating corruption can be divided into two aspects: (a) greater managerial autonomy and (b) ability to pay higher wages.

Is greater autonomy an effective remedy for corruption? Granting autonomy to revenue authorities is usually justified on the grounds of greater managerial flexibility and control of political interference and patronage. These are good bases to design an effective anticorruption strategy for the tax administration agency. On the other hand, as just pointed out, autonomy could be used as a way to circumvent the deficiencies of public administrations and thus void comprehensive reform of the entire civil service.[121] Another concern is that autonomy could be abused to avoid regular channels of control. The latter would facilitate corruption in SARAs vis-a-vis regular or "unreformed" tax administrations. However, there is not much evidence that too much autonomy by SARAs has led to any of these perverse effects. In fact, it has been quite common for SARAs to struggle to reach some minimum level of autonomy from the Ministry of Finance. The Ugandan Revenue Authority (URA) is a good example of how the interference of the Ministry of Finance and absence of real autonomy led to the limited reduction of political patronage (see Box 5.6). Two recent studies by Taliercio (2000, 2004) show there is a strong positive correlation between SARAs' overall performance (including the control of

---

[120] See Taliercio (2004).
[121] See, for example, Taliercio (2004) and McCarten (2003).

corruption) and their degree of autonomy. In particular, Taliercio high-lights the success of the institutions in Peru and Kenya based on their high levels of autonomy.

Can freedom or increased flexibility to set wages for tax administrators work as an effective anticorruption tool? In general, the answer is yes, since low wages make it harder to recruit and maintain skilled disciplined workers and low wages also provide incentives to engage in corruption. However, there are some potential problems associated with this strategy. First, as the recent case of Ghana shows (World Bank, 2000c), pay hikes for tax revenue officials may cause unrest and complaints from the rest of civil servants in government. In Ghana, this situation finally translated into a general salary increase for all civil servants, matching the increases in the revenue department. Thus, wage differential strategies within the public service apparatus are not necessarily stable and may turn into pressures for the government to incur unaffordable personnel spending. Second, if wage differentials between the revenue department and the rest of the civil service persist, envy can lead to problems with interagency cooperation (Taliercio, 2004). Third, higher wages in the revenue department can raise the stakes for political capture and corruption in the appointment of staff. For example, in 1991, the new URA was separated from the Ministry of Finance and was granted the rights to hire its personnel outside the regulations of the rest of the civil service. The relative high salaries for URA's were devised as a pivotal instrument to enhance the quality of recruitment and to avoid future corrupt behavior. Although recruiting decisions were in theory to be independent of the rest of the executive, in practice, both the Ministry of Finance and other government agencies managed to effectively interfere with URA's hiring and firing policies (see Box 5.6).[122]

All things considered, SARAs have been somewhat successful in combating corruption in developing nations, especially in the first few years after their creation. However, their overall effectiveness is still in question.

Large taxpayer units. An especially sensitive area for corruption in tax administration is the monitoring and collection of tax payments from large taxpayers. The size and scope of tax payments by large corporations – and the potential financial gain resulting through bribes – are generally mul-tiples of the salaries of individual tax collectors. Thus, a very tempting bribe in most of these cases can just be a very small fraction of the taxes owed.

---

[122] For instance, several high-ranked officials working previously at the revenue office were provisionally transferred directly to the URA. However, most of these positions were legit-imized soon after. It is also reported that after 1996, the recruitment for administrative positions started to grow faster (Therkildsen, 2004).

> ### Box 5.6.   Revenue authority with 'limited autonomy' in Uganda
>
> The Ugandan Revenue Authority (URA) was established in the early 1990s with the goal of improving tax administration management and results and, among other things, to fight corruption. To these ends, the URA was to hire its staff outside the strict regulations for the general civil service, and to have flexibility in hiring, firing, and pay compensation policies. The main problem with the Ugandan reform was the level of actual autonomy granted to the URA. In practice, some of the autonomy prescribed in the legal framework was never put in place, and the Ministry of Finance has continued to take unilateral decisions that affected the URA's operations. Despite the existence of a legal provision regarding a permanent and predictable level of funding for this authority, the Ministry of Finance gained the power to change that level each year. The annual approval of the URA's budget also has provided a vehicle to politicians to exert power over URA's high-ranked officials.
>
> Source: Therkildsen (2004), Fjeldstad *et al.* (2003).

The creation of LTUs can play an important role in a country's anti-corruption strategy. LTUs are special divisions within the tax administration apparatus that focus on a reduced share of taxpayers, sometimes just in the hundreds, but which may represent up to two-thirds of total collections (see Box 5.7).[123] Due to their considerably higher tax liabilities, large taxpayers are more likely to have incentives to evade and to seek the cooperation of corrupt tax officials than are smaller taxpayers. The potential for corrupt relationships between large taxpayers and tax officials is likely to be higher if the large taxpayers are assigned to "regular" tax officers. This is because regular tax officers are likely to have lower salaries,

---

[123] Large Taxpayer Units represent an "enclave approach" that allows the tax administration authorities to concentrate resources, to more closely monitor tax inspectors, and to exercise greater managerial flexibility in a smaller unit vis-a-vis the overall tax administration. In addition, LTUs have been used as a pilot group to test new and more sophisticated tax administration procedures such as electronic filing and self assessment of liabilities, which can then be rolled out to the general population (Baer *et al.*, 2002). For example, the application of customs services specifically designed for large taxpayers has increased administrative efficiency and compliance in several transitional and developing countries (McCarten, 2003).

Box 5.7. **The large taxpayers monitoring system in the Bureau of Internal Revenues of the Republic of the Philippines**

Following a significant increase in the fiscal deficit in the late 1990s, the government of the Republic of Philippines introduced reforms directed at improving the revenue base and tax effort. As such, the Bureau of Internal Revenue (BIR) proceeded to put in place programs that, although mainly intended to enhance revenues, also address corruption through the use of information technology. These programs included electronic transmission of tax payments, an automated tax verification system as well as the computerization of all data pertaining to large taxpayers.

This last measure, the computerization of data on large taxpayers, was a part of establishment of the Large Taxpayers Monitoring System aimed at closely monitoring the tax compliance of the country's large taxpayers. Besides technological improvements there also were efforts on the administrative side: in November 1999 the BIR went through organizational restructuring that aimed, among other things, to strengthen administrative control over large taxpayers.

These measures allowed a significant improvement of the tracking of the value-added tax audits. According to the Deputy Commissioner and Head of Large Taxpayer Operations Group, in just 1 year approximately PHP 70 billion (US 1.4 billion) in under-declarations were uncovered. One of the initial projects that the BIR undertook was to concentrate on the correct declaration of VAT by large corporate taxpayers, in particular the electronic matching of purchases and sales and the fraudulent use of VAT credits. A further advantage of computerizing the data on large taxpayers was that, since it has phased out human intervention, it was possible to employ what was called the "no contact audit". The assessment and collection of taxes were accomplished without using human resources, which reduced corruption and also saved money and time as fewer people had to make site visits.

Sources: SAS-Business Intelligence (2004).

---

to be less closely monitored, and may not be trained to deal with strong pressures that large payers can exert. In contrast, LTUs personnel can receive advanced training, have at their disposal advanced equipment and better facilities, and because they are highly skilled, they tend to have higher salaries.[124] In addition, opportunities for engaging in corruption are limited by the improvement of automated control systems. LTU's managers also have a greater ability to monitor the activities of lower level functionaries, if nothing else because LTU's officials are fewer in number.

LTUs are more able to address the "depth" of corruption (the size of the bribes or gains from corruption) than the "breadth" (how widespread corruption is in number of corrupt acts or corrupt individuals.). The more careful identification and monitoring of large taxpayer compliance is an effective mechanism to control the type of corruption that offers potentially larger bribes and also larger revenue-collection loss. [125] Hence the introduction of LTUs in highly corrupt systems can help bring a sharp increase in tax revenue collections. Moreover, curtailing corruption and bribery at the top is not only important in terms of the avoided losses in revenues, but also for the demonstration effect that this can have on the rest of the tax administration disposition toward corruption. Thus, LTUs may also have an effect on the breadth of corruption as this demonstration effect helps reduce corruption among the large number of small taxpayers.

However, it must be clear that LTU's staff is not immune to corruption, and in some ways have even greater risks of being "captured" by tax evaders than regular tax administrators. Some potential disadvantages are easily noticeable. First, LTU's tend to control the significantly larger percent of tax revenues of the country and thus this position offers much higher levels of potential gains from corruption. Second, LTU's tend to offer greater possibilities of interaction between tax officials and taxpayers. Often the largest taxpayers receive LTU's special personal services and particular tax administrators may be assigned to specific taxpayers. Third, the smaller number of employees at LTUs may facilitate the multiparty concealment of corruption (that is necessary for corrupt acts to occur in settings where personnel are separated according to tax functions).

It appears that the ultimate effects of LTUs in curbing corruption depend on the continuity of the financial and technical support that they receive from the central government, and in developing countries from donor organizations. There are countries where, when this support faulted, a large share of the nation's revenues has fallen prey to corruption. Such has been the case in Ecuador's LTU, which was riddled by corruption at the end of 1990s, and in which rents (from corruption) were so high

---

[124] However, some of the failures of LTUs in developing countries are attributed to limitations in technical assistance, budget support, and external funding after the initial stages (Terkper, 2003).

[125] See Mocan (2004).

that LTU positions were bought from corrupt administrators (Baer *et al.*, 2002).

5.2. Reducing corruption on the expenditure side of the budget

Whereas anticorruption activities on the revenue side of the budget are largely limited to monitoring the activities of tax collectors and their interactions with taxpayers, the nature of corruption – and hence, anticorruption approaches – on the expenditure side of the budget are substantially more varied.

In some sense, the basic dimensions of anticorruption activities on the expenditure side of the budget are the same as on the revenue side, notably efforts to reduce the motivation for corruption and efforts to reduce the windows of opportunity for corruption. The discussion of different approaches to limit the opportunities for corruption in this section further distinguishes between opportunities for administrative or bureaucratic corruption and opportunities for political corruption. Our own empirical analysis, reported in Annex 5.A, reveals that characteristics of budget process institutions, which signal a priori greater opportunities for corruption, are correlated with higher levels of political and administrative corruption.

5.2.1. Reducing motivations for corruption in government spending

Although the incentive or motivation to engage in corruption is identical on the revenue and expenditure sides of the budgets, and the general nature of the possible policy responses are quite similar, the effectiveness of the various responses to reduce corruption are in some ways quite different on the expenditure side of the budget. On the other hand, the available policy instruments to reduce the motivation for public officials to engage in corruption on the expenditure side of the budget are quite similar to those reviewed above for corruption on the revenue side and they include creating a culture of ethical behavior among government officials, establishing mechanisms of reporting and detecting corruption, increasing and enforcing penalties for corruption, and increasing wages in the public sector. Let us review these policy measures briefly, with a focus on responsiveness and effectiveness.

5.2.1.1. Political will, and instilling honesty and ethics. A key prerequisite for an effective anticorruption strategy in any country is a clear indication that public officials are expected to conduct themselves in an ethical manner. Creating a culture of ethical behavior in the public sector is easier said than done, especially in countries that have a tradition of closed government and hierarchical social relationships. As previously mentioned, many of the issues faced on the revenue side of the budget are far more cumbersome on the expenditure side, if nothing else because of the sheer number of civil servants related to the expenditure side of the budget.

Instilling honesty and ethics among civil servants is one these issues.[126]
Yet, there are many practical steps that a country can take to promote a
"culture of honesty" in the civil service. In Section 5.1.1 above we discuss a
variety of strategies designed to increase ethics among tax officials, including morals-building campaigns, the introduction of a Code of Conduct, and corruption purge campaigns. The challenge of the expenditure
side is how to reach the considerably larger number of people involved in
service delivery.

Several approaches have been used to address this need. One strategy
consists of using the mass media to recognize public servants who stand
against corruption. For example, the government of Argentina has officially named June the fourth as *Anticorruption Day* in honor of Alfredo
Mara Pochat, a lawyer murdered after more than a decade of fighting
corruption at Argentina's Central Bank and as the head of the Corruption
Control Program of the National Postal Service. This type of recognition
not only demonstrates the gratitude of a country to those who denounce
and combat corruption, but also educates the population by spreading a
*"powerful example of how one individual can create resistance to corrup-
tion."*[127]

It is widely accepted that no anticorruption policy can be successful
without a strong political will and commitment from the top to enforce and
promote anticorruption policies. As such, the effectiveness of anticorruption efforts is greatly undermined when the leadership of a country is itself
perceived to be corrupt. This is because government officials at all levels
believe that little effort will be dedicated to the enforcement, revision, and
follow-up of anticorruption programs and policies.

The question is how to generate political will? Where political will is
weak, the international community may exert pressures on high levels of
government to take specific anticorruption measures. IFIs have taken an
active role in this regard. For instance, this kind of pressure was displayed
in 1997, when the IMF suspended a 220 million loan to Kenya after President Daniel Arap Moi failed to establish an anticorruption authority
(Wittig, 2000, p. 9). Similarly, other multilateral organizations and individual donor countries have conditioned aid resources to minimum anticorruption measures by recipient countries.[128] To date there is no good
analysis or evidence on the effectiveness of foreign pressures in curbing
corruption in developing countries. However, the "carrot approach"

---

[126] Some reasons for this are discussed in Chapter 4.

[127] See *"Alfredo Mara Pochat has received the Integrity Award from Transparency International
in year 2000."* Transparency International Web Page/Integrity Award Winners.

[128] Section 5.5 below discusses the anticorruption pressure exerted by the European Union on
Cote d'Ivoire, Denmark on Burkina Faso, Britain on Sierra Leone, and Denmark and Britain
on Malawi.

currently used by donors is likely to capture the attention of political leaders, especially when foreign aid is a significant part of the budget of developing countries. An important difficulty is that, at least in the shorter run, it is difficult to discern whether or not anticorruption reforms are actually applied in practice or are just part of a cosmetic cover to comply with donors' demands.

Civil society organizations can be significant substitutes when political will is lacking. In particular, the OECD (2003) reports the important role played by several NGOs in generating political will that led to significant intergovernmental agreements against corruption in issues such as the criminalization of international bribery.[129]

5.2.1.2. Establishing mechanisms of reporting and detecting corruption. Although experiences vary from country to country and region to region (as discussed further in Chapter 3 of this study), the most common and pervasive form of expenditure corruption is likely to be petty corruption, including "petty theft" of government property, petty fraud (e.g., illicit diversion of government resources), "petty bribery" in order to assure the delivery of government services, or other "petty" illicit activities. The fragmented nature of the corrupt activity, the relatively small amounts involved (per corrupt act), and the pervasiveness throughout the system, complicate the effective detection and prosecution of administrative corruption. A wide variety of government responses that promote greater transparency and accountability procedures in the provision of public services can contribute to a more open public sector, and one that is less tolerant of corrupt practices.

In addition to the reliance on regular sound public expenditure management practices and public expenditure controls (which are discussed below in Section 5.2.2), there are two specific approaches to monitoring administrative corruption, and thereby increasing the probability of getting caught (which in turn should provide a negative incentive to engage in corruption).

First, systematic vertical "top–down" monitoring of government officials represents a potentially effective first step in curtailing corrupt practices. For instance, the Ministry of Health officials could monitor that medicines are disbursed to regional health institutions as intended, while regional officials should have a hierarchical supervisory relationship with the district health officials, and so on. In addition to the regular hierarchical monitoring, it is effective to have additional monitoring mechanisms to prevent the collusion between two links in the chain. For instance,

---

[129] The OECD report highlights the effective work of the Business and Advisory Committee to the OECD, the Trade Union Advisory Committee to the OECD, the International Chamber of Commerce, and Transparency International.

inspectors from the Ministry of Health may wish to (physically) verify the stocks of medicines actually received by district health offices. Such direct inspections (rather than relying exclusively on hierarchical monitoring) increase the openness and unpredictability of the monitoring process and increase the probability of detection of corruption.

A second approach to detecting administrative corruption is to rely on "bottom-up" or "grass-roots" monitoring and reporting administrative corruption. This involves establishing reporting mechanisms such as an ombudsman or an autonomous anticorruption office, where citizens can report corrupt activities. For instance, this would enable residents to report when they are forced to make illicit copayments in order to receive medicine from a public clinic, or would provide parents with an avenue to report teachers who fail to show up at their schools, and so on. Of course, it is crucial that the reporting mechanism be seen as fair, quick and effective at correcting the corrupt practices, while protecting whistle-blowers from potential retribution by the corruption official or "the system." In many countries, the limited effectiveness in practice of such reporting mechanisms results from the limited enforcement authority yielded to the "autonomous" anticorruption officials.

The effectiveness of both approaches to monitoring and reporting types of petty corruption are often tied to the social and geographic mobility of a country. Particularly in highly centralized developing and transitional countries, the cost of top–down monitoring – beyond the hierarchical monitoring of one's immediate subordinates – can be prohibitively expensive. For instance, due to the limited transportation and telecommunications infrastructure in Bangladesh, central government officials in Dhaka are barely able to supervise the activities within the 64 districts, let alone directly observe whether resources in fact make it down to the Thanas (approximately 500 rural subdistrict government units). Likewise, district level officials are unable to directly observe whether resources make it down to the service delivery units at the community level. Thus, if a local headmaster or doctor acts in cohorts with Thana officials, local residents would have to go either to the District Headquarters or to Dhaka to effectively register a complaint with the knowledge that likely no corrective action will be taken (World Bank, 1997, 2002a).

The fight against political corruption should be carried out by institutions such as the parliament, supreme external audit institutions, civil society organizations, and media. Although these institutions have an important role in overseeing government actions, it must not be forgotten that these institutions themselves are often also important stakeholders in the political process through political appointments and other links. Thus, it is desirable to rely on a variety of institutions and watch for mechanisms that preserve their independence from policy makers.

Parliament is the highest representation of civil society and, as such, is empowered to monitor the executive branch and hold it accountable.

Legislators have the responsibility for containing corruption at the policy-making level (political corruption or state capture) through the monitoring and approval of the budget. Hence, strengthening the capabilities of legislative bodies to effectively perform this role is a pivotal step in anticorruption policy (see Box 5.8). Some advances in this mater can be seen in several countries.

Recent studies show that more parliament bodies have been strengthening their capabilities and taking active roles in budget oversight,[130] with direct beneficial effects on curbing corruption.[131] Parliamentarian committees may be delegated responsibility to oversee public accounts and general audit reports, and maintain hearings and investigations through anticorruption commissions. In order to be effective and maintain credibility, these commissions should not only be formed by members of the governing party, but also members of opposition or independent members of the parliament. More generally, in order to preserve transparency and accountability of parliamentary activity, anticorruption policy should aim to decrease political parties' ability to compel legislators to act for the benefit of narrow party interests (Schick, 2002). In order to increase accountability of parliamentarians to the constituents they represent, civil society should have the ability to follow and scrutinize parliamentary debates as well as parliamentary voting. This may be possible by the broadcast of parliamentarian proceedings and transparency in the legislative decision-making mechanisms.[132]

5.2.1.3. Enforcing penalties and prosecution of corruption. All efforts of detection, investigation, and oversight are useless if corruption culprits remain unpunished after their wrongdoing is detected. However, the enforcement of prosecution for corrupt acts on the expenditure side is subject to different restrictions than on the revenue side. For example, on the revenue side we discussed the policy response of firing the entire staff of a tax administration and then requiring that all personnel reapply for their positions. Such an approach is unlikely to be feasible or successful if applied to the rest of the public administration, even under the most endemic corruption situations. The sheer number involved makes it also difficult to undertake the criminal prosecution of petty administrative corruption (such as requiring illicit payments in exchange for health services). In addition, the dismissal of corrupt civil servants is often hard to enforce. If enforcement were done randomly, this would severely limit the ability to dismiss public officials on the grounds of the unfairness of the system.

---

[130] See OECD (1998), World Bank (2003), and Santiso and Garcia-Belgrano (2004).
[131] See World Bank (2002b), OECD (1998), and Santiso and Garcia-Belgrano (2004).
[132] Secret ballot voting mechanisms undermine transparency of the decision-making, and, thus accountability of legislators to voters.

Box 5.8. Support to parliamentarian development

The wave of democratization in the past decade has turned legislative bodies around the world into essential pieces of the puzzle for curbing corruption. Multilateral and bilateral aid organizations such as the World Bank and USAID have recognized that steps must be taken to support the performance of parliamentarians and to increase their capabilities in the governance process. For example, the World Bank has developed a program for parliaments to strengthen their capacity to oversee the allocation and use of public funds, to better represent the interests of the poor in the policy process, to support learning networks on the development of key policy issues. This kind of support motivates parliamentarians to exert effective oversight of the executive and also to promote effective anticorruption legislation. Similarly, USAID supports programs on democratic governance, legislative strengthening, and corruption reduction. In 2002, for instance, USAID's legislative program focused on building Ghana's Parliament institutional capacity, increasing stakeholder input on policy and legislation, and empowering selected Parliamentary committees. NGOs have also been involved in these activities. For example, the National Democratic Institute (NDI) recently assisted the South African and Turkish parliaments with the adoption of codes of ethics and has held symposiums on ethics and transparency in Paraguay and Southern Africa.

Anticorruption efforts by legislators can benefit from the experiences of other countries. Associations and networks of legislators across countries such as the Global Organization of Parliamentarians Against Corruption (GOPAC) are organized to build integrity and to promote effective parliament oversight. The GOPAC serves as the global point of contact for information sharing between parliaments, best practice research provision and as a liaison with other international organizations. Other examples of parliamentarian associations that have addressed corruption issues include the African Parliamentarians Network Against Corruption (APNAC), the Interparliamentary Forum of the Americas (FIPA), and the Parliamentary Centre.

Sources: USAID (2001), World Bank (2004b, c).

Furthermore, public employees are usually under the protection of powerful unions such as teachers and health workers unions. Another factor working against enforcement is political patronage and "protection" by higher echelons in the political hierarchy.

Here again, there are two aspects that need to be considered in order to strengthen the effectiveness of prosecution in a country: anticorruption legislation and the judicial system. The number of reported cases of corruption that end up prosecuted may be low due to loopholes in the legislation regarding rules of evidence. For instance, when the legislation places very strict standards of burden of proof on the prosecution, it considerably limits the ability of the judicial system to ensure convictions. This appears to have been a difficulty in recent times in Thailand, the Philippines, and Indonesia.[133]

The effectiveness of the criminal legislation to guarantee successful prosecution is a crucial point for anticorruption efforts. Singapore and Hong Kong provide good examples of effective anticorruption legislations. On the other hand, anticorruption legislation may also go too far. For example, in Hong Kong and Tanzania there are special corruption rules that reverse the ordinary burden-of-proof rule, significantly favoring the prosecution's work.[134] In these countries, a public official accused of illicit enrichment is not presumed innocent until proven guilty, but rather presumed guilty until he/she is able to demonstrate the legal origin of his/her wealth. Of course, this relieves the prosecution of the burden of providing evidence of the corrupt act itself.[135]

At any rate, revisions of the current legal system should determine if the legislation is suited to support the investigation of reported or suspicious cases. At the other end, some country legislations impose formidable obstacles to investigative actions. For example, the Philippines maintains laws that protect the secrecy of bank accounts. In other countries, such as Ukraine, investigative journalists and other investigative organizations require the prior approval of the individual under investigation.

Criminal prosecution of high-ranked officials charged with political corruption commonly faces greater hurdles than those faced against petty corruption. In particular, effective prosecution of political corruption is often limited by legislation regarding immunity of president/prime minister and sometimes senior political figures.[136] This is a difficult area because some degree of immunity is required to protect political leaders, while conducting duties of national interest, from charges that very often

---

[133] See Transparency International (2003).

[134] In Hong Kong, the Prevention of Bribery Act and in Tanzania the Prevention of Corruption Act.

[135] In Tanzania, for example, "For a prima facie case to be established against the accused, it is enough for the prosecution to establish that the accused was a public officer; that, in that capacity, he or she acquired property or obtained the benefit of services, and that there are reasonable grounds to suspect that he or she corruptly acquired property or obtained the benefit of services, as the case may be." (Ofosu-Amaah *et al.*, 1999, p. 58).

[136] Two recent prominent cases illustrating this point are those of the President of France, Jacques Chirac and former Prime Minister of Italy, Silvio Berlusconi.

can be politically motivated. Yet, when immunity clauses are too broad and generous they have been used as shields against prosecution of corruption and thus to circumvent political accountability. For example, until recently it was not uncommon in the Russian Federation for indicted businessmen to run for a parliament seat in some far-flung region, often showering the electorate with unrealistic promises, to gain political immunity.[137]

Another potential problem with the prosecution for corruption and the enforcement of penalties is that when corrupt behavior is detected by external audit institutions in many countries these agencies have no prosecutorial powers. While either parliament or the court system in these countries is supposed to follow up with the proper prosecution of the case, this does not always happen because of the blockage by dominant coalitions in parliament or because of the lesser independence of the courts. Thus an important aspect of enforcement of penalties for corruption is to provide supreme audit institutions with prosecutorial powers. However, there are some other problems associated with this latter arrangement. In order to prosecute a former president or prime minister on grounds of corruption, it can sometimes be necessary to turn to the highest political decision-making body in the country. Effective judicial process against political corruption also requires the existence of extradition agreements, in order to prosecute corrupt politicians who leave the country. Extradition agreements, such as the European Arrest Warrant signed in year 2001, are important steps forward to enable transnational prosecution. While agreements extend to more countries, bilateral agreements can be useful for the prosecution of most important cases of political corruption (see Box 5.9).

The lack of independence and probity of the court system can also severely hinder the prosecution of corruption cases. For example, there is a list of countries, which includes Mexico, Malaysia, Philippines, and Thailand, where very few cases of reported corruption end up being prosecuted, mainly due to bribery of judges.[138] Several measures can be taken to control endemic corruption of the judiciary. One remedy is the closer monitoring of case results by the Ministry of Justice, parliament, and NGOs. In the case of political corruption judges may be manipulated not only through bribery but also through strong influences and some times harassment.[139]

Even when the right anticorruption legislation is there and the court system is able to enforce the law, it is important to ask whether a punitive

---

[137] For some example, see Russian Regional Report (1999, 2002).
[138] More on this issue is discussed in Chapter 3.
[139] See Chapter 3 for several examples of manipulation of judges and harassment of investigative journalists.

Box 5.9. Extradition and political corruption: Argentina's request of extradition for former President Carlos Menem

The controversial Peronist, former President of Argentina Carlos Menem, in power from 1989 to 1999, ended his mandate under accusations of corruption and several investigations linked to his time in office. Menem spent seven months under house arrest in Argentina in 2001 after allegations that he headed an "illicit association" which sold Argentine weapons to Croatia and Ecuador in defiance of United Nations weapons embargoes in the 1990s. After withdrawing his candidacy for a third presidential term in 2003 he left for Chile. He faced two extradition requests filed in April 2004. The first extradition was requested by Argentine federal magistrate Norbert Oyarbide for allegedly undeclared funds in a Swiss Bank account. The second extradition was requested by Argentine federal Judge Jorge Urso after Menem repeatedly failed to appear in court about alleged misuse of funds allocated for the construction of two jails during his administration.

One of the key issues for Menem's extradition requests was that Chile and Argentina have very different legal systems. Moreover, there is no existing bilateral treaty on extradition between the two countries. However, they are both part of the regional Montevideo Convention on Extradition treaty in force since 1933. In order for the Montevideo Extradition Treaty to be enforced some conditions must be met: the allegation for which an arrest warrant and extradition are requested must be considered a crime in both nations; the allegation must deserve imprisonment greater than 1 year; and the allegation must still stand. In this case, a Chilean judge must review all conditions and consequently the defendant's attorneys have the right to an appeal, which can then be transferred to a penal court. On May 28, 2004, Chilean Judge Humberto Espejo rejected the first extradition request filed by Judge Norberto Oyarbide stating that Menem's extradition is inadmissible since he has not been formally charged in Argentina, as is required by Chilean law. The second extradition request filed by Judge Urso was cancelled in September 2004, after Menem retruned from his self-imposed exile. He is currently working on a possible candidacy for 2008.

Sources: Mercosur. Chilean justice blocks Menem extradition, Mercopress, May 28, 2004, The Associated Press, Menem extradition bid turned down, BBC News UK Edition, May 28, 2004, The Associated Press, Argentina Requests Extradition for Menem, Washington Post, April 30, 2004.

strategy is an effective tool in fighting corruption. While the overall effects of prosecution and penalties are difficult to measure, convictions are, at least, an effective way to isolate corrupt agents from the system and prevent them from continuing. Yet, prosecution even at the highest levels may not be effective without the application of simultaneous prevention strategies such as an appropriate system of incentives and instilling ethics. For instance, the dismissals and indictments of the Primer Ministers of South Korea and Pakistan for several consecutive terms highlight a commitment to combat corruption at high levels of government, but it also reveals that this cycle can continue indefinitely if there is not a change in the predisposition to engage in corruption of political leaders and public servants in general.

5.2.1.4. Wages and incentive-compatible compensation systems. Just as they can be used to curb corruption among tax administrators, higher wages and incentive-compatible compensation schemes can be used to curb corruption on the expenditure side of the budget. It seems obvious that when public officials such as teachers and doctors and government accountants are paid a "fair" competitive wage, their incentive to engage in corrupt practices to supplement their income is reduced. But, even though this policy response has been quite common in efforts to reduce revenue corruption, it is rarely discussed in the policy debate to reduce administrative corruption. And there are probably good reasons for that. The consideration of a broad increase in the wages of public officials including "front-line providers" (e.g., health care providers) in developing and transitional countries is often highly unrealistic, since many governments are simply unable to generate the necessary resources.[140] In short, in an ideal world, performance-based compensation may be used to reduce incentives for corruption. Yet, the scarcity of public resources and the complex nature of public services make this option unfeasible in many cases. It is often the case in developing countries that administrative services are over-staffed with poorly paid and low-skilled personnel. The obvious policy – reducing the number of public employees while increasing wages and required skills – runs the risk of reforming the entire civil service of the country, an overwhelming task that very few governments are willing to consider. This issue is further discussed in the next section.

---

[140] This high cost of fair wages is particularly true for public officials that are expected to work in poor and rural areas. Front-line providers request higher wages to be willing to reside in these areas. For example, the World Bank (2003, p. 97) reports that a doctor in Indonesia would require multiples of current pay levels to live in the remote province of West Papua.

5.2.2. Reducing the opportunities for administrative corruption in government expenditures

There exist a number of strategies to reduce opportunities for bureaucrats to engage in corrupt practices. Among the most prominent ones we have the following:

(i) Improving systems of public service spending control and public financial management.
(ii) Introducing best practices in public procurement mechanisms.
(iii) Designing adequate mechanisms of civil service control.

5.2.2.1. Improving systems of public service spending control.   Budget implementation processes and practices have been the subject of significant improvements and innovations that have improved the overall efficiency of budgets and have also contributed to reducing opportunities for corrupt behavior among bureaucrats (see Box 5.10).[141] Accountability and transparency are needed to assure that the budget is executed as planned, without any leakages. This requires in turn strengthening the budget legislation, mechanisms and procedures for accounting, internal and external auditing, control and monitoring of the budget implementation, budget reporting, budget evaluation and performance monitoring practices.[142] In a recent publication Schaeffer (2002) lays out important dimensions that should be taken into consideration to reduce opportunities of corruption within the financial management system of a country. The adequacy of the financial management system in place can be examined by means of diagnostic surveys (Table 5.1).

It is clear that financial information is a key input for all the aforementioned controls; and that data integrity and legitimateness is a precondition for their effectiveness.

Integrated Financial Management Systems (IFMSs)are computerized software applications that enable external and internal appraisal activities to retrieve financial information in a timely and consistent way for diverse report applications, institute automated controls, historical policy analysis, and integrated networking for expenditure tracking.[143] Modern IFMSs and accounting systems facilitate tracking of public spending and the matching of information from alternative sources (see IFMSs programmatic responses for further discussion on this topic). It is important to note, however, that effective implementation of IFMSs is conditioned by

---

[141] For example, Schiavo-Campo and Tomassi (1999) present detailed and comprehensive guidelines for improving expenditure management and budget implementation.
[142] Several studies in this topic are collected in Schiavo-Campo (1999).
[143] Also cited as Integrated Financial Management Information Systems (IFMISs).

Box 5.10.   The separation of functions in budget execution

In the budget execution phase, public resources are to be used in accordance with the budget formulation, and it is typically the responsibility of the Treasury system. Although the budget execution process varies substantially among countries, broadly speaking the process has the following stages: (i) commitment stage, when purchase orders are placed or contracts are signed; (ii) verification stage, when the spending agencies confirm the delivery of the goods and check the bill; (iii) payment authorization, in which a public accountant authorizes the payment; (iv) payment stage, when the bill is paid by cash, check, or electronic transfers; (v) accounting stage, when all transactions are recorded in books.

Corruption may arise in any of these stages or it may entail an interaction of them. For instance, a corrupt official may sign a verification with the help of another agent who created a ghost purchase order. To avoid such occurrences, in modern Treasury systems each of the aforementioned functions is undertaken by separate units. The separation of budget implementation functions to different units not only limits possibilities of corruption collusion within the administration but it also allows the collection of different records of data from each institution and the application of rigorous controls in each stage of the budget execution, reducing the opportunities for corruption. Internal audits, financial reports (generated by agencies for future monitoring and evaluation), and external audits are also important instruments of the budget implementation control.

Source: IMF (2001, 1999), Allen and Tommasi (2001).

---

the institution on supporting reforms on existing institutional structures embedded on the processes and procedures followed by all parties involved, including: the Ministry of Finance, the Treasury, the Central Bank, line ministries, spending agencies, the revenue administration agency, and the accountant general, as well as in the overarching legal and organizational framework of these parties.[144]

---

[144] Supporting reforms include the consolidation of all government accounts under the control of the Treasury, the harmonization of expenditure classification – typically following the GFS format, the integration of the IFMS with elements of e-governance, establishing network applications for information disclosure.

Table 5.1. **Example of a diagnostic questionnaire for public financial management systems**

Diagnostic area	Question
Budget legislation	Provides a clear and comprehensive definition of public money? Establishes the following elements of intergovernmental fiscal relations?
	1. Basic principles of supervision, intervention, and audit responsibilities?
	2. Budget accounting classifications are coherent and common to all levels of government?
	Establishes the definition of budget deficit and surplus, which excludes borrowings from receipts and excludes repayments for principal from expenditures
	Provides a legal basis for management (internal) control and internal audit?
	Defines the authorities and responsibilities for issuing and reporting on government guarantees?
Scope of the budget	Clearly defines appropriation and spending authority?
	All transactions of statutory extra-budgetary funds are defined?
	All fiscal transfers to subnational governments for general and specific purposes are defined?
	Does the budget document include:
	1. Fiscal policy objectives?
	2. Complete information on past and projected spending?
	3. Complete information on financial plans and operations of statutory extra-budgetary funds?
	4. A statement of contingent liabilities?
Budget execution and monitoring	Are there laws, regulations, and procedures that:
	1. Ensure that all public revenues are directly deposited?
	2. If separate bank accounts are permitted, who is responsible for opening, monitoring the banking operations?
	The Ministry of Finance/Treasury controls cash balances daily relative to borrowings?
	There are procedures to report and correct overspending?
Legal and policy framework	Are there laws, regulations, or policies that:
	1. Limit and define the authorities at each level of the administration for transferring funds within the approved budget?
	2. Prevent transfers between personnel costs and other subheads of the budget?
	3. Specify how budget funds that are unspent at the end of the fiscal year should be treated?
	4. Establish sanctions for overspending?
	5. Bind all persons responsible for spending money to implement management control practices?

(*Continued on next page*)

Table 5.1   *(Continued)*

Diagnostic area	Question
Performance monitoring	Does the government foster an environment that supports and demands improved performance by organizations and individuals? Is performance information on easily measured activities collected and used by spending units? By the Ministry of Finance? Are managers who are responsible for government programs and projects given clear short- and/or long-term operational goals and targets?
Evaluation	Is there an evaluation capacity sufficient to respond to the demands of the public sector/accountability?
Accounting and reporting	Is there an unified accounting and budgeting classification system regulated by the Ministry of Finance/Treasury? Are the final accounts produced, audited, and tabled in parliament shortly after the end of the fiscal year? Does the system provide for the recording commitments (obligations) as well as cash transactions?
Internal audits	Are internal audits established in line ministries? Does the mandate for these units include: Financial audit? System audit? Procurement audit process? Review of management internal control arrangements?
External audits	Is there an external auditor established by law with independence from government? Does the external auditor have authority to audit/clear all public and statutory funds and resources?
Organization and capacity for reform	Is there a coherent written strategy for bringing public financial management systems into line with general accepted standards? Does this strategy have the support of the Ministry of Finance? Are there training programs to complement any reform process?

Source: Schiavo Campo (1999) adapted by Spector (2005).

Public Finance Management (PFM), as a thematic concept, pervades almost every aspect discussed along this study, and so, it cannot be discussed as an independent item on this anticorruption checklist. One of PFM's conceptual components, the budget formulation approach, is of vital importance for corruption control. This is because all subsequent facets along the budget implementation are inevitably dependent on the quality of the budget formulation, and hence, dependent on the approach followed on the budget formulation process. Accountability and transparency are enhanced when the budget document establishes clear linkages among specific allocations and the programs they finance, the expected outcomes/results, the performance targets and indicators of progress, and the representatives or managers being accountable for the results. The performance-based budgeting (PBB) or budgeting for results approach has these characteristics.[145,146] The PBB approach is effective in combating corruption by allowing the disclosure of budgetary information in a transparent manner, and transforming the budget document into a binding commitment with civil society. Thus, society becomes an active control agent in the budget implementation process. PBB may help to reduce corruption through its effects on several fronts:

- increasing transparency in the allocation of resources among specific policy goals and objectives and the programs whereby the government expects to reach them;
- making representative and program managers accountable to citizenry in both the money spent (reducing fiduciary risks) and the results attained (achieving efficiency or value for money is rationally incompatible with corruption); and
- making higher level bureaucrats accountable to those responsible for determined programs, who will demand the full amount of funds allocated to them in the budget documents, minimizing the possibilities of those resources being lost in-route to those agencies.

Modern integrated accounting systems facilitate tracking of public spending and the matching of information from alternative sources. The most effective tool for control and internal audit of budget implementation is the introduction of a modern Treasury system where only items authorized in the budgets can be authorized for expenditure and the actual commitments of the spending units are checked for approval and finally disbursed by deconcentrated offices of an independent Treasury, which operates separately from the budget implementation units.

External audit organizations are also part of the process of public service spending control, but in this case the control is done in an ex-post fashion, intervening after the budget has been actually implemented. In order to guarantee an optimum level of audit quality, international audit standards should be required by law. The ultimate objective of audit reports is to be used as an evaluation tool and lead to corrective action if necessary. In order to accomplish this mission, audit reports should be made public and regularly revised by the legislature.

Although the audit of budget and accounting records is the main tool of spending control, its use as a tool for corruption oversight has limitations. A promising complementary approach for public spending control is the

---

[145] A superior anticorruption budgeting approach than line-item budgeting, and a greater focus on results vis-a-vis program-based budgeting, increasing accountability a step further than the latter.

[146] See Andrews and Shah (2004) for a discussion of subnational Citizen-Centered Budgets.

analysis of spending outcomes. In a recent study of Uganda, Ablo and Reinikka (1999) and Reinnika and Svensson (2004) point out that "actual service delivery (output) is much worse than budgetary allocations would imply because public funds (inputs) do not reach the intended facilities as expected, and hence outcomes cannot improve." More often than not, corruption translates into poor quality services. Thus, most mechanisms designed to monitor and improve the quality of public services can also be useful in uncovering or preventing corruption in public spending. The checks and balances needed to improve service delivery, such as greater accountability, also help decrease the opportunities for corruption.[147]

Public Expenditure Tracking Surveys (PETS) have become important instruments of expenditure control and anticorruption tools. These PETS are mechanisms of data collection based on field observation of physical public goods and public service characteristics and attributes, such as inputs actually used (e.g., labor and drugs), quality of services, outputs (e.g., enrollment rates, numbers of patients treated), and so on. The use of PETS for corruption control has already attained some encouraging results. Reinikka and Svensson (2003) report the successful case of Uganda, where a PETS in 1995 found that an average of 80 percent of public education funds were captured or misused by district public officials. This information was then widely covered in the media and several oversight mechanisms were put into place. The central government started to publicize monthly funds transferred to lower tiers of government in newspapers and primary schools were required to make public all of the information on the resources they received, in particular to parent–teacher associations. A subsequent PETS conducted in 2001 found that public resources captured or misused were on average equal to 20 percent of education funds, a drastic reduction from the previous 80 percent found in 1995. Following this success, several other country teams at the World Bank have started to conduct PETS in countries such as Albania, Ghana, Honduras, Macedonia, Mali, Rwanda, and Zambia.

5.2.2.2. Introducing best practices in public procurement and tendering mechanisms. Public procurement involves all government purchases of goods and services from the private sector. This is a key area in budget execution where there can be ample opportunity for corrupt behavior unless procurement procedures are transparent and explicitly stated. Transparency in the procurement process requires that relevant information is made available to participants in timely manner. Procurement process should have the objective of purchasing the right items, of a stated quality level at the minimum price. Clear and transparent biding and tendering process should guarantee equal opportunities for private companies and decisions need to be based on known standard rules.

---

[147] See, for example, the World Bank Development Report 2004.

Corrupt practices in public procurement involve the collusion of public officials with bidders in order to rig the award decision. This may include selective leaks of sensitive information, which may affect the final decision. Information leaks may involve the facilitation of bidding related information to a given contractor regarding the selection process, which is not made available to other competitors.

Internal and external procurement quality controls and independent auditing should be performed regularly to oversee the transparency of the system. Wittig (2000) presents a comprehensive description of contexts under which corruption arises in the procurement process, the respective corrections that may be applied, and relevant laws and regulations used in specific countries. The following discussion draws on Wittig's work.[148]

One first step to keep corruption out of public procurement is to prevent higher level officials from influencing procurement decisions. Thus, clear mechanisms are required to guarantee the independence of public officials in charge of procurement. The prevention of patronage and the promotion of independence and integrity by procurement officials require strong institutional support. A second step is to have clear regulations about responsibilities and clear delineations of what is considered ethical interaction among procurement officials. Third, measures need to be taken to prevent collusion between buyers and sellers. To this end it can be quite effective to separate the operational staff responsible for the different procurement duties such as budgeting, receipt and storage of bidding documentation, purchasing, dispute settlement, payments, and so on. Staff rotation may also be used to prevent sellers from establishing contact with procurement officials in charge of the process.

Fourth, it is equally important to safeguard procurement professionalism through merit-based recruitment and training programs. Procurement specialists may be required to satisfy international standards through international certification requirements.[149] Fifth, appeal procedures should allow competing firms to protest and dispute procurement procedures and award decisions. Conflict resolution mechanisms should include a first instance of internal review and self-evaluation. However, in cases for which internal evaluation results are in disagreement with the claim, contractors should have the right to appeal to alternative independent institutions or to a higher judiciary level. Sixth, the existence of a procurement office aimed at supervising and supporting ethics in the entire executive branch of government is an essential element for transparent procurement operations.

---

[148] See Klitgaard *et al.* (2000) for an alternative discussion on procurement policy remedies for a stylized procurement process.

[149] Some institutions that provide professional procurement certification and training are the National Association of Purchasing Managers (NAPM) and the Chartered Institute of Purchasing and Supply (CIPS).

The evidence suggests that education and training and discussion of ethical matters is important in controlling corruption. Seventh, the records of companies that competed, bidding prices and characteristics of the product offered must be made publicly available. Eighth, financial disclosure reports of public officers in charge of procurement in line ministries, departments, and public agencies are a cornerstone of public integrity and transparency. In order for financial disclosure reports to be fully effective to deter corruption, they should be coupled with illicit enrichment legislation. This should establish as an offense any increase in assets of government officials that cannot be explained by their public lawful earnings. Ninth, whistle-blowers of contractor abuses or fraud to the government should receive protection under the law and governments might even offer incentives such as offering a fraction of resources recovered by the government from legal action against offenders. This mechanism is used, for example, in the United States where any person is authorized to sue in the name of the government and receive up to 30 percent of the amount recovered as a result of the suit. Other countries with whistle-blower protection legislation include Australia, Great Britain, and New Zealand.[150] A step further in encouraging public officials and private agents to report corruption practices is to make reporting corruption mandatory and impose heavy sanctions on offenders (Klitgaard, 1991).

Corruption arises where procurement laws are outdated or inadequate given the structure of control mechanisms in place. The United Nations Commission on International Trade Law (UNCITRAL) has published a model procurement law.[151] Ofosu-Amaah *et al.* (1999) notes the importance of structuring public procurement procedures by law as opposed to regulations. Structuring procurement procedures in a law, as opposed to simply listing them in government regulations, makes it less likely that the procedures would be modified to suit particular interests. In other words, procedures stated in a law tend to be more transparent and make it less likely that the process will be "captured" by interested parties. Some countries have gone even further. For example, South Africa has made explicit basic procurement principles in its constitution, explicitly addressing expectations on procurement transparency and the commitment to curb corruption in this process. At the other extreme, there are countries, which still govern the procurement process by tender boards functioning according to regulations, the latter usually designed by the Ministries of Finance.

---

[150] See Groeneweg (2001) for a comparative analysis of whistle-blower protection legislation in Australia, United States, and the United Kingdom.
[151] United Nations. UNCITRAL Model Law for Procurement on Goods, Construction, and Services, New York.

Besides the application of standard procedures and other best practices mentioned so far, transparency in government procurement may be enhanced by the use of the internet (e-procurement). Information technology and internet use in government activities (e-government) and also business (e-commerce) operations offer several advantages. Some examples of procurement over the internet include diverse users, such as the case of municipalities in Campo Elias in Venezuela, Limpio in Paraguay, and Obnisnsk in Russia (de Gonzales, 2000). Good examples of countries that have introduced e-procurement systems at the national level are South Korea and Mexico (see Box 5.11).[152] Although there is no concrete hard evidence that these reforms have led to lower levels of corruption, the transparency of procurement processes has increased notably and casual observations suggest a noticeable decrease of corruption opportunities (see Box 5.11). For example, the e-procurement systems have reduced personal interaction between public officials and bidders, have broadened participation of bidders, and have helped create a database of contractors' performance (Ibarra-Estrada, 2002; Hyun Yum, 2003).

However, e-procurement also introduces new challenges, as new forms of security are needed to control possibilities of leaks of sensitive data in electronic form (e-corruption). These issues are already being discussed in countries that manipulate sensitive information electronically. It is important, for instance, to create and capacitate procurement officials in the use of clear and detailed procedures for data management, such as the manipulation of files via email, deletion of electronic documents, disclosure or encryption of passwords, and the like.

5.2.2.3. Designing adequate mechanisms for civil service spending control. A weak and out of control civil service creates an atmosphere ripe for corrupt practices. On the expenditure side, civil service management should focus on the optimization of the resources used to pay the civil service. Mechanisms of civil service control and personnel management should aim for detection of absenteeism and ghost workers through audits and computerization of records, and control of unnecessary recruitment (control of overstaffing).

Public Expenditure Tracking Surveys (PETS) are also useful instruments in identifying ghost workers as was demonstrated in studying Honduras and Uganda service delivery (Dehn *et al.*, 2003). Besides decreasing corruption in a direct way by preventing the embezzlement of public funds, identifying ghost workers may increase available resources, which can in turn be used to increase public sector wages (Klitgaard, 1989). The amounts of diverted funds can be significant. Dehn *et al.* (2003)

---

[152] Other countries that are already using this approach include Argentina, Chile, Malaysia, Brazil, New Zealand, Philippines, and Bulgaria.

Box 5.11.   E-procurement in Mexico and South Korea: enhancing transparency

Compranet, the Mexican government e-procurement initiative was introduced in April 1996 by the Unit of Electronic Government Services within the Mexican Ministry of the Controllership and Administrative Development (MCAD). Prior to the introduction of *Compranet*, the Mexican Federal Government had little or no information pertaining to item acquisition, procurement prices, and government suppliers. In general, acquisitions were overpriced and the process was costly and imbued with corruption. Most suppliers were concentrated in the Mexico City area. By April 2002, around 3,000 procurement units from different government agencies, including municipalities, had posted their requirements and had received proposals from suppliers online. Suppliers have expanded to include small/medium enterprises from outside the capital region. Compranet's has helped to make the procurement process more efficient and transparent. Automated control and auditing mechanisms have improved, and costs have decreased by nearly 20 percent. In addition, Compranet provides citizen involvement through their accessibility to the government procurement process.

South Korea is one of the participants of the World Trade Organization Public Procurement Agreement (WTOGPA). As such, it was required to ensure the use of international government procurement procedures by 1997. Procurement functions have been an important contributor to corruption activities in South Korea, allegedly due to personal interaction between officers and bidders in the former procurement system. Starting in January 2001, all government purchases were made through the new internet-based system. The new system ensures the opening of contract specifications at the same time for all bidders as opposed to the former practice of releasing information in advance to selected bidders. It was previously observed that government suppliers were often the same; hence market competition was limited. The internet-based system broadens the range of companies that participate in the procurement process allowing national and international companies to participate. This led the number of participating companies in each bid to increase threefold. Another important aspect of e-procurement has been the creation of a database of suppliers and recording their performance in delivering their products to public agencies – thus effectively allowing the system to prequalify or disqualify bidders based on previous performance. This is a significant step forward in curbing corruption since in the past, suppliers with bad performance and even corruption allegations continued often to win new contracts.

Sources: Hyun Yum (2003), Kang (2000), Ibarra-Estrada (2002).

report that approximately 20 percent of the wage expenditures in Uganda were paid to ghost teachers. If those resources would be distributed among real teachers their wages could increase by as much as 25 percent. While there is no evidence of the effectiveness that disclosing PETS information has in decreasing the number of ghost employees, PETS' results are already increasing awareness among policy makers and citizens in several countries.

5.2.3. *Reducing the opportunities for political corruption*

In Section 5.2 above, we saw there are two main avenues for political corruption. First, state capture may take place when some politicians exert excessive control over budget formulation, whereby they can favor projects or individuals in return for financial favors. Second, political corruption can also arise in a variety of ways in the process of budget execution.

In order to decrease opportunities for state capture, an anticorruption strategy should work to reduce discretionary control by some groups or individuals over the budget allocation process. Several measures are available to this end, including:

(i) Assuring political representation and electoral accountability.
(ii) Systematic and comprehensive formulation of the budget.
(iii) Transparent regulation of rent-seeking activities.

5.2.3.1. Assuring political representation and electoral accountability.   The overall political system determines how closely politicians are accountable to the electorate. Are executives directly elected, or indirectly? Who determines the candidate lists: primaries or party selections? Are there recall procedures for corrupt politicians? The more accountable politicians are to their constituents, the potentially smaller their window for corruption.

A variety of political institutions play a role in holding politicians accountable. The process of "participatory planning" can help obtain greater responsiveness of politicians to their electorate and limit unnecessary political discretion. Participatory planning generally pursues two objectives: (a) greater consistency between budget allocations and true national/subnational objectives and priorities, (b) greater surveillance and evaluation of public policy.

(a) Greater consistency between allocations and priorities requires a clear definition of roles and responsibilities in the budget formulation process. The prioritization of public spending should be made public and public debate of alternative options should allow the design of more participatory budgets. Australia is a country that has a long tradition of making the medium-term costs of competing policies public and submitting them to consultation and debate.[153] To enable civil society to follow the process, parliamentary discussions and voting should be made public or broadcast. Where it is compatible with the constitution, national or local consultations (referenda) should also be used to decide controversial issues. In addition, the draft budget and historical budget information should be made publicly available in citizen information centers or posted on government web sites.

(b) The recipe for more effective civil society participation in public surveillance has two main ingredients: relevant public information and an active and motivated citizenry. Relevant information consists of audits, evaluations, and surveys conducted by external supreme audit institutions and independent consultants, and a vast array of other public records. A particularly useful tool is citizens and business perception surveys on corruption issues. These surveys provide information on the occurrence of corruption in the provision of public services and utilities, or extortion in tax and custom administration. These surveys not only identify key sources of corruption, and thus the need for reform on these areas, but also provide a benchmark measurement of corruption that can be used to assess the effectiveness of anticorruption policies and institutional reforms in the future. Public access to different types of institutional information is also required for increased transparency and accountability. This institutional information may include court decisions and court trial records, parliament sessions and parliamentarians voting, high-level officials assets disclosure, tendering and procurement procedures, public acquisitions, and public registering of political campaign contributions.[154]

However, information is only useful where there is a motivated and active civil society to scrutinize it. Motivating the active participation of civil society is, in most cases, a hard challenge. The creation of specialized units that provide public spaces and services such as internet access to public information available in government or other public institutions websites may sometimes help.[155]

---

[153] See World Bank (1997).

[154] For further discussion on this topic see World Bank (2000a) and Gonzales de Asis (2000).

[155] Section 5.5.3 below discusses further strategies aimed at strengthening civil society and private sector participation in the fight against corruption.

5.2.3.2. Making public budgets comprehensive. The use of extra-budget-ary and off-budget accounts propitiates some types of political corruption because generally these funds are not subject to a high level of public scrutiny. An effective anticorruption rule is to require that all government activities are reflected in the general budget document, including spending of line agencies and special spending units, and revenues collected from user fees, or resources financed by external sources. If this is not entirely possible, the transactions that are not covered in the main body of the budget should include budget annexes (Allen and Tommasi, 2001; Allen *et al.*, 2004).

5.2.3.3. Regulation of rent-seeking activities. A distinction must be made between legitimate and illegitimate lobbying. Legitimate lobbying involves industries or specific companies that advocate publicly their need for pref-erential treatment from the government by exposing their strategic con-tribution to public welfare or the economy as whole. These cases do not imply corruption or loss of efficiency since they may be assessed in a transparent way by computing and weighing the costs (including the effects on competing industries or companies) and the benefits of adopting the preferential treatment policy being lobbied. On the contrary, illegitimate lobbying does not involve public demonstrations or weighing cost and benefits to society, but rather bribing public officials.

One of the most evident forms of rent-seeking behavior is the private funding of political campaigns.[156] In many democracies in the world, electoral campaigns are financed primarily from contributions from the private sector. Campaign financing regulations are a necessary instrument in order to protect countries from political corruption (state capture). Making political party advertising expenditure information publicly avail-able has proven to be an important step in increasing awareness of this issue and the possible pervasive effects of it.[157] Campaign finance regu-lations can be quite helpful in drawing a line between legal and illegal practices in rent-seeking behavior. The guidelines suggested by Transpar-ency International (2004) address the following issues: (1) bans on certain types of donations, (2) contribution limits, (3) spending limits for political parties and presidential candidates, (4) public subsidies, (5) indirect public funding and in-kind subsidies, (6) comprehensive disclosure and reporting

---

[156] For example, see Rhodes (1997) for an analysis of corruption in financing political parties in Italy.

[157] A good example is presented by Transparency International's Report (2001), about the role of "Poder Ciudadano" in the Argentina chapter on the disclosure of political campaigns spending. Reporting on campaign spending is becoming a more common practice in the developing countries: awareness and debate are growing with respect to this issue.

regulations, and (7) penalties. In parallel, similar rules and public disclosure standards are of course needed for lobbying activities in parliament. A number of countries have made significant advances in campaign legislation reforms, yet others seem to have taken steps backwards in the fight to contain political corruption (see Box 5.12).

5.2.4. Programmatic responses to reducing corruption on the expenditure side

Although an anticorruption strategy based on the piecemeal application of some of the policy responses reviewed above is possible and can be quite effective, it has become more common to design anticorruption programs that encompass several integrated policies and that simultaneously pursue several objectives.[158] Here we review several alternative forms of integrated anticorruption programs, or programmatic responses to corruption:

- Introduction of IFMSs.
- Creation of Independent Audit Institutions (IAIs)/Strengthening of the Controller-Accountant-General Office.
- Creation of Fiscal Analysis Units (FAUs).
- Initiation of Public Expenditure Tracking Surveys (PETS).

5.2.4.1. Integrated financial management systems. The implementation of computerized IFMS has benefits that go beyond the improved accounting and control of budget implementation and a Treasury system. The implementation of IFMS can help to reduce corruption on a variety of fronts. Better tracking and matching of sources by computerized information is quite helpful in detecting ghost workers and identifying irregularities in procurement processes.[159] The improved audit capacity introduced by the IFMS also adds transparency to other processes such as the audit of funds used for electoral campaigns, which in turn can reduce the occurrence of state capture and inform the complex process of industrial rent seeking.[160] Given their potential beneficial effects, capacity building programs for modernized accounting systems are often supported by bilateral donors (e.g., USAID) and international financial institutions (e.g., the World Bank and the IMF). One case in point is USAID's support for the implementation of an IFMS in Bosnia and Herzegovina (see Box 5.13).

---

[158] See, for example, USAID (2000).
[159] An example of these outcomes is reported within the result of the Regional Financial Management Improvement (RFMI) I, Latin American Countries (USAID, 2000).
[160] See USAID (2000).

Box 5.12. Transparency International: a selection of the year's legislation on political party governance, funding, and disclosure

Positive developments

Brazil: Legislation approved in February 2002 requires candidates to present their campaign donations and expenditure statements electronically. Previously, such statements were presented only in paper format, making it virtually impossible to organize and aggregate the data or make it available to a broader public.

Canada: Amendments to the Canada Elections Act approved in June 2003 introduced strict limits on political donations. To compensate for the loss of private financing, parties will receive state financing in proportion to the number of votes received.

Costa Rica: The constitutional court ruled in May 2003 that bank secrecy privileges do not apply to political party assets. All accounts held by political parties at state or private banks or any non-bank entity must now be made available to the general public.

USA: The Bipartisan Campaign Reform Act (BCRA), otherwise known as the McCain-Feingold-Cochran Bill, was passed in March 2002. Proponents consider it a major step toward reducing corruption in US politics by putting an end to 'soft money' and restricting candidate specific 'issue' advertising. However, the legislation has shortcomings and has already been subject to legal challenges and efforts to circumvent it.

Mixed developments

Kenya: The Public Officer Ethics Act of May 2003 requires all public officials, including members of parliament, to declare their wealth. It does not provide public access to the information, however, nor does it provide a framework for inspecting declarations.

Uganda: On the positive side, the Leadership Code 2002 requires elected politicians and senior public officials to declare income and assets or face a penalty, and provides for their declarations to be made public. Nevertheless, the Political Parties and Organizations Act 2002 bars political parties from campaigning for office, limits their freedom to hold public meetings and stops them from operating outside the capital. The law's constitutionality is still being challenged.

Negative developments

Azerbaijan: Adopted by referendum in August 2002, a constitutional amendment allows ordinary courts to close down political parties; formerly, only higher level courts could ban parties. A second amendment increases the term for official confirmation of election results from 7 to 14 postelection days, which gives incumbents a better opportunity to falsify results.

Kazakhstan: The July 2002 law on political parties controls donations, but, critically, also increases the number of members required to set up a party from 3,000 to 50,000 people. As a result, the number of parties in existence was reduced from 19 to 7, of which only one is an opposition party.

Zambia: In March 2003, the president refused to give his assent to the parliamentary Political Parties Fund Bill, which would have funded political parties in proportion to their number of members of parliament.

Sources: Extracted from Transparency International (2004, p. 28).

5.2.4.2. Independent audit institutions. Audits are basic instruments to foster accountability of governmental units. IAI[161] are watchdog agencies whose main function is to audit (attest to and verify that) all the accounts of the executed budget presented by the executive branch of government and deliver the results to parliament for review and final approval. These types of audits are known as financial audits. Yet, audits of different types can undertake more comprehensive roles. Compliance auditing, for example, verifies the consistency between budget procedures and ultimate objectives of the government and whether the audited government department budget is in compliance with current laws and regulations. Performance auditing is a type of audit that is based on the assessment of an advisory committee of experts that evaluate the performance of budget agencies vis-a-vis ex ante objectives and indicators (Dye and Stapenhurst, 1998).

However, IAIs financial oversight roles can be extended to several other areas. Recent reforms in Bulgaria illustrate the broad range of areas that Supreme Audit Institutions can oversee (see Box 5.14).

In most countries, IAIs play a crucial role in fostering the credibility and independence of external audit management and financial control. In some

---

[161] At the central government level it also receives the name of Supreme Audit Institution.

Box 5.13.   Corruption and anticorruption responses in Bosnia and Herzegovina

Bosnia and Herzegovina is a country that has recently come out from a 4-year armed conflict between three ethnic enclaves. Negotiations involving the Republics of Croatia, the Federal Republic of Yugoslavia, and the United States led to the signature of the Dayton Peace agreement in 1995. The state of Bosnia and Herzegovina was founded by this agreement comprising two highly autonomous entities: the Serbian Republika Srpska (RS) and the Muslim-Croat Federation (FBiH). The case of Bosnia offers a replicable example of public expenditure management reform in transition economies and middle-income countries, which can be instrumental in controlling many important aspects of fiscal corruption.

Corruption and concentration of groups of power followed the communist style of government of the former Yugoslavia. For example, in 1999 the New York Times reported that up to a billion dollars disappeared from international aid projects based on an investigation of a national Anti Fraud Unit. There is currently a widespread perception that corruption levels are getting worse. In the words of High Representative, Lord Ashdown "the grip of criminality and corruption is strengthening" (Transparency International, 2003). Likewise, survey data reveals that more than 50 percent of the general public, public officials, and enterprise managers perceive that corruption in BiH is very widespread (World Bank, 2001c). Political corruption is also entrenched in BiH. Illegal party financing often leads to the granting of monopoly powers in key productive sectors via excessive regulatory burdens and barriers to entry. Surveys of enterprise managers show that unofficial payments to political parties represent as much as four percent of their company's profits.

Corruption trends in Bosnia and Herzegovina

Question: when did corruption reached the highest level?

	Public officials (percent)	General public (percent)	Enterprise managers (percent)
Before the war, prior to 1992	1	3	1
During the war, 1992–1995	9	13	10
After the war 1996–1998	22	22	28
From 1998 till now (2000)	36	34	26
It was the same in all these periods	32	28	35

Source: World Bank (2001c).

One of the determinants of corruption, prior to year 2001, was BiH's outdated financial management system composed of three payment bureaus that controlled public expenditures and also state revenues. In previous years when most firms were state owned, the tax collection process was, for the most part, an accounting exercise between public accounts. These structures were not designed to work in a privatized economy. Thus tax administration monitoring and enforcement units were not capable of performing their functions once the new private sector emerged. The Payment Bureau system was not only inefficient but it also undermined the development of a market-oriented banking system. The system was also prone to corruption mainly due to monopoly power in the management of public budget accounts. The elimination of the three payment bureaus was, therefore, an important inroad against corruption in public funds management.

The revenue functions of the Payment Bureaus were transferred to three tax administration agencies (one in the Federation of Bosnia and Herzegovina, on in the Republic of Srpska, and one in the District of Brcko), with each one attempting to enforce different tax legislations. To fight corruption in the new tax administrations employees were given a Code of Conduct. The idea was to foster ethical behavior and define issues of conflict of interests. Yet, not much has been done yet regarding the enforcement of regulations (Mayville, 2003). Thus despite these changes corruption in the tax revenue agencies is still a problem. Among other indicators, the corruption level is revealed by survey results of public employees' perceptions regarding the extent of corruption in different public institutions which rank tax authorities in third place (out of 11 options), just after customs and local authorities (World Bank, 2001c).

The tax system is complex and the existence of three sets of tax laws offers wide opportunities for corruption. Moreover, BiH's tax system resulted often in double taxation and produced several economic distortions that generate incentives for corruption (Gallagher and Bosnic, 2004; Office of the High Representative, 2004). High tax burdens (e.g., the social fund payments and wage tax in the Federation reaches a total of 69 percent of salaries) generate incentives for under-reporting actual wages paid, for keeping business in the underground economy, or for bribing tax officials. It has been said that the extent of inconsistencies and economic distortions in the tax system is such, that if the tax system were fully enforced it would nullify the possibilities of private sector economic development (Gallagher and Bosnic, 2004).

In the recent reforms, the expenditure functions of the Payment Bureaus were transferred to 13 Treasury systems: one in the Federation, one in the Republic of Srpska, and in one in each of the Federation Canton governments (each one part of their respective bureau of finance). The new Treasury system appears to have had immediate positive results. These include better control of budget spending, improved management of public funds, and greater overall fiscal discipline (Gallagher, 2004). Information from these separate treasuries has been centralized into a new Integrated Financial Management Information System (FMIS) allowing for the automatization and integration of the most relevant Treasury information. The FMIS has been particularly useful in controlling corruption in cases of atomization of the public management responsibilities such as the case of BiH.

countries, IAIs also evaluate budgets to ascertain how well objectives have been achieved, which further enhances the transparency of government actions. Therefore, the creation or strengthening of IAIs constitutes currently a main policy objective of many international assistance programs.[162]

Dye and Stapenhurst (1998) offer an insightful analysis of the role of Supreme Audit institutions in fighting corruption. These authors identify four main factors for IAI's success: a clear mandate, independence protected by legislation, adequate funding and staff, and sharing knowledge and experience with analogous international agencies. Having a clear mandate is vital to ensure that the IAI meets the requirements of the parliament and that it is empowered with enough authority to fulfill its duties. There must also be clear mechanisms for the selection of the Auditor General and for ensuring his immunity from liability.

In order to be effective in controlling corruption, IAIs need to be fully independent from the executive branch of government. This is because the IAIs' role is to audit most government departments, and so being subordinated to them would generate a conflict of interests. In some

---

[162] This is, for example, the case of the joint OECD-EU SIGMA program. SIGMA provides assistance and the assessment of several reform issues regarding IAIs to eight new EU Member States and three EU candidate countries. Sigma also generates a variety of material on high accounting standards and best practices of IAIs.

Box 5.14.   Strengthening and broadening the roles of Bulgaria's Supreme Audit Institution

In December 2001, Bulgaria's National Assembly instituted a new National Audit Office Act. This new act extended the mandate of the Supreme Audit Institution in Bulgaria (Smetna Palata, or SP), to include the right to audit budget expenditures of the Bulgarian National Bank; management of the state debt; allocation and budgeting of profits from privatization and concessions, execution of international treaties, contracts and covenants; and auditing resources funded by the EU's Phare Programme (which provides assistance to the EU applicant countries). Furthermore, the SP oversight authority was extended to new areas, such as the scrutiny of political party revenues and expenditures (as established by the Law of Political Parties, enacted in 2001). Additionally, a proposal is currently in progress to extend the SP's mandate to include the audit of municipal debts. While assuming these functions the SP has benefited from the support of the National Audit Office of the United Kingdom, the European Court of Auditors, and the Open Government Initiative Project to the fight against fraud and corruption, funded by USAID. These institutions were crucial to increase SP's credibility and technical capabilities.

It is now widely perceived that the SP has made significant progress in the last few years. Although there are no formal measures of success, according to Transparency International's Corruption Perception Index Ranking, Bulgaria has improved from 66th place in year 1998 to 45th place in year 2002.

Sources: Sigma (2002, 2003).

---

countries, the IAI is fully independent and does not even report to parliament, and in other countries it does report. These reports should be made publicly available. The main objective of the reports is to reveal cases of conflict and irregularities in public accounts. As a result, and in the same vein as many other cases in which wrongdoing is revealed, the main policy challenge is to develop mechanisms by which legislators can take appropriate and timely actions to prevent further wrongdoings in the future.

IAI activities should respond to some degree to the concerns and interests of the parliament as well as of civil society. Furthermore, IAIs should follow up on the implementation of remedial actions and update the parliament when they are not applied (SAICEEC, 2001).[163] Quite clearly, an independent and strong IAI is a powerful tool to fight corruption in all its manifestations, from administrative to political corruption.

5.2.4.3. Parliamentary fiscal analysis units. Parliamentary FAUs have been supported by the international donor community, especially USAID, to enhance parliamentary oversight capacity over the budget process in a number of countries such as Croatia, Kyrgyz Republic, and Ukraine. Although the primary function of the FAU is to provide analytical capabilities and better information to the members of parliament, these institutions have proved to be quite helpful also in enhancing transparency of all public dealings using or costing fiscal resources, and thus have contributed to reducing opportunities for political and administrative corruption. See Box 5.15 for an account of the impacts of the FAU in the Kyrgyz Republic.

5.3. Reducing quasi-fiscal corruption

5.3.1. Corruption and privatization

The privatization of state assets, especially in the case of massive privatization processes, such as those conducted in transitional countries during the 1990, present enormous opportunities for corruption. The presence of corruption opportunities in the privatization of state assets is influenced by several factors including the choice of privatization method, the implementation phase, and the legal framework.

The influence of the choice of privatization method and the implementation phase on corruption have been studied by Kaufmann and Seigelbaum (1997) for the transition economies of the FSU and CEE. These authors discuss six privatization methods and the order in which these schemes are more likely to be affected by corruption during the program implementation phase. Starting with the method that is the least prone to corruption, these are the schemes:

(1) *Voucher-based mass privatization,* in which the Government sells vouchers to the population, which can be used to purchase shares of state assets being privatized. Sometimes private "privatization funds" are used as intermediaries.

---

[163] A study on the relations between Supreme Audit Institutions and parliamentary committees describes extensively the role and practices in 14 countries in accession process to the EU. This study presents a comprehensive list of suggestions to enhance the responsiveness of parliamentary committees to IAI's reports (Supreme Audit Institutions of the Central and Eastern European Countries, 2001).

Box 5.15. Parliament fiscal analysis unit in the Kyrgyz Republic

Since independence, the Parliament of the Kyrgyz Republic has struggled to fulfill its role as an assembly representing the people and exercising "checks and balances" over the executive branch of government. The establishment of the Parliament's Fiscal Analysis Unit (FAU), with support from USAID, has proven to be an effective step in enabling the Parliament to carry out its duties. The FAU has improved parliamentarians' access to fiscal information, enabled them to better oversee public funds, and increased transparency of the budget process.

Since the FAU's creation in May 2000, Parliament adopted two major tax law changes, removing what had been cited as special tax breaks adopted by the previous Parliament to benefit a few of its members. Thanks in part to the FAU, the new Parliament has also shed its reputation as a rubber stamp institution. On several occasions, Parliament significantly modified and even defeated ill-conceived proposals from the executive, including a flawed system of SME taxation and a proposed transfer of legislative authority to set tax rates.

The FAU serves as a think tank and research organization for parliamentarians so that members can objectively evaluate issues in the broader context of what is best for the country. As a result of the FAU, MPs have access to reliable statistics, economic, and budgetary information and analysis and no longer rely solely on subjective interpretation or estimates to make critical decisions. The FAU has helped legislators to consider each policy change in the context of its impact on spending, on taxpayers and on the economy, allowing MPs to make enlightened decisions that better represent the needs of citizens. Through fairer, more beneficial policies, Kyrgyzstan's citizens are reaping the rewards of a more responsive legislature. The general result has been a more transparent budget process and a reduction of opportunities for different forms of corruption in the public sector.

Source: Extracted from USAID (2002).

(2) *Liquidation*, in which enterprises with financial problems are dismantled and sold by parts.
(3) *Initial public offerings*, in which shares are openly offered in the domestic capital markets.

(4) *Tenders and trade sales which are also referred as case-by-case method of privatization*, in which the privatization strategy is particular to each enterprise and enterprises are privatized one at a time.

(5) *Management and employment buyouts*, in which enterprise shares are sold to their own management and staff.

(6) *Spontaneous privatization*, which is basically the direct transfer of public assets to private parties (managers, bureaucrats, or politicians) through the abuse of power, rather than a privatization process in the proper sense.

Kaufmann and Sieguelbaum's categorization is based on the degree to which each privatization method relates to the following corruption factors:

- *Speed of the process*: Quick processes are likely to offer less opportunity to arrange corrupt transactions than slow-paced processes.
- *Level of administration discretion*: Administrative discretion and bureaucratic clearances often lead to abuse and corruption as they grant power and *control rights* to public officials.[164] Hence lower levels of administrative discretion can lead to lower opportunities for corruption.
- *Transparency of the process*: This refers to the degree of public and open disclosure of process information, evaluation procedures, and results of the privatization process.
- *Independent administration of the program*. The implementation process is likely to lead to a more transparent process if it is conducted by a new or independent agency. This reduces considerably opportunities of capture of the process by government bureaucrats and politicians.

The importance and desirability of each of these factors varies considerably. For instance, speed of mass privatization may largely reduce opportunities for corrupt schemes, which require some preparation time. Mass privatization is likely to be an effective method when radical privatization needs to be conducted rapidly and at a low cost.[165] On the other hand, a case-by-case privatization method can pay closer attention to policy issues and allow for appropriate corruption controls which are likely to be decisive when privatizing strategic and large enterprises (Welch and Fraemond, 1998). For example, in order to minimize corruption in a second phase of privatization in countries from the FSU and CEE, Kaufmann

---

[164] Control rights refer to the decision power over the use and management of state assets, including transactions such as transfer of property (Grossman and Hart (1986); Boycko *et al.*, 1996).

[165] For instance, a case-by-case privatization of close to 16,500 small and medium sized enterprises during 1993–1994 would be an unimaginably complex and also quite likely corrupt process.

and Sieguelbaum suggested the implementation of "speedy mass privatization techniques resulting in full transfer of the interest sold, without special deals for insiders and without attaching lingering investments or employment obligations." (1997, p. 26).

Combating corruption does not only depend on the appropriate selection of the type of privatization method but also on the implementation process. The implementation agency should spend enough time preparing to ensure transparency and the minimum scope for corruption during the execution of the privatization process. Implementation best practices tend to be specific to each method of privatization.[166]

The existence of an appropriate legal framework is also quite critical for the success and transparency of privatization processes. Often, privatization requires timely reforms of the legislation, many of which are geared to minimize corruption. Legislation reforms may also focus on the promotion of greater competition by enacting laws designed to reduce country risk investment, such as in the case of laws and regulations related to the protection of foreign investors (contract enforcement, securities regulations, and so on).[167]

5.3.2. Market regulation

Excessive government regulation and the absence of market institutions are often the source of discretionary government intervention and ultimately of corruption. This has led many economists to suggest lower levels of government intervention and, on the other hand, increasing the liberalization of markets. In the words of Rose-Ackerman, "if the state has no authority to restrict exports or license businesses, there is no opportunity for bribes. If a subsidy program is eliminated, the associated bribes will also disappear. If price controls are lifted, market prices will express scarcity values, not bribes. If a parastatal that is the locus of corrupt payoffs is moved into the private sector, those payoffs will end." (1996, p. 3).

Getting rid of regulations to cut the level of corruption may sound a bit like the story of the old man that solves the problem of children constantly stealing his apples by cutting the tree. It is obvious that the elimination of regulations is not always possible since they are needed to protect consumers and ensure competition. The message here is that governments should, to the extent possible, minimize the number of regulations

---

[166] See, for example, Salacuse (1998) and Ofosu-Amaah *et al.* (1999) for a discussion of the factors that can ensure a transparent case-by-case privatization method. The following is compiled from several sources, such as Salacuse (1998) and Ofosu-Amaah *et al.* (1999)
[167] See Salacuse (1998).

through market liberalization and especially through the reduction of import controls. Each and every regulation in the functioning markets and private-agent activity opens windows of opportunity for corruption by public officials. In turn, the higher the number of clearances needed in the process of authorization is an extra opportunity for corruption.

Empirical studies have indeed found liberalization reforms to be effective in combating corruption. For example, based on a cross-country dataset of institutional reforms in transition economies, Broadman and Recanatini (2001) find evidence that a reduction of protectionist measures, price, and production liberalization reforms are useful tools to curtail corruption. Likewise, results from Treisman (2000) and Gurgur and Shah (2000) suggest that greater openness to trade and a competitive structure is correlated with lower levels of corruption.[168]

Some multilateral and bilateral organizations have engaged in programs designed to minimize opportunities for corruption in the regulatory process. For example, a combined effort of USAID and the World Bank has supported the Investor Road Map Project, which is designed to reduce the number of clearances needed to obtain business licenses, and working permits to a "one-stop" process.[169] USAID (2000) reports that the number of authorizations required in order to obtain work permits and start a business in Tanzania has already been successfully reduced.[170] Yet not much is known regarding the reform's effects on corruption in these processes.[171]

5.3.3. Pricing of public utilities and natural resource exploitation

In most countries, citizens have limited, if any, choice among providers of public utilities such as telecommunications, electricity, gas, water, transportation, postal services. Thus, utility providers have varying degrees of monopoly power over large parts of the population. To counterbalance those powers, governments create regulatory agencies, which are charged with the regulation of prices and other aspects of the services with the aim of protecting public interests. Corruption may arise if the regulated firms are able to capture the regulatory agencies, and thus maximize rents at the expense of utility users.

In general terms, pricing regulation strategies usually try to rely on the industry's costs of production, but the real costs typically are only known

---

[168] These results may have problems of endogeneity, as Treisman notes: openness to trade may reduce corruption, but corrupt officials may create protectionist measures with the expectation of extracting illicit rents.

[169] See USAID (2000).

[170] USAID has also started a program for support service sector liberalization and advancement: Trade Enhancement for the Services Sector (TESS).

[171] The case of Tanzania is discussed in Chapter 6.1 of this report.

to producers. Thus, in order to determine prices, regulatory agencies often collect cost account records from service producers relying on audits to verify their accuracy. Anticorruption strategies focused on the monitoring of auditing procedures may help reduce the opportunities for collusion between those regulated and the regulators (cost auditors or regulation policymakers).[172] Broadman and Rescanatini (2001) have stressed the importance of the establishment of independent regulatory agencies to reduce capture of regulation. Independent agencies that promote transparency and accountability in regulation by means of public hearings and elections of regulators, or term limits, tend to be more effective in curbing corruption.

In terms of natural resources, the issues are quite similar. In Chapter 4 of this study we discussed how natural resource exploitation can generate considerable rents, a situation which in turn may lead to corruption. The main target of anticorruption efforts regarding natural resources is to increase the accountability of high-level officials for the revenues generated from natural resource exploitation. International donors often exert pressures on government leaders of countries rich in natural resources in order to improve accounting records. These organizations often also exert pressure on multinational firms that participate in the exploitation of natural resources with allegedly corrupt governments. For example, in 2004 after constant pressures from the World Bank, the IMF, and the British government, the government of Angola (whose officials had been repeatedly accused of having embezzled oil revenues) agreed to disclose payments it receives from the oil company ChevronTexaco, estimated as high as US $300 million.[173] Although the enforcement of these types of agreements raise many challenges, the agreements, themselves, constitute a first step to increased accountability, and their use should be further explored.

5.4. Decentralization as a programmatic response to corruption

Decentralization, among other things, brings government closer to the people and can empower citizens to require more accountability from government officials. Thus, in theory at least, a decentralized system of government can be one where there is less corruption. However, a fundamental question in this regard still lingers in the literature on corruption: Which level of government is more corrupt, the central government or the

---

[172] See Beato and Laffont (2002) who discuss the issue of pricing policies most prone to corruption.
[173] New York Times (2004b).

local governments? Opposing arguments have been raised in the literature. Opponents of decentralization often provide arguments suggesting that local government officials tend to be *more* prone to corruption than central government officials.[174] Theoretical explanations for this assertion can be summarized as follows:

- *Lower ability of central-level monitoring:* Decentralization reforms may lead to less monitoring of public officials because central governments do not have the capacity to monitor local officials as effectively as they do central government officials (Rose-Ackerman, 1978).[175]
- *Greater possibilities of capture at the local level:* In decentralized systems there are many more transactions and points of contact between public officials and citizens, which may also create more opportunity for corrupt behavior. Local interest groups that are too weak to influence a centralized system may be strong enough to capture the local government apparatus. Moreover, Bardhan and Mookherjee (2000) argue that local voter ignorance and lack of political awarness may also contribute to local government's ability to clientelism favoring local elites. Litvack *et al.* (1998) posit that local elites' capture arises from weaknesses in the democratic systems in developing countries. Similarly, Prud'homme (1995) posits "local bureaucrats are less independent from local politicians than national bureaucrats are from national politicians." (p. 211).
- *Greater possibilities of corruption at the local level:* The interaction between taxpayers and public officials is closer and more frequent at the local level. This type of argument has been advanced by Prud'homme (1995) and Tanzi (1995).
- *Higher incentives for corruption at the local level:* The system of incentives for engaging in corruption may be greater for local officials. First, because local government officials are often more poorly compensated than their central government counterpart and career prospects are so much poorer at the local level. Second, because local public officials are generally less educated and may have a lower "sprit de corps" than central administrations bureaucrats.
- *Intergovernmental bribe-cascading:* Decentralization may lead to a bribe-cascading effect whereby the total amount of bribes paid is greater than under a centralized system. Shleifer and Vishny (1993) and Treisman (2000), posit that a higher number of bribes may be extracted

---

[174] Some have argued that, between the two devils, local corruption may actually be preferable than centralized corruption. For example, decentralized corruption gains may be better distributed than those from centralized corruption (Prud'homme, 1995).

[175] Supporters of this argument seem to ignore the ability of local governments to monitor their own staff.

when different tiers of governments share tax authority over common tax bases.

Without denying the occurrence of corrupt behavior at the local government level, there are a number of reasons why these previously mentioned arguments may not represent the entire story. Contentions that corruption is higher at the local level may be influenced by perception distortions. First, small corrupt acts by local government officials may simply be more visible to the local community than central government corruption. While this would lead to a perception of greater corruption of the local level, this does not mean that local officials are indeed more corrupt. In fact, the visibility of local corruption would suggest that local corruption is easier to address than central government corruption. It needs to be mentioned also that often what is interpreted as "local" corrupt officials in developing and transition countries are in fact central government employees working in deconcentrated central government offices (see Box 5.16). The question also remains: does a system of petty

---

Box 5.16.   Local corruption in Bangladesh?

The problem of corruption in public service provision in Bangladesh is systemic. The severity of the problem is illustrated by a survey on corruption in public service delivery conducted by the Bangladesh chapter of Transparency International. This was collected from persons receiving services at the various institutions. The results of this survey show that 74 percent of the respondents used "extra regular methods" for admission of their children into school. Likewise, for health services, 39.4 percent of the households reported paying higher than normal registration fees at the outpatient department. A common perception in Bangladesh is that local governments are highly corrupt because local public servants are regarded as local employees, despite the fact that local staff is hired by the central government. In order to hold local governments accountable for the corrupt behavior of local government officials, it is necessary to provide local governments with considerable administrative decentralization, including the ability to hire and fire and set salary levels. This is usually taken for granted by traditional decentralization analysis, but is actually absent in practice in several countries. In all, corruption of centrally managed local personnel should not be regarded as local government corruption.

Sources: World Bank (2001a), Ahmad (2003).

corruption by many local officials generate lower or higher levels of corruption (however measured), and what are the impacts of the two types of corruption?[176]

Do central governments indeed have less ability to monitor local public servants? This might be the case in highly centralized countries, where the hierarchical lines of accountability are stretched thin, allowing locally posted government officials to operate with little or no effective central oversight. In more decentralized countries, an effective response to monitoring local public servants is to generate "horizontal" accountability mechanisms, by empowering local communities and their elected representatives at the local level to play a more important role in this area. In decentralized settings, the "distance" traversed by the funding flows is generally shortened, thereby reducing the opportunities for corrupt leakages. More direct accountability may be arguably more effective on both the revenue side and the expenditure sides of the budget, as local communities are in a better position – and have a greater incentive – to monitor the financial operations of their local authorities. Furthermore, perceptions in relation to which levels of government are more corrupt also vary from country to country. For example, Azfar *et al.* (2001) find that household perceptions in Uganda and the Philippines are that corruption in the central government is higher than corruption in the local government.

What does the empirical evidence show? In all, the opinion on whether or not corruption is higher at the local level is far from a consensus. The literature studying the relationship between decentralization and corruption is relatively young, and suffers from a variety of measurement problems (in addition to the challenges of measuring corruption itself). The available empirical literature on this topic presents also mixed results. Gurglur and Shah (2000), Arikan (2004), and Fisman and Gatti (2002a) find that decentralization reduces the overall level of corruption, suggesting that structural decentralization reforms that improve participatory governance and accountability have the potential for also being effective in the fight against corruption.[177]

Fisman and Gatti (2002b) examine the relationship between decentralization and corruption, from a different perspective. In their study the degree of decentralization is defined as the mismatch between local own-revenue generation and local expenditures and measured as the share of

---

[176] Alternative hypothesis in favor of decentralization support the belief that interregional competition in an economy with decentralized governments helps to reduce corruption and leads to increase private investment (Tumennasan, 2004).

[177] Huther and Shah (1998) also find a positive relation between fiscal decentralization and governance, when governance is measured by an index, which, among other variables, includes reduced corruption.

federal transfers in state and local expenditures. They find that transfers are positively correlated to corruption. This is, according to Fisman, because local public officials are prone to the abuse and misuse of resources from program-based federal transfers (assuming they face a soft-budget constraint).[178] These results suggest that in order for expenditure decentralization to be fully effective as an anticorruption tool it must be coupled with effective revenue decentralization and lower dependency on central transfers.

On the other side of the spectrum, Treisman (2000) finds corruption to be higher in federal (as opposed to unitary and supposedly more centralized) countries. This result is partially supported by Gurgur and Shah's results (2000). While these authors find a negative correlation between corruption and decentralization, they also find that the negative effects of decentralization on corruption are greater in unitary countries than in federal countries. Some of the aforementioned arguments against decentralization may explain this relationship. Treisman states that, presumably, the extraction of bribes by different levels of government may lead to an "overgrazing of the commons" (p. 401).

An additional point to consider in analyzing the effects of decentralization on corruption levels is that these effects can be asymmetrical across local governments. In this regard, Reinikka and Svensson (2004), who study the determinants of the degree of local capture, find that the share of resources actually received by schools in relation with what they should have received is positively correlated with the income level of the local community. They attribute this relation to a higher bargaining power in richer communities, which, in turn, suggests that, regardless of the de jure characteristics of the resource allocation mechanism grant among schools, corruption may cause education spending to be regressive. If that is the case, and it is also assumed that the leaked resources are indeed locally captured (as opposed to being captured at a higher level), decentralization may lead to increases in corruption in low income local governments while having a smaller or nil effects in high income ones. Based on firm-level data on bribing activity and harassment in Indonesia, Henderson and Kuncoro (2006) conclude that the overall level of corruption declined after decentralization. Yet, according to this study, the effects of decentralization are asymmetric across districts, as those districts that elected non-Islamic parties experienced relative increases in corruption.

Whether or not decentralization is an effective programmatic response to fight corruption is a question that will need much more research to be answered categorically, if ever. However, the institution of powerful

---

[178] This type of argument is not applicable to block grants, which may generate lower incentives for overspending or abuse.

decentralization reform programs around the world, such as in Bolivia, Indonesia, Mexico, or even the Russian Federation, has been justified because of the need to reduce the overall level of corruption in those countries, among other reasons.[179,180] The case of Bolivia is discussed in Box 5.17.

The remaining discussion in this section focuses on a number of direct effects on corruption of moving from a centralized to a decentralized government system. The discussion will separately consider the impact of expenditure decentralization on corruption; the relationship between revenue decentralization and corruption; and the use of formula-based intergovernmental grants as an anticorruption tool.

5.4.1. Expenditure decentralization

Despite the potential benefits of expenditure decentralization in curtailing corruption, poorly designed or poorly implemented decentralization reforms could actually increase the overall level of corruption. In order to minimize opportunities for corruption by local government officials, the framework for decentralized local governance should incorporate several features that increase the transparency and accountability of local government operations:

(i) Define clear roles of each tier of government.
(ii) Strengthen technical capacity in local financial management.
(iii) Promote participatory planning and surveillance.

5.4.1.1. Define clear roles of each level of government. Accountability, clarity, and transparency in the assignment of expenditure responsibilities among levels of government are of crucial importance. Unclear mandates would allow public officials at different levels of government to "pass the buck" to each other. As such, the decentralization framework should aim to streamline the legislative and regulatory system pertaining to intergovernmental relations. It is common to find contradictory regulations and spending assignments that overlap among two or even three levels of government. Such is the case for health and education in many developing countries.

---

[179] See Shah and Thompson (2004) for a review of several motivations for decentralization in a broad group of countries and regions.

[180] Furthermore Arze *et al.* (2003) find that decentralization reforms have an influence in the composition of public expenditures by increasing the share of social spending (education and health). This finding coupled with evidence that military spending is positively correlated with higher corruption (Gupta *et al.*, 2001), suggests that decentralization may indirectly reduce corruption through its effect on the composition of public expenditures.

Box 5.17.   Decentralization promotes citizen's voice in Bolivia

In 1994, Bolivia initiated a series of decentralization efforts to increase transparency and accountability at all levels of government, increase citizen participation, and strengthen local governance. Bolivia implemented a strong and comprehensive decentralization reform with the enactment of the Law of Popular Participation (LPP) and the Law of Administrative Decentralization (LDA). These laws devolve public spending responsibilities to municipal governments, assign revenue sources to local governments, and redistribute central government resources.

One part of the strategy within the LPP was to fight corruption by promoting citizens' voice. This was accomplished by creating mechanisms that allowed social organizations to participate in the planning and execution of budgets and to monitor overall municipal performance. The LPP law tackles the problem of multiethnicity by recognizing peasant communities, indigenous communities, and neighborhood groups as legal representatives of territorially based organizations (OTBs). Each OTB elects democratically a Vigilance Committee (CV), which is responsible for the legitimacy of the participatory planning process, approving strategic planning along with municipal councils, and most importantly, monitoring the formulation and implementation of the municipal budget.

The CVs can legally request financial information, review projects, and initiate the process of removal of corrupt officials in municipal governments. The CVs are also empowered to report irregularities to the Ministry of Finance, which in turn, has the duty to investigate and report these demands to the Senate within 30 days. If the irregularity is verified by the Congress, all municipal funding is frozen indefinitely until the Comptroller's Office conducts an audit of its accounts. This system has received some criticism on the grounds of the inability to find technically qualified CV members and the capture of OTBs by political groups. But there is also consensus that, in practice, local transparency has improved where CVs are most active.

Sources: Gray-Molina et al. (1999), Behrendt-Adam (2002).

5.4.1.2. Strengthen local financial management regulations and practices. Improvements in local financial management regulations and the financial management practices at the local level reduce the ability of local governments to engage in corrupt practices. The first line of defense against diversion of local funds to local politicians should be the improvement of local budget practices, better auditing and greater oversight by central financial authorities. While such corrupt misallocations can take place at every level of government, simple but well-designed expenditure management techniques can easily be put in place at the local level to prevent such diversions of funds.

Another common "trick" applied by local governments is to over-estimate budget revenues. As this increases the budget envelope, it allows overspending on no-priority items and pet projects by local politicians until the belt has to be tightened.

A good local budget is structured in order to maximize transparency. For instance, local budgets should categorize spending in a meaningful way, for monitoring purposes. In order to prevent ghost workers and the like, personnel expenditures should be itemized by service delivery post, allowing communities to monitor whether employees are, in fact, at their post. Additional simple steps, such as posting budgets on bulletin boards at the district headquarters, promote a culture of transparency. These simple measures often receive insufficient attention.

5.4.1.3. Promote participatory planning and surveillance at the local level. Mechanisms to promote and enhance the effectiveness of participatory planning were discussed earlier, particularly in Section 5.2 of this chapter. It must be stressed that participatory planning mechanisms have particular benefits in the context of local governments, offering the potential to utilize public hearings for the elaboration of participatory budgets in citizen forums, something that seems implausible at the national level. de Gonzales (2000) describes a typical participatory budgetary mechanism, which starts with a preliminary budget presented by the mayor, continues with workshops held in each territorial organization (e.g., Ward) to select the projects or programs that are priorities and discuss them with technical specialists that assess feasibility and costs. Proposed projects are, finally, gathered from each neighborhood association to be selected by an auditing commission and included with the final budget.[181] The existence of community-based organizations or administrative subdivisions (such as wards or villages within a larger local government jurisdiction) is a key factor for the success of participatory planning and local oversight. The powers and duties of these organizations and institutions should be made explicit by law and their participation and reports reviewed by central authorities. A good example of mechanisms used to strengthen civil territorial organizations and public oversight of local budgets is the case of Bolivia (see Box 5.17).

---

[181] de Gonzales (2001) describes the success of Porto Alegre (Brazil) in the use of participatory budgeting mechanism.

5.4.2. *Revenue decentralization*

The advantages and disadvantages of revenue decentralization – assigning revenue sources to regional and local government levels – are many and have been widely discussed in the economic literature (McLure, 2000; Bird, 2001). A decentralized revenue assignment might help curb corruption by increasing the accountability of subnational governments to constituents – a more direct link between the payment of local taxes and fees and the benefits of locally provided services. In this context, revenue decentralization decreases the possibilities of local tax revenues being misused or embezzled en route from local tax collectors to central tax administrations. Hence greater revenue decentralization is per se a mechanism able to reduce opportunities for corruption.

There are two main reasons to believe that local taxpayers have a better chance to hold subnational (as opposed to national) authorities accountable. First, there exists a better link between specific taxes and specific expenditures at the subnational level. Where resources are collected at the central level, they are usually not associated with the provision of specific goods or services, thus not allowing taxpayers to indirectly scrutinize the use of tax revenues by central governments. Second, constituents of local governments have greater power to vote their authorities out when there are doubts about their honesty. The power of the vote is greater at the local than at the national level. Small groups of voters are more likely to cast the decisive vote in local elections and particular issues are less likely to get buried in broader "packages" of policy issues, as is the case at the national level.

Accountability of public revenues requires that citizens have free access to public information. The importance of revenue decentralization vis-a-vis a centralized system is that this information is more manageable at the local level (if nothing else for the smaller quantity of information to be scrutinized). As noted earlier, however, this presumes that mechanisms for disclosure of local revenue collections are explicitly mandated by central government laws and regulations. The following revenue information should be timely and publicly available: budgets, mechanisms of disbursement, and the criteria used for the distribution of resources. To be useful to citizens, the public information available should be relevant, complete, and legitimate.[182]

5.4.3. *Intergovernmental transfer system*

The third pillar of decentralization, the design of a country's intergovernmental transfer system, can have a significant impact on opportunities

---

[182] See *State Capture and Participatory Planning* for further information that should be made publicly available in order to increase accountability.

for corruption. The high degree of central government discretion in the distribution of public resources among local jurisdictions – which is common among more centralized countries – offers extensive opportunities for corruption practices, both at the central as well as the local government level.

At the central level, discretion over horizontal allocations and conditions gives the opportunity for extorting bribes. Anecdotal evidence abound regarding local officials meeting behind closed doors with officials from the Ministry of Local Government or the Budget Commissioner responsible for local governments, whereby larger transfers are negotiated in return for private gain. Likewise, if sector ministries are given the responsibility to certify that local governments have met certain regulations or conditions, it provides the opportunity for arbitrage on the part of the approving official.

At the local level, the absence of transparency of actual funding flows limits the degree to which local officials can be held accountable. Publication of actual disbursements of grants, as is increasingly common in many African countries, enables local bureaucrats to hold the Local Treasurer accountable, whereas local residents and community leaders are able to hold service providers accountable. Likewise, annual publication and analysis of local government finances in the form of an Intergovernmental Fiscal Review provides an informed overall picture of local government finances. The documentation provided by South Africa's Treasury on intergovernmental finances provides a good example of a well-documented and transparent system of intergovernmental grants.

5.5. Other programmatic responses to corruption

In their fight against corruption, governments can engage in a number of other broad responses with a noticeable impact on the fiscal sphere. Like in the case of decentralization, multinational organizations (such as UNDP) or bilateral donors, such as USAID, have often provided technical assistance and material support for these other initiatives.

5.5.1. Anticorruption commissions or bureaus

The most immediate, and perhaps the most common, response to perceived corruption in governments is the establishment of an autonomous "anticorruption commission" or an "Anticorruption Bureau" charged with identifying and sometimes prosecuting all forms of corruption in government. In some cases, these commissions are given the task of coming up with proposals for administrative and political reforms that can eliminate or reduce systemic corrupt practices.

Despite the proliferation of anticorruption commissions or bureaus, the effectiveness of such organizations varies greatly among countries. Critics have argued that many of these efforts are just window dressing or just paying lip service to the issues. The effectiveness of anticorruption bodies depends on the exact legal mandate of the commission, the level of autonomy of the commission, and the energy and resources available for the effort. Independent prosecutorial power seems to be an important – albeit not sufficient – ingredient for a successful anticorruption body. Examples of anticorruption commissions are abundant. For instance, a successful case is the Independent Commission against Corruption in Hong Kong (see Box 5.18). A not so successful case is the "Prevention of Corruption Bureau (PCB)" of Tanzania established in 1991 as part of the President's Office.[183]

5.5.2. Legislative and judicial responses

Another broad strategy in the fight against corruption is to concentrate on legislative responses. In this context, governments can strengthen the legal framework through the creation of specific anticorruption laws. In this book, we have analyzed several anticorruption instruments such as Codes of Conduct for public servants, open records legislation, legislation requiring financial disclosure for politicians and senior civil servants, extradition agreements, party financing legislation, and so on. New legislation needs to be revised to ensure that it does not introduce obstacles to anticorruption efforts, in particular issues such as the use of immunity as protection against corruption charges, legislation restricting the disclosure of bank account information, or legislation restricting investigative rights of anticorruption bureaus or investigative journalism.

Naturally, a sound legislative and regulatory framework for corruption is a necessary but not a sufficient condition; legislative responses can be indicative of tokenism if the legislation or regulation is not actually implemented. Likewise, anticorruption may be pursued by policies aimed at broadly strengthening the rule of law, and more particularly, strengthening the judiciary system by streamlining the court system's procedures (i.e., enforcement of time limits on hearing cases, preventing judges' overload of cases, disallowing litigant selection of judges, and electronic archiving of case information) which in some cases requires the implementation of computerized systems.[184] Other measures to ensure judges' probity and competence include building professional capacity of judges, replacing a judge when necessary, recruiting on the basis of merit, and increasing judges' salaries.

---

[183] The case of Tanzania is discussed in greater detail in Chapter 6.
[184] This is has been supported, for example, by USAID in Sri Lanka (USAID, 2000).

Box 5.18. Independent commission against corruption in Hong Kong

During the 1960s and 1970s, corruption was a major social problem in Hong Kong. The severity of corruption was widespread in most public institutions and especially in the police. "Vivid examples included ambulance attendants demanding tea money before picking up a sick person and firemen soliciting water money before they would turn on the hoses to put out a fire. Even hospital amahs asked for "tips" before they gave patients a bedpan or a glass of water." (IACA website History Gallery).

However, things have changed drastically during the last three decades. Hong Kong is now considered one of the least corrupt countries in the world. One single institution has played a crucial role in Hong Kong's success against corruption: the Independent Commission Against Corruption (ICAC). The ICAC was created in 1974 with the objectives of promoting education and the investigation and prevention of corruption in Hong Kong. The ICAC has currently more than 1,300 staff members who are educated by means of a dedicated training school and learning resource center. The ICAC has powers of investigation and prosecution, which are independent from the police. Indeed one of the first tasks of the ICAC was to clean up corruption in the police department.

The ICAC publishes a series of reports with the aim of informing the public of the ICAC activities: corruption reports, election-related corruption reports, and statistics regarding prosecutions. The Community Relations Department of the ICAC provides support to government departments, public bodies, and private organizations in corruption prevention programs. This includes the arrangement of seminars on legislation covering corruption in Hong Kong, corporate system controls, ethical decision-making at work, and managing staff integrity. Survey data shows a dramatic change in the public's perceptions of corruption from 1977 to the present and a widespread belief that the ICAC was and continues to be a key factor of this change.

Sources: ICAC Website, World Bank (1997).

5.5.3. Strengthening the role of civil society and the private sector

A well-informed civil society is the anticorruption watchdog on a large scale. "Any process or decision that is required to be open to public scrutiny acquires thousands, if not millions of unpaid auditors." (Kaufmann and Siegelbaum, 1997, p. 9). Several country cases have proven that citizen-led groups, NGOs, and other civil society organizations (community groups, chambers of commerce, churches, and so on) are able to effectively contribute to controlling corruption, even when high-level government officials are involved (see Box 5.19). Such anticorruption efforts can be

---

Box 5.19. Bangalore: report card on public services

In 1993 a small group of people in Bangalore, concerned about the city's deteriorating standards of public services, initiated an exercise to collect feedback from users. User perceptions on the quality, efficiency, and adequacy of the various services were aggregated to create a 'report card' that rated the performance of all major service providers in the city. The findings presented a quantitative measure of satisfaction and perceived levels of corruption, which, following coverage in the media, not only mobilized citizen and government support for reform, but also prompted the rated agencies themselves to respond positively to civic calls for improvement in services. This exercise was repeated in 1999, and has been replicated in at least five other Indian cities, as well as the State of Karnataka in the interim.

The report cards have forced the public agencies at least to listen and react to citizen concerns. Quantification of perceptions has brought a credible indicator that lays down the extent of dissatisfaction and allows interagency comparison, triggering internal reforms. There was substantial response to the innovation: of the eight agencies covered in the report card in 1993, four did make attempts to respond to public dissatisfaction. The worst-rated agency, The Bangalore Development Authority (BDA), reviewed its internal systems for service delivery, introduced training for junior staff, and, along with the Bangalore Municipal Corporation, began to host a joint forum of NGOs and public agencies to consult on solving high-priority problems such as waste management. The Karnataka Electricity Board, too, formalized periodic dialogues with resident associations to garner feedback from users. Two others agencies also tried to strengthen their grievance redress systems.

Sources: Extracted from World Bank (2003a).

---

supported by governments, donor agencies, and international organizations by providing support, among others, for training community-based groups, academics, and journalists.

Effective anticorruption policy needs to design mechanisms whereby independent units are enabled to collect citizen complaints and seek remedial action (see Box 5.18). An active and free media may provide coverage of complaints channeled through these units in order to pressure governmental institutions to find solutions. Thus, policies targeted to strengthen the independence and ability of the media can be important anticorruption instruments. This strengthening may be done, for example, by supporting training programs with focus on ethical reporting and investigative journalism.[185] The effectiveness of mass media as an anticorruption tool is supported in the empirical literature. For example, in a recent study entitled "A Free Press is Bad News for Corruption" Brunetti and Weder (2003) present solid evidence of a negative correlation between press freedom and corruption.

Similarly, business associations can be important agents in the fight against corruption in government. The creation of coalitions between private and public sectors, NGOS and international organizations generates synergies that have proven successful in the fight against corruption. Several coalitions of this type are becoming active in several countries. Some successful examples can be found in Bulgaria, Dominican Republic, Paraguay, and Russia.[186] Coalition 2000 (2005) is, for example, an association of Bulgarian NGO's that also received the support of USAID. This institution is designed to increase awareness of corruption among the citizenry.

5.5.4. Monitoring and evaluation of anticorruption systems

In this section we review potential instruments of anticorruption control and evaluation. Several dimensions need to be considered in the diagnostics of those instruments: government institutions (processes, resources, products/output), public perception, and the national anticorruption strategy. Figure 5.1 presents a general framework that highlights potential instruments of diagnostic. The framework distinguishes between the nature of the object being monitored, the organizational and institutional context, and the nature of the sources of information.

5.5.4.1. Government institutions. Government activities are the fundamental source of corruption. The Public Financial Management System

---

[185] One such example of anticorruption policy by strengthening the media is the creation of the Latin American Journalism Center in Panama, which focuses on instruction in the ethics of journalism and the fight against corruption (USAID, 2000).
[186] See among others Coalition 2000 (2005), de Gonzales (2001), and Business Week (2002).

Figure 5.1.   Monitoring and evaluation of corruption

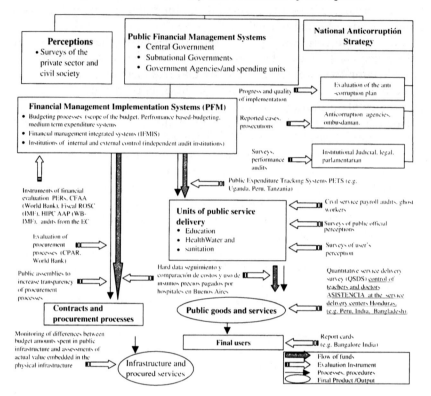

(PFMS) is an instrument of particular interest, comprising the preparation and implementation of the budget through the management of public revenues and expenditures. An evaluation of the PFMS can cover one, or more, of the following aspects:

- Processes, procedures, and organizational structure; for example, evaluation instruments conducted by International Finance Institutions such as the World Bank's Public Expenditure Reviews (PERs); Country Financial Accountability Assessment (CFAA) of member countries; IMF's Report on the Observance of Standards and Codes (ROS); BM-FMI HIPC Public Expenditure Tracking Assessment and Action Plan (HIPC-AAP); European Community audits; Country Procurement Assessment Reports (CPARR); and other tools of regional development banks and unilateral development agencies.
- Flow of resources, control mechanisms for disbursement and the administration of funds for identifying fraud; for example the comparison of input prices for health clinics or the tracking of resource flows across

different levels of government, such as in the case of Public Expenditure Tracking Surveys (PETS) in Uganda, Peru, and Tanzania.

• Quality control of goods and services produced by agencies or public governmental service units (schools, health posts, etc.) or by private agents delegated by tendering or direct contract; for example, the use of report cards for the evaluation of public services by final users in Bangalore, India, and results collected by its Public Affairs Center (Paul, 1995);[187] or the systematic collection of input data from service centers (medicines, medical equipment, educational materials, personnel absenteeism), characteristics of quantity and quality of outputs (number of medical consultations per day, school enrollment rates, test scores, etc) – quantitative service delivery surveys (QSDS) in Honduras, Peru, India, Bangladesh, Uganda, and Zambia (Reinikka and Svensson, 2002); or user satisfaction surveys in service delivery units with the objective of identifying the quality of the service and the presence of any requests of illegal payments for public services (Ensor, 2004).

5.5.4.2. Perceptions. As discussed previously, public perception is a powerful instrument of evaluation. Surveys of the public sector and civil society can help reveal the effectiveness, de facto, of reforms in the governmental system. Their validity depends on the degree that the surveyed agencies have contact with the object of the reform, being an organizational unit (tax administration, customs, judicial system, etc.), a process (tendering process for provision of public services, business license applications, etc.), or a flow of resources (disbursement of funds under tendering or direct public contracts). For example, surveys targeted to the private sector are conducted periodically by international organizations and NGOs, such as in the cases of: the WBES, the BEEPS, and the Global Competitiveness Report (GCR).[188] The examples include aggregated indicators (computed on the basis of various sources of perception surveys); among the best known are the Corruption control (Kaufmann *et al.*, 1999, 2003), and the CPI by the NGO Transparency International.

5.5.4.3. National strategy and framework for anticorruption control. The fundamental component here is the evaluation of the National Anticorruption Plan. Good examples include the report of the status of the implementation of the anticorruption strategy in South Africa, or the evaluation of the corruption in the legislative and judicial system in Bulgaria conducted by a civil organization (Coalition, 2000).

---

[187] See "Training Kit on the Report Card Approach" Public Affairs Centre, Bangalore.
[188] See the webpage of the World Bank Institute for other examples.

5.6. Concluding remarks

In this chapter we review policy responses that have been used around the world to combat all different forms of fiscal corruption. Some policy responses concentrate on attacking the symptoms of corruption by detecting and punishing public officials who have already made a decision to partake in corruption, while other policies concentrate on preventing corruption by removing opportunities and eliminating perverse behavior incentives. Of course, both types of remedies are necessary in any effective anticorruption strategy.

In our discussion we identify three different levels of comprehensiveness in anticorruption policy design: piecemeal strategies designed to attack specific determinants and forms of corruption, programmatic policy interventions designed to address several of these issues simultaneously, and broad-based governance reform required for the long-term comprehensive control of corruption.

One main goal of this section has been to assess the relative effectiveness of the different policy responses that are being used to fight corruption. Admittedly, this is a complex task. In many cases the results of anticorruption policy responses have been mixed. In some other cases, the results seem to be successful but only for a short period of time. The relevant question becomes: is the brief duration of the effect an intrinsic result of the strategy itself or rather an exogenous result of a decrease in commitment and political will needed to sustain the effort over time? In general, we need to be watchful against accepting 'one-size-fit-all' policy responses without taking into account the unique characteristics of individual countries.

From a policy standpoint the main contribution of this section is to show that, despite our current difficulties in devising anticorruption campaigns with guaranteed success, there are many practical approaches to containing and reducing the different manifestations of corruption. Belief in the possibility of success in the fight against corruption is a key step in generating a positive can-do attitude among policymakers and civil societies. The main conclusion is a positive one: corruption is by no means invincible. It is quite feasible for any country to fight it effectively.

Annex 5.A.

Revenues from tax collection were delegated to the SUNAT (see Table 5.A.1).

Table 5.A.1. Peru: Tax ratios, 1990–2003

Year	All taxes	Income	VAT[a]	Excises	Import duties	Others[b]	Social security	SUNAT-collected taxes[c]
1990	11.75	0.66	1.44	4.28	2.08	2.37	0.92	7.84
1991	12.86	0.94	2.56	4.55	1.33	1.66	1.82	9.05
1992	13.87	1.67	3.60	3.94	1.44	1.34	1.88	10.10
1993	13.91	2.03	4.95	2.37	1.75	1.07	1.74	10.06
1994	14.76	2.56	5.50	2.34	1.70	1.13	1.53	11.45
1995	15.19	2.88	5.72	2.09	1.74	1.22	1.54	11.88
1996	15.59	3.64	5.62	2.05	1.66	1.15	1.47	12.46
1997	15.70	3.63	5.61	2.17	1.55	1.28	1.46	12.69
1998	15.55	3.53	5.50	2.07	1.79	1.30	1.36	12.39
1999	14.08	2.92	5.08	1.98	1.66	1.16	1.28	11.13
2000	14.13	2.77	4.96	1.86	1.60	1.22	1.72	10.81
2001	14.34	2.99	4.76	1.89	1.48	1.49	1.73	11.13
2002	13.86	3.03	4.86	2.11	1.25	0.94	1.67	10.93
2003	14.63	3.76	5.16	2.13	1.20	0.73	1.65	11.78

Source: Extracted from Mann (2004).

[a]Net of refunds; includes the VAT on both domestic transactions and imports.

[b]The principal taxes included here are the payroll tax (impuesto extraordinario de solidaridad), taxes on small taxpayers (regimen unico simplificado), fines, road user fees (impuesto al rodaje), and the tax on public companies (impuesto a las acciones del estado).

[c]Income, VAT, excises, payroll, and others. The main exclusions are social security and import duties. Although the SUNAT began collection of social security taxes (health and pensions) in 1999 and import duties in 2003 (with the fusion of SUNAT and the formerly semi-autonomous customs agency, to generate a consistent data series from 1990 to 2003 these two levies are excluded. To be completely consistent, the VAT and excises collected on imports should also be excluded, given that they were a function of imports; this was not done.

Annex 5.B. Budget institutions and corruption

In this annex we use cross-country data to empirically explore the relationships between some dimensions of corruption (*general* and *type-specific* aggregate corruption composites) and specific budgetary practices (mainly entailing budget execution and audit). As it is discussed in Section 5.2 of this study, the most commonly used measures of corruption are the TI's CPI and the Corruption Control Index computed by Kaufmann *et al.* (2003). Yet, other available data sources, such as the Global Competitiveness Report, provide cross-country information suitable for the quantification of specific types of corruption, such as political and administrative corruption. In this annex we aggregate selected survey questions from the GCR to construct two composite indexes. The questions used for the generation of these composites and their correlation are shown in Tables 5.B.1 and 5.B.2.

Table 5.B.1.   *Correlation among administrative corruption variables*

Survey question	Q1	Q2	Q3	Q4	Q5
$V1$. Irregular payments in exports and imports	1.00				
$V2$. Irregular payments in public utilities	0.93	1.00			
$V3$. Irregular payments in tax collection	0.91	0.92	1.00		
$V4$. Irregular payments in public contracts	0.93	0.89	0.83	1.00	
$V5$. Diversion of public funds	0.88	0.85	0.80	0.94	1.00

Note: Computed with data from Global Competitiveness Report (2004).

Table 5.B.2.   *Correlation among political corruption variables*

	$V1$	$V2$	$V3$	$V4$
$V1$. Irregular payments in government policymaking	1.00			
$V2$. Irregular payments in judicial decisions	0.95	1.00		
$V3$. Prevalence of illegal political donations	0.85	0.78	1.00	
$V4$. Policy consequences of legal political donations	0.78	0.74	0.85	1.00

Note: Computed with data from Global Competitiveness Report (2004).

An aggregation of these variables can be useful in the analysis of the determinants of specific types of corruption. To this end, we apply the principal components methodology to construct the two composite indicators of corruption. Each of these indicators is built as a linear combination of the largest eigenvalues of the correlation matrix of these variables (the first component). The composites' indexes so generated account for 86.91 percent of the variance of the four questions used to measure political corruption (Table 5.B.1) and 91.12 percent of the variance of the five questions used to measure administrative corruption (Table 5.B.2). The composite weights used are:

$$\text{Political corruption} = 0.51566 \times V1 + 0.49852 \times V2$$
$$+ 0.50061 \times V3 + 0.48473 \times V4.$$

$$\text{Administrative corruption} = 0.45640 \times V1 + 0.45089 \times V2 + 0.43740$$
$$\times V3 + 0.45172 \times V4 + 0.43935 \times V5.$$

The descriptive statistics of the two constructed composite indexes are shown in Table 5.B.3. The administrative corruption composite and the political corruption are highly correlated, $r \approx 0.89$ (see Table 5.B.4). As a check on the validity of the principal component composites constructed here, it is useful to look at how well-correlated these indexes are with other indexes of (general) corruption in the literature. Our composite for administrative corruption is more closely correlated to TI's CPI and Kaufmann's *et al.* (2003) Corruption Control measures ($r = 0.94$ and -0.91, respectively) than our composite for political corruption ($r = 0.85$ and -0.82, respectively). Nevertheless, the correlation is high in both cases.

Table 5.B.3. **Descriptive statistics composite index of administrative and political corruption**

Variable	No. of observations	Mean	Standard deviation	Minimum	Maximum
Administrative corruption	102	3.76 E-09	2.13	−4.18	4.19
Political corruption	102	2.42 E-09	1.86	−4.15	2.94

Source: Computed by authors based in survey scores from Global Competitiveness Report (2003–2004).

Table 5.B.4. **Correlation matrix**

	1	2	3	4
1 Administrative corruption	1			
2 Political corruption	0.8887	1		
3 CPI 2001	0.9368	0.8546	1	
4 Corruption control 2002	−0.9151	−0.8219	−0.9703	1

Source: Computed by authors based on survey scores from Global Competitiveness Report (2003–2004).

Some recent studies have identified historical and institutional determinants of corruption (Gurgur and Shah, 2000; Treisman, 2000). But corruption in the expenditure side of the budget can also arise from particular budgetary practices, which offer opportunities for certain forms of corruption. Unfortunately, budget processes are complex and often country specific. For these reasons, comparable data on budget processes across countries are for the most part inexistent. However, the OECD/World Bank Budget Practices and Procedures Database provides a unique source of information on budgetary practices across countries. These data are collected by surveying 30 OECD Member countries and 30 non-OECD countries, of which close to data for 40 countries are already available. Seven variables in this dataset allow us to measure the "appropriateness" of important budget practices, such as: capital investment management ($V1$ and $V2$), the comprehensiveness of the Treasury system ($V3$), procurement regulations and audit ($V4$–$V5$), and external audit practices ($V6$–$V7$). We recode the variables to take a value of 1 if the practice in question is suited for corruption control objectives and 0 otherwise (see Table 5.B.5).

Table 5.B.5. Variables: Budgetary institutions

Variable label/ WB survey code	Question	Coding
$V1$/(3.2.a.5)	More generally, are transfers permitted between capital investments or transfer programs (social security pensions, etc.) and operating expenditures?	There can be no such transfers = 1. Otherwise = 0
$V2$/(3.2.b.3)	Is it possible to carry-over unused appropriations for investments (building construction, etc.) from 1 year to another?	No = 1, Otherwise = 0
$V3$/(3.3.b.1)	Are ministries/government organizations allowed to maintain cash accounts separate from the Treasury?	No = 1, Otherwise = 0
$V4$/(3.4.f)	Are compliance with procurement regulations audited?	Yes in full = 1. Otherwise = 0
$V5$/(3.4.j)	Is there a minimum threshold value above which "open and competitive" tender procedures must be used?	Yes = 1, Otherwise = 0
$V6$/(4.5.b)	Is there a central Supreme or National Audit Office?	Yes and reports to either Legislative or Judiciary = 1. Otherwise = 0
$V7$/(4.5.e)	How would external audit arrangements be described?	Independent of the Executive = 1. Otherwise = 0

Source: OECD/World Bank Budget Practices and Procedures Database (recoded).

In order to preserve degrees of freedom, given the small number of observations available on the budget dataset, and to reduce multicollinearity among these variables, we proceed to aggregate several of the variables in Table 5.B.5 into a single composite index. To construct the composite index of budgetary institutions we use canonical analysis. That is, we construct a linear combination of the variables such the composite to be obtained maximizes its correlation with the dependent variable (one composite index is estimated for each one of the models to be estimated). This composite is aimed to capture variations in the budget institutional framework across countries. Each specification also controls for standard explanatory variables for corruption (variables and sources of the data are reported in Table 5.B.6).

The canonical weights estimated are:

$$Bud1 = -0.838V1 + 1.439V2 - 0.166V3 - 0.923V4$$
$$+ 0.400V5 - 0.340V6 + 0.606V7 \quad (1) \quad \text{Dep. Var. CPI.}$$

$$Bud2 = -0.840V1 + 1.152V2 - 0.464V3 - 0.977V4$$
$$+ 0.895V5 - 0.196V6 + 0.886V7 \quad (2) \quad \text{Dep. Var. CC.}$$

$$Bud3 = -1.060V1 + 0.914V2 \pm 0.273V3 \pm 1.146V4$$
$$+ 0.217V5 + 0.178V6 + 1.14V7 \quad (3) \quad \text{Dep. Var. Adm. C.}$$

$$Bud4 = -0.875V1 + 1.354V2 \pm 0.111V3 \pm 0.994V4 \pm 0.014V5$$
$$\pm 0.069V6 + 0.799V7 \quad (4) \quad \text{Dep. Var. Pol. C.}$$

Table 5.B.6.   Data sources

Variable	Source
GDP per capita	World Bank (2003b)
Log Population	World Bank (2003b)
Industrialized	World Bank (2003b)
Legal English Origin	La Porta *et al.* (1998)
Ethnic Fractionalization	Alesina *et al.* (2003)
Budget Institution Composite	OECD/World Bank Budget Practices and Procedures Database
Pubic Service Competence	World Economic Forum (2003)
Freedom of the Press	World Economic Forum (2003)

The estimation results from four different models are reported in Table 5.B.7. Given the aggregated nature of both the dependent variables and the budgetary institutions independent variables these results should be only considered as suggestive and some caution should be exercised in its interpretation. We must also notice the small sample size ($n = 29$) with which we need to work. Given that each estimated equation has a different dependent variable, the magnitudes of the coefficients across equations are not comparable. Despite the caveats, the results in Table 5.B.7 show that the estimated coefficient signs for most explanatory variables are consistent with those found in the previous empirical literature. Gross Domestic Product (GDP) per capita and freedom of the press are significant predictors of lower corruption at a 5 percent level of significance. A larger population is significantly associated with higher levels of corruption. A

Fighting Corruption in the Public Sector

common legal system (inherited by British colonies) and ethno-linguistic fractionalization are not statistically significant in any of the models. Public service competence takes a negative coefficient and statistically significant at the 10 percent confidence level in the administration corruption and political corruption equations.

Table 5.B.7. Determinants of alternative corruption types

	Corruption perception index	Corruption control	Administrative corruption	Political corruption
GDP per capita	−6E-5[+]	2.7E-5*	−1.6E-5	−1.5E-5
	(3.3E-5)	(1.2E-5)	(3.1E-5)	(4.27E-5)
Log Population	0.3594**	−0.1411**	0.2764*	0.256
	(0.1207)	(0.0454)	(0.1123)	(0.1553)
Industrialized	−1.019	0.316981	−0.6137	−0.892
	(0.8528)	(0.3182)	(0.7893)	(1.099)
Legal English Origin	−0.6289	0.30422	−0.3906	0.4683
	(0.5211)	(0.1962)	(0.4851)	(0.6705)
Ethnic Fractionalization	−0.2969	−0.12188	0.1954	−1.642
	(1.134)	(0.4343)	(1.092)	(1.469)
Budgetary Institution	−0.4061*	0.2452**	−0.2182	−0.5489*
	(0.1780)	(0.0669)	(0.1704)	(0.2327)
Pubic Service Competence	−0.6078	0.2311	−0.7142[+]	−0.9069[+]
	(0.3987)	(0.1483)	(0.3681)	(0.5158)
Freedom of the Press	−0.4603	0.2493*	−0.8283**	−0.6257
	(0.2824)	(0.1057)	(0.2637)	(0.3656)
Constant	2.7111	0.1884	1.8630	2.711
	(3.8841)	(1.130)	(2.796)	(3.884)

Note: Robust standard errors reported in parenthesis.
**denotes significance at the 1 percent level.
*denotes significance at the 5 percent level.
[+]denotes significance at the 10 percent level.

More importantly from our perspective, Table 5.B.7 shows a negative (and statistically significant) correlation between the budget institutions composite and three of the four corruption measures estimated (administrative corruption is negatively correlated with the budget composite but not statistically significant). These results suggest that corruption is not only determined by historical factors deeply engrained in the history and culture of countries but it is also determined by budget practices and institutional controls that are, at least in principle, subject to policy reform.

The small sample size of the dataset used for the estimations in Table 4.B.7 is a limiting factor, so is the use of a single source of information in the construction of the corruption composites. Nevertheless, this empirical exercise is useful in drawing some preliminary conclusions as well as in identifying the need for further empirical analysis on the relation between specific types of corruption and budget institutions and practices.

While the finding that "bad" budget practices are associated with higher degrees of corruption may not come as a surprise to students of corruption, we believe it to be of vital importance that empirical studies start identifying and narrowing down practices and institutions that are statistically associated with higher corruption levels. In this way, empirical studies of corruption will become of practical help to policymakers designing anticorruption strategies.

CHAPTER 6

A Case Study in Corruption and Anticorruption Responses

While Chapter 5 and the previous chapters in this book provide numerous specific real-world examples of corruption and specific anticorruption responses, the breadth of the topic has prevented us thus far from presenting a specific in-depth case study of a country's experience with the problem of corruption and its anticorruption policy responses.

This chapter provides a specific country case study in corruption and anticorruption responses, with an overview of Tanzania's corruption challenges and its anticorruption policies over the past decade.

Considering the case of Tanzania in greater detail provides a number of benefits. First, Tanzania has faced – and in many aspects continues to face – a wide variety of challenges on the corruption front that are more or less typical of lesser-developed economies. Second, the country's policy responses suggest that – although it may be impossible to stamp out corruption completely – it is possible to make substantial improvements in limiting corruption if a comprehensive policy approach is taken. As such, the anticorruption responses taken in Tanzania – both its successes and failures – provide valuable lessons for the development of anticorruption strategies elsewhere. Third, the case of Tanzania further emphasizes the ongoing challenge of keeping anticorruption efforts center stage in the management of the public sector.

6.1. Corruption and anticorruption responses in Tanzania

Over the past decade a transformation has taken place in Tanzanian policy circles with regard to the public sector's attitude toward corruption and the fight against corruption (Sundet, 2004). As one of the least developed economies in Africa, Tanzania suffered so badly from endemic corruption in the public sector in the 1980s and early 1990s that a number of international donors froze disbursement of aid in 1994 in protest against massive irregularities in the granting of tax exemptions. From this low point, Tanzania has made a convincing policy reversal by integrating anticorruption efforts as an important component of its overall governance agenda.[189]

6.1.1. A synopsis of corruption in Tanzania

Anecdotal evidence suggests that corruption in Tanzania can be divided roughly into two periods. During the first period, starting at independence in 1961, the degree of corruption in Tanzania gradually increased over time. Policy factors during this period that contributed to making corruption a progressively important governance problem included: the expansion of the public sector (following the nationalization policies of 1967); the gradual erosion of compensation levels for government officials; the resulting erosion of ethos in the public service, which was hitherto based on public servants as national role models; increases in discretionary powers accorded to public officials; the decline in transparency and accountability mechanisms; and the fading of the line separating politicians and the private sector (Muganda, 1995).

Although the nature of corruption in Tanzania is typical in many ways of corruption in developing economies throughout Africa, Tanzania has been relatively more corrupt than many of its neighbors (see Box 6.1). Despite intermittent anticorruption efforts by the government, as a result of the gradual erosion of ethical standards in the public sector, by the early 1990s a number of large corruption scandals were brought to light by the media that seriously brought into question the government's commitment to good governance. In response to the domestic and international outcry over corruption in Tanzania, anticorruption and good governance became important themes championed by Benjamin Mkapa in his election platform in 1995. The election of President Mkapa signaled the beginning of a period of systematic focus on the problem of corruption and the introduction of a series of anticorruption policies.

A Presidential Commission of Inquiry on Corruption – known as the Warioba Commission – was appointed by President Mkapa in 1996 with the task of identifying the scope of the corruption problem and mapping out the country's overall anticorruption strategy. In its deliberations, the Commission identified and considered two different types of corruption, namely "petty corruption" and "grand corruption" (President's Office, 1999). While closely related to the concepts of bureaucratic (administrative) corruption and political corruption, respectively (as discussed earlier in this study), the two types were distinguished by motive: while petty

---

[189] The United Republic of Tanzania is divided into two entities: Mainland Tanzania and Zanzibar. The current discussion focuses on corruption in Mainland Tanzania. Zanzibar is deemed considerably more corrupt that the Mainland, and has only recently begun to take steps toward reducing corruption in the public sector.

Box 6.1. Corruption in Tanzania: trends and comparisons

Systematic information about the level of corruption in Tanzania is limited. By all accounts, Tanzania was and continues to be one of the more corrupt countries in Africa. However, based on the available quantitative analyses, it is unclear whether corruption has improved, remained constant, or in fact worsened in recent years.

Based on Transparency International's Corruption Perception Index (CPI) in 1998, Tanzania was ranked one of the most corrupt countries in Africa, ranking 16th out of 18 African countries for which comparable data were available (receiving the same score as Nigeria). While CPI is statistically not comparable across different years, the perception index of corruption in Tanzania – both in nominal terms as well as relative to other African countries – has improved slightly in recent years. Corruption in Tanzania continues to be perceived as above average for the region, but Tanzania's CPI score of 2.5 assured an improved rank of 11th (out of 18 countries).

However, the World Bank's Corruption Control Index (Kaufmann, 2003), which also is statistically not comparable across different years, suggests the level of corruption in Tanzania is essentially unchanged over the period 1998–2002, but its relative ranking does suggest a slight relative improvement vis-a-vis other African countries.

In contrast, a recent Public Service Satisfaction Survey conducted in Tanzania found that 50 percent of the respondents felt that corruption was increasing in Tanzania against only 33 percent who thought it was decreasing (Sundet, 2004).

Year	Tanzania CPI	African average CPI	Tanzania CPI ranking	Tanzania CC	Tanzania CCI ranking
1998	1.9	3.6	16	−0.96	42
1999	1.9	3.5	16	–	–
2000	2.5	3.5	14	−1.01	40
2001	2.2	3.3	14	–	–
2002	2.7	3.4	11	−1.00	35
2003	2.5	3.1	11	–	–

Note: The African average reflects 18 countries for which consistent data were available. Based on CPI data by Transparency International (2004), data were available for 18 countries for the period under consideration. The World Bank's Corruption Control Index (Kaufmann, 2003) covers 49 African countries. The table is based on data prepared by Sundet (2004).

corruption is engaged in "as a means of supplementing their meager income," grand corruption is perceived to be driven by "excessive greed for accumulation of wealth."

While the Warioba Commission found petty corruption to be pervasive in the public sector (see Box 6.2), the government chose to first address highly visible forms of corruption, based upon the belief that ethics in the lower echelons of the public sector could not be restored without a clear example and commitment by the country's political leadership

---

Box 6.2.   *Petty corruption in Tanzania*

Petty corruption is identified as corrupt acts by public officials who seek or receive bribes because of their low incomes and standard of living. This type of petty corruption is rampant throughout the public sector in Tanzania. Examples of petty corruption in public expenditures and the delivery of services include:

- Bribes are demanded and given during the registration of children in schools; to enable pupils pass examinations, or to enable students obtain placement in secondary schools and colleges. Moreover teachers give bribes in order to be promoted, to be transferred, and to be placed.
- Patients are forced to offer bribes at hospitals in order to be treated, X-rayed, and allocated a bed in a ward or to be operated upon. Health staff sells publicly provided medical supplies for personal gain.
- Absenteeism by government officials is high: they are absent in order to generate additional income through alternative employment.
- Trade officers solicit and accept bribes from businessmen who trade without licenses; and they demand bribes when issuing trading licenses.
- Land officers demand bribes during the surveying and allocation of plots, valuation of crops, and issuing certificates of Title.
- Forest officers receive bribes to give permission for felling more trees than allowed in the licenses or to free culprits who are caught poaching or with unauthorized forest products.
- Public utility employees demand bribes in order to establish new connections.

Sources: Prevention of Corruption Bureau (2004), Hosea (1999), Muganda (1995).

(President's Office, 1999). As such, the first priority was given to (largely political) grand corruption, particularly in the administration of government revenues.

As discussed in detail below, the first two major interventions taken in the fight against corruption were the strengthening of the institutional anticorruption framework (both legislative and organizational), and a major overhaul of the tax administration, achieved with the establishment of the Tanzania Revenue Authority (TRA) in 1996. This emphasis on political corruption and corruption in the revenue side of the budget was not coincidental. Since Tanzania ranks quite consistently on the lower end of the spectrum in national revenue performance, any further reduction in tax revenues (whether due to direct theft of tax payments, increased tax evasion condoned by corrupt tax officials; or reduction in taxpayer compliance due to loss of trust in the public sector) posed a direct threat to the government's ability to function, and compromised its relationship with international financial institutions and the international donor community. The discussion in more recent years – to the extent that corruption still features broadly on the government's agenda – seems to have shifted more toward addressing corrupt practices on the expenditure side of the budget.

Based on this chronology, the discussion of Tanzania's anticorruption efforts in the remainder of this section is broken down into four main segments:

• Strengthening tax administration and revenue collections.
• Anticorruption efforts on the expenditure side of the budget.
• Improvements in the system of local governance.
• Strengthening the anticorruption framework.

In Chapters 4 and 5 of this book we make an effort to clearly differentiate between determinants of corruption and potential strategies that can be employed to reduce the consequences of those determinants. It would be important for policymakers to realize that what is being targeted by any given of the discussed strategies is a specific determinant of corruption, rather than corruption itself. Why is this important? When considering corruption strategies, it is tempting to skip the intermediate step (the determinant of corruption) as an object of analysis, and instead just focus directly on the potential effects of the strategy in terms of corruption. But when this happens, the objectivity of the analysis is undermined since, in practice, this type of approach would ignore the mechanism by which the strategy is expected to reduce corruption in the first place.

The assessment of the Tanzania anticorruption strategies in this chapter seeks to identify the degree of success of given anticorruption strategies in tackling the specific determinants of corruption, and when successful, in turn, in decreasing corruption itself. As noted previously, not all anticorruption strategies are suitable for all countries as one strategy does not fit all. Thus, it seems more appropriate to analyze the effectiveness of policies that were undertaken by the Tanzanian government as opposed to running a checklist against the menu of anticorruption strategies introduced in Chapter 5. This gives the benefit of the doubt to the Tanzanian authorities as to what may be the most fitting anticorruption strategy in that country. Of course, there is the possibility that there may have been a different and more effective strategy.

6.1.2. Strengthening government revenue collections

Within the larger anticorruption and good governance strategy pursued by the Government of Tanzania starting during the mid-1990s, a concerted effort was made early on to reduce corrupt practices in the collection and administration of government revenues. With support from the World Bank and the donor community, a key product of Tanzania's anticorruption strategy was the establishment in 1995 of the semi-autonomous TRA, and its subsequent institutional strengthening.

The tax administration reform program formulated around the establishment of the TRA combined a number of specific interventions aimed at structurally reducing corruption in the collection of government revenues: TRA was given greater autonomy over hiring and firing decisions, with the objective of reducing political influence over appointments, increasing the probability of termination when caught in corrupt practices, and thereby increasing the overall opportunity cost of engaging in corruption.

The creation of a SARA was identified in Chapter 5 as a programmatic response to corruption because it can address simultaneously several determinants of corruption. Besides the creation of the TRA, the government of Tanzania undertook additional anticorruption strategies on the revenue side. Some of these are discussed below.

The creation of the TRA, at least in theory, contributed to decreasing the opportunities for corruption. In particular, granting some degree of autonomy to the TRA and introducing merit-based recruitment allowed the depoliticization of tax officials and the reduction of patronage. As an autonomous government authority, the CEO of the TRA is appointed directly by the President and the management of the TRA is supervised by a TRA Board. The increased level of autonomy assures greater political independence for the organization and assures that TRA's senior leadership is generally considered to be clean. At the same time, the institutional set-up of the TRA seems to have increased the distance between the staff and the executive management team.

In order to break the previous culture of corruption in the tax administration agency, all former staff members were dismissed and had to reapply for a position in the new TRA with a 1-year probationary period. During this process, more than a third of the staff was rejected on evidence or suspicion of misconduct. Yet, perhaps most importantly, the tax administration reforms failed to structurally break the corruption networks within the tax administration. Anecdotal evidence suggests that middle managers informally required new applicants to pay "speed money" to have their applications considered – allowing managers to identify applicants willing to collude, but also suggesting that applicants continued to be willing to pay for a possibly lucrative position within TRA.

Thus, despite its de jure autonomy, the TRA did not manage to achieve either the objective of meritocracy or depoliticization of the hiring process.[190]

Another key element of the administrative reform was to pay salaries that would enable TRA to attract and retain highly qualified and honest staff. This involved dramatic initial increases in pay rates – for some categories of staff up to ten times higher than corresponding positions in the civil service. As discussed in previous chapter, this strategy was expected to decrease corruption levels through one of the two effects: either by allowing public servants to afford being honest or by increasing the perceived opportunity cost of being caught. The affordability effect was likely more effective during the first year, but it lost its effectiveness as the real value of wages decreased over time due to inflation, since the initial nominal wages remained frozen from 1996 until 2000.

At the same time, the discouragement effect arising from higher opportunity costs of loosing a job that pays well is present only if there is a credible probability of getting caught and losing the job. This became more unlikely in the face of the corruption evidence found within the internal investigation monitoring unit (IIMU), as discussed further below. As a result, higher wages may have served only as an additional income to the resources obtained through bribes rather than a substitute of it.[191]

Changes in the Prevention of Corruption Act (PCA) in 1993 also aimed at changing the incentives for corruption by increasing the probabilities of detection via strengthening the ability to monitor the TRA's staff. Stronger internal oversight mechanisms were put in place through the establishment of a new unit for IIMU, thereby ostensibly increasing the probability of detection. Yet, once again, the effectiveness of this strategy was thwarted by internal corruption within the IIMU. In 2000, 24 members from this unit, including its head, were dismissed over corruption charges (Fjeldstad,

---

[190] Other thing may have gone wrong. After the creation of the TRA politically allocated tax exemptions to private companies increased considerably leading the share of tax exemptions from total tax revenue collections to increase from 15 percent in 1996 to 37 percent in year 2000 (Mokoro Ltd., 2001).

[191] This reasoning is consistent with the theoretical model presented in Section 2.2, which reveals that whenever the probability of detection of the corruption act equals zero, a positive value of corruption will increase a public official's expected income regardless of the public wage level.

2002). The infiltration of corruption in monitoring agencies is not an uncommon problem, for which it is often suggested to combine monitoring efforts with reports gathered directly from private companies, which may have an incentive to report corruption (Mookerjee and Pung, 1992).

Thus, the important question is whether the anticorruption strategies taken on the revenue side of the budget were successful? In a strict sense, it is very difficult to judge the success or failure of any given anticorruption strategy because its effects are not easy to perceive and they are much harder to measure in any objective way. However, as noted in the previous paragraphs, many of the strategies followed in Tanzania failed to have a practical effect on addressing the determinants of corruption within the revenue agency, and therefore pretty much failed to reduce corruption on the revenue side of the budget. Other studies have reached the same conclusion, even though some of them emphasize the success that reached the first year after the establishment of the TRA. A taxpayer survey by PriceWaterHouse Coopers (1998), for example, reports that corruption decreased during the first year of TRA existence. Yet, Osoro *et al.* (1999) report that after experiencing an initial decrease during the first year, the level of corruption started to increase thereafter. Similarly, a recent study of the TRA by Fjeldstad *et al.* (2003) concludes that, while some improvements in revenue administration resulted as early as 1996–1997, overall the introduction of the TRA has not lived up to its expectations. Revenue collections seem to have followed a similar pattern to that of corruption. While a modest increase of the tax revenue ratio was experienced in year 1996/1997 (the first year that the TRA was fully operational), later years saw decreases through 1999–2000. The tax ratio has slighted improved since then (Table 6.1).

Why were these strategies not more successful? There are several reasons. The attempts to increase ethics and clearly define corruption offenses and penalties through the PCA were neutralized by corruption in the judicial system, which failed to ensure convictions. The establishment of the TRA allowed targeting simultaneously several determinants of corruption. Yet, revenue corruption continues to persist despite the substantial pay increases received by TRA officials, confirming that pay level is only one of several factors affecting the behavior of tax officers. Despite efforts to increase the effectiveness of staff monitoring by the creation of a special monitoring unit, this very unit engaged in corruption decreasing the de facto monitoring abilities of the agency. It may be posited that in an environment where the demand for corrupt services is extensive and monitoring is relatively ineffective, wage increases may simply end up forming an extra bonus on top of the bribes taken by corrupt officers. This observation is also consistent with empirical results from Di Tella and Schargrodsky (2003). These authors find that the degree of audit intensity determines the effectiveness of the wage level as an anticorruption tool. Their study finds that the effects of higher wages on corruption when audit

Table 6.1.   Tanzania tax revenue collections

Tax revenue GDP ratio						Real tax revenues	
Fiscal year[a] All taxes	Income	VAT[b]	Excises	Import duties	Other taxes	Deflated total tax revenues[d]	Index (1994/ 1995 = 100)
1991/1992	12.49	3.27	3.65	2.49	1.72	1.36	328,394	109.5
1992/1993	9.46	2.94	2.66	1.31	1.05	1.50	250,291	83.5
1993/1994	10.95	2.91	3.14	1.44	1.41	2.05	220,360	94.3
1994/1995	11.28	3.26	2.00	0.80	NA	NA	299,900	100.0
1995/1996	11.31	3.31	2.78	2.07	1.81	1.34	317,149	105.8
1996/1997	12.15	3.17	2.88	2.16	1.85	2.09	366,496	122.2
1997/1998	11.01	2.91	2.69	1.97	1.68	1.76	357,414	119.2
1998/1999	10.27	2.71	3.47	1.40	1.46	1.23	360,724	120.3
1999/2000	10.13	3.00	3.28	1.30	1.28	1.27	382,290	127.5
2000/2001	10.74	2.52	3.92	2.01	1.24	1.05	434,992	145.0
2001/2002	10.88	2.65	4.08	2.06	1.03	1.06	471,597	157.3
2002/2003	11.58	2.89	4.44	1.96	1.11	1.18	531,697	177.3
2003/2004[c]	12.09	2.92	4.73	2.13	1.21	1.10	583,234	194.5

Source: Mann (2004).
[a]The fiscal year for the TRA and tax statistics runs from July 1 to June 30. The denominator value (GDP) employed to calculate these tax ratios represents 2-year calendar averages, given that Tanzania's GDP is estimated on a calendar year basis.
[b]The VAT was introduced at the beginning of FY 1998/1999. Prior to this date, the taxation of consumer expenditures was levied via a multirate (turnover) sales tax.
[c]Estimated.
[d]Millions of Tanzanian shillings.

Table 6.2.   Expected effects of wage increases

Audit intensity	Low	Intermediate	High
Corruption	High	Medium	Low
Effect of wages on corruption	Nil	Negative	Low

Source: Extracted from Di Tella and Schargrodsky (2003).

levels are low are nil, but negative when audit levels are intermediate, and paradoxically negative but lower in magnitude when audit levels are high (Table 6.2).[192] These results suggest that positive incentives should be complemented by negative incentives, that is, "carrots and sticks should be viewed as complementary tools in fighting corruption" (Di Tella and Schargrodsky, 2003, p. 3). This dual strategy is also recommended by anticorruption strategy for tax revenue administrations developed by the World Bank (1999).

---

[192]The latter effect is however, not statistically significant.

This contention also helps to explain why the TRA reforms were more successful during the program's first year. First, most employees were working on a probationary basis (which sends a message that their behavior is or will be assessed to make a permanent hiring decision). Second, during this first year tax officials were unable to assess the risk of getting caught, as they had yet to learn how the new internal auditing systems worked or whether they could collude with members of IIMU.

Finally, as noted before, the effort to improve the quality of staff and the attempt to depoliticize the hiring process through merit-based recruitment of the TRA were undermined by irregularities in the management of the application process. In fact, the high turnover in TRA may have supported the development of the corruption network outside TRA, as former tax administrators and customs officials dismissed from the organization (but with extensive knowledge of tax regulations and loopholes) found employment as tax accountants in the private sector. This increased the window of opportunity for the remaining TRA officers to work in collusion with their former colleagues now in the private sector.

Another weakness of the anticorruption approach in Tanzania on the revenue side of the budget has been the absence of appropriate strategies aimed at controlling the demand for corruption from taxpayers. As noted in Chapter 4 of this study, high tax burdens increase the incentives for corruption for tax officials as they are often approached or even harassed by taxpayers eager to decrease their tax liabilities. While personal income tax rates are considered moderate in Tanzania, corporate tax rates are perceived as relatively high (Miles *et al.*, 2004). Moreover, despite ongoing tax reform efforts in Tanzania, its current tax laws and regulatory framework are complex and outdated. Strategies to reduce this window of opportunity by the simplification of tax laws and regulations have been weak, if not absent. In all, a combination of (perceived) high tax rates and a complex legal and regulatory tax system motivates taxpayers to collude with tax officials and at the same time it allows tax officials to negotiate tax liabilities via the discretionary interpretation of the law.

6.1.3. *Reform of expenditure management*

Although much of the early work on anticorruption reforms in Tanzania focused on the revenue side of the budget, systematic steps were also taken to secure improvements in expenditure management and reduce the opportunities for corruption in government spending.

An important element in Tanzania's strategy to assure improved government control over public expenditures has been the reform of the budget execution process through the treasury by successfully introducing a computerized IFMS, which became fully operational in 2001 (Ministry of Finance Tanzania, 2001). The computerized system, known as Epicor, is responsible for processing all central government disbursements, thereby assuring that all disbursements are made only to registered vendors, as approved by the appropriate government accounting official, and in accordance with the approved budget estimates. By introducing a single, transparent accounts mechanism that links budget implementation with the government's spending plan, Epicor has clearly reduced the window of opportunity for government officials to access public funds at will and spend them inconsistent with their intended purpose.

Although the introduction of Epicor has widely been acknowledged as a technical and logistical success, there is a need to acknowledge limitations on the scope of any computerized IFMS system to counteract corruption (Schiavo-Campo and Tommasi, 1999). While the system provides certain accounting controls to assure that resources are not directly diverted for illicit purposes, the system is simply an accounting tool and, as such, for instance not able to verify that the goods or services for which payments are made were actually delivered to specification. Although the Epicor system makes government payments more transparent and systematic and assures areas of spending are in accordance with the government's spending priorities, the system in itself provides no guarantee that government officials do not demand bribes before issuing payment orders, or that civil servants entered into the system are actual workers (as opposed to ghost workers), or that contractors do not bribe the approving officials to sign off on incomplete, shoddy, or non-existent work. Furthermore, the coverage of the Epicor system is not universal; the system does not track local government expenditures beyond the stage of disbursement to Local Government Authorities, and a variety of donor-funded capital development activities flow outside the scope of Epicor.

6.1.4. Local government reform

The years following independence in Tanzania were characterized by highly centralized, planned control over the economy and the public sector. During this period, elected local governments were abolished and the accountability of public servants to their local communities was lost. Even the architect of these policies – President Nyerere – belatedly recognized the importance of subnational authorities in a participatory and accountable public sector.[193] In recognition of this fact, the government reestablished elected local authorities in 1982 and has been pursuing a gradual process of decentralization reforms. As a result of these efforts, over 20 percent of government spending – including all spending for basic

---

[193] Ngware (1999) quotes President Nyerere stating in 1985 "There are certain things that I would not do if I were to start again. One of them is the abolition of Local Government.... We had ... useful instruments of participation, and we got rid of them."

education, basic health care, and a variety of other typically local services –
are devolved to the local level (Boex and Martinez-Vazquez, 2006).

Due to the increased fiscal prominence of the local government sector,
local government (finance) reform has been an increasingly important
component of public sector reforms. In fact, despite a period of relative
inaction since the "first wave" of local government reforms in the 1980s, a
renewed "second wave" of decentralization reforms was initiated in 1999
with the establishment of the Local Government Reform Program. The
main objective of the reform program is to improve the quality of local
government services by improving governance structures and by improving
the financing of local authorities. As such, reducing corruption in the various aspects of local government finance is an important ingredient in local
government reforms. Reduced fiscal corruption and improved local governance are pursued through a variety of reform activities:

- *Improved local financial management.* Although public expenditure management at the national level was strengthened significantly with the introduction of an IFMS at the National Treasury, the treasury only tracks
  gross disbursements to local authorities. Once within the accounts of local
  authorities, supervision over the financial management of local government
  resources becomes the mandate of the President's Office-Regional Administration and Local Government (PO-RALG). Through the Local Government Reform Program, PO-RALG is seeking to strengthen the ability
  of local government officials to monitor and control local expenditures by
  introducing computerized financial management systems at the local government level. Meanwhile, a number of public expenditure tracking surveys
  performed since 1999 suggest that significant outflows occur in local
  spending (see Box 6.3).
- *Rationalization of local revenues.* Local government revenue collections
  have long been recognized as a window of opportunity for corruption in
  Tanzania. For instance, in a recent survey on local taxation almost half
  of the respondents indicated that the dishonesty of local tax collectors
  was a major problem in local taxation. In response to these problems, the
  Ministry of Finance has reduced the revenue sources assigned to the local
  government level; the local Development Levy was abolished in 2003
  along with several other "nuisance taxes" that were hard to administer
  and therefore easily open to corruption.
- *Introduction of* formula-*based grants.* In February 2004, Tanzania's
  Cabinet approved the introduction of a system of formula-based block
  grants to local authorities, replacing a system a discretionary local government allocations. The introduction of formula-based grants has increased the equity of the system of local government finances while
  reducing the opportunity for corruption at the central level (generating
  bribes in return for larger allocations) as well as at the local level (where

---

Box 6.3.   Public expenditure tracking in Tanzania

Tanzania conducted its first Public Expenditure Tracking Surveys (PETS) in 1999 and 2001 (Dehn *et al.*, 2002; Sundet, 2004). As in neighboring Uganda, there was a strong suspicion that serious problems existed in the flow of funds from the central government via the local authorities to frontline service facilities.

The first Tanzanian PETS, which was limited to 3 districts, 45 primary schools, and 36 health facilities, pointed to qualitatively similar problems observed in Uganda a few years earlier. It was found that local councils diverted a large part of funds disbursed by the center for non-wage education and health expenditures to other uses (i.e., to sectors other than education and health), or used the resources for private gain. Leakage was estimated at 57 percent in education and 41 percent in health care. Salaries appeared to be less prone to diversion, but payrolls suffered from ghost workers and frontline staff from delays in salary payments.

The second Tanzania PETS also tracked flows of money and materials from the central government via regional and local governments to basic service delivery points, using a combination of existing documentation and records and facility visits and interviews. The sectoral focus was on health and education, while some information was collected on other pro-poor expenditures (rural roads, water supply, judiciary, and HIV/AIDS). The survey covered five districts, considering four primary schools and four clinics in each district.

Although the findings of the two PETS were disseminated during the national budget consultations, unlike in Uganda, they have not had as strong a catalytic effect on central government oversight or transparency arrangements. The treasury has initiated regular dissemination of itemized local government budgets to members of Parliament and regular publication of budget allocations for the selected pro-poor spending programs both in Swahili and English language newspapers, covering allocations for ministries, regions, and local authorities. Yet no substantial awareness campaign was undertaken to promote these new transparency measures, and despite government regulations, only a few local authorities displayed budgets on public notice boards.

greater transparency due to the introduction of formula should result in greater accountability).

6.1.5. Others responses: Strengthening of the anticorruption framework

The first thrust of the government's anticorruption strategy during the mid-1990s was to signal a clear attitude change in government, by demonstrating that the government was serious about tackling this issue. In 1991 the PCB was established by restructuring and renaming a previously existent Anticorruption Squad, which had been created in 1975. The PCB forms part of the President's Office and its Director is appointed by the President, to whom the Bureau is accountable. The fact that the PCB is accountable only to the President and not to the Parliament (as is the case in other countries, such as Uganda), have raised concerns about the effectiveness of this organization to hold the executive accountable (Sedigh and Muganda, 1999). Furthermore, there are no clear instructions for holding the PCB accountable for its performance.[194]

The amendment of the PCA in 1993 (enacted originally in 1971) was another attempt to instill ethics and define moral standards in the public service. This act also defined and established penalties for broad forms of bribery. In addition, illicit enrichment regulations made it an offense for public officials to be in the possession of pecuniary resources, property, or to have a standard of living that was not in proportion with present or past legitimate emoluments. In these cases, the PCA shifted the burden of proof from the prosecution to the accused, which now must provide true account for the income used for the acquisition of these assets, goods, or services. This type of rules of evidence for corruption offenses, which is also applied in other countries, such as Hong Kong, reflects a much stronger commitment to ensure convictions over corruption charges.

The PCA also aimed at introducing strong incentives against corruption by establishing high penalties for corruption offenses, which include imprisonment up to 2 years for failure to account for property under illicit enrichment, as well as the confiscation of pecuniary property and resources under the control of the accused, and imprisonment up to 14 years depending on the seriousness of the offense.[195]

In summary, the PCA aimed to instill ethics, strengthen the anticorruption legislation, and stiffen penalties against corrupt acts. Yet, despite the strong commitment against corruption reflected in PCA, the effectiveness of

---

[194] Anticorruption Bureaus in other countries, such as the Independent Commission Against Corruption in Hong Kong, have dealt with this problem by creating a specialized Committee that receives complains from the public about the Anticorruption Bureau, and their practices and procedures.

[195] See Ofosu-Amaah *et al.* (1999).

this law has been de facto greatly undermined by corruption within the judicial system and weak enforcement of its regulations. Thus, in theory, corruption cases could be identified more effectively by the comprehensive and strong regulations contained in the PCA. However, a good piece of legislation is easily rendered useless unless there are solid institutions behind it that can guarantee their enforcement. It is still alleged in Tanzania today that even when the most obvious cases of illicit enrichment are identified and brought to courts, judges can be bribed to avoid confiscation of assets or imprisonment.[196]

Beyond the enactment of the PCA, the more rigorous pursuit of anticorruption by the PCB, and the prominence accorded to the issue in policy speeches, another concrete step was taken to strengthen the legal and institutional framework for anticorruption policies. The *Leadership Code of Ethics*, which was enacted in 1995, was designed to curb improper conduct of public leaders in higher echelons by preventing conflicts of interest and requiring the public disclosure of assets. Another specific action taken to strengthen the legislative framework included the strengthening of procurement and tender legislation and regulations.

As already noted, one of the first major policy initiatives put in place shortly after Mkapa assumed the presidency was the establishment of a Presidential Commission of Enquiry into Corruption. Based on the Commission's findings and in close concert with its donor partners, a National Anticorruption Strategy and Action Plan (NACSAP) was adopted in November 1999 and a Good Governance Coordination Unit (GGCU) was set up in the President's Office to oversee the implementation of NACSAP. As part of NACSAP, virtually all government ministries and departments have gone through a thorough consultative process to develop their own Anticorruption Action Plans, on the basis of which they report quarterly to the GGCU in the President's Office. These reports provide data on the number of complaints of corruption received as well as on the administrative and legal action taken against employees suspected of corruption.

Although the Government of Tanzania continues to be committed to the fight against corruption and the implementation of NASCAP, the public focus on corruption in Tanzania seems to have declined in recent years as other public sector reforms have assumed a more central role. In addition, while the implementation of NASCAP in itself has been encouraging, implementation of the strategy has not lived up to its potential (Sundet, 2004). Concerns include the fact that the capacity of the GGCU remains low, the production of quarterly monitoring reports is chronically behind schedule, and the government has not seized the opportunity to generate significant publicity around NACSAP.

---

[196] See Fjeldstad (2002).

6.2. Conclusions

The Tanzania's anticorruption strategy, actions, and results constitute a
useful example for the study of anticorruption policy and fiscal reform.
The Tanzanian government has taken several of the "right steps" to reduce
corruption: it has introduced a SARA; introduced a computerized treasury
system, strengthened its anticorruption legislation, established an Anticorruption Bureau, and is pursuing a comprehensive local government
reform program. Yet, despite the dedication of significant political attention and public resources to good governance and anticorruption efforts
(see Box 6.1), and the national and international perception of progress
and success, the reality seems to be that the corruption problem in Tanzania has not improved significantly, if at all over this period.[197] And
unfortunately, despite the fact that the corruption problem certainly has
not yet been resolved, attention to good governance and to fighting corruption both on the part of the government as well on the donor community seems to be waning.

Should we conclude that Tanzania's anticorruption strategy has failed?
Before answering this question it is important to note that despite the
millions spent on anticorruption programs, conferences and policy making, available evidence suggests that corruption is generally getting worse,
not better, across the African continent. In the context of this rather
gloomy picture, perhaps the fact that Tanzania has been able to stop the
further deterioration of corruption may be considered a qualified
victory. Thus, in a broad sense it is not proper to categorize Tanzanian
anticorruption efforts as a failure. However, the Tanzanian anticorruption
strategy cannot be considered a success either, since there is evidence
that on several occasions it failed to achieve their most direct intended
objectives.

Why did these strategies fail? As noted through this study a successful
anticorruption strategy is based not only on a structure of appropriate
systems and best fiscal practices, but also on the existence of a broad range
of institutions, which are strongly interdependent. This interdependence
makes it possible for the entire strategy to falter even if only one of these
institutions is weakened by corruption.

Langseth *et al.* (1997) describe policy responses to corruption in the
context of a National Integrity System as a framework for analysis that
compares these responses to a platform sustained by eight integrity institutions (pillars): political will, administrative reforms, watchdog agencies,
parliaments, public awareness/involvement, the judiciary, the media, and

---

[197] It is also important to acknowledge the limitations of these indicators for comparisons
across time (see Section 2.3 for details).

the private sector.[198] If any of these pillars is weakened by corruption the others receive excessive pressure, the platform tilts, and the "round ball of sustainable development rolls off". The role of these integrity pillars and their effects on the incentives and opportunities for corruption have been identified in different sections of this study as interdependent components.

Was there genuine political will against corruption in Tanzania? This is a hard question to answer here with the information we have. By some accounts there seems to have been. As Sundet (2004) points out, the regional reports from Africa in Transparency International's Global Corruption Report (2003) suggest that the impressive array of national anticorruption strategies across the continent has little to do with any real commitment to fight corruption and all to do with the need to placate donors by putting wished-for strategies and institutions in place. Cosmetic reforms are unlikely to make any real difference mainly due to the lack of a genuine political will to follow the process closely enough to guarantee its proper implementation.

It is also worth noting that many of the anticorruption interventions in Tanzania have been rather "top–down" in nature and have had a rather limited scope. On several occasions the key question seems to have been: who guards the guard? Some of the very institutions aimed to control corruption allowed corruption to thrive within their structures. Unfortunately, a weak demand for accountability from the bottom-up in Tanzania has allowed the presence of several leakages during the implementation of the anticorruption reforms. The absence of mechanisms empowering civil society institutions to oversee the probity of the anticorruption agencies and to hold the executive and parliament accountable left those guards without a guard. The relatively weak demand for accountability from the bottom up should not come as a surprise given that most of the anticorruption initiatives in Tanzania targeted relatively small groups of actors, such as senior politicians, tax collectors, and government accounts officers.

The Tanzanian anticorruption strategy has been marked by insufficient support in building public awareness and media participation. It has also failed to reinforce the judicial system. As a result, the efforts to strengthen the government's administrative systems and to put in place meaningful watchdog agencies were greatly undermined if not nullified.[199] As argued by the Transparency International Regional Report (2001, p. 29), "without judicial support, watchdogs can bark, but not bite". Furthermore, anticorruption policies have clearly been less successful in tackling broader

---

[198] The concept of a National Integrity System composed by these eight pillars was first introduced by Ibrahim Seushi, President of Transparency International Tanzania.

[199] Several nations share the same type of issues, such as Thailand, Malaysia, Philippines, and Indonesia, suggesting that strengthening the judicial systems should be a first and necessary step in the fight against corruption.

corruption challenges, such as addressing administrative corruption at various levels of government, eliminating corruption networks, and restoring an ethos of public service. It is also clear that fewer systematic efforts have been undertaken to control corruption on the expenditure side of the budget.

With this in mind, the government and its international partners should consider exploring ways of targeting more support to the "demand side" of accountability in ways that feed more directly into the ongoing reforms, including strengthening the capacity of civil society, media, and parliament (Muganda, 1995; Sundet, 2004). These efforts may serve to strengthen the existing institutions and generate the political will needed to reduce the gaps between the institutional de jure framework and de facto realities that have undermined the effectiveness of the anticorruption process. The Tanzanian government should also broaden the anticorruption strategy by increasing efforts in reducing the demand for corruption from the side of taxpayers through tax policy reforms as well as continue to undertake strategies aimed at reducing corruption levels on the expenditure side of the budget.

CHAPTER 7

Summary, Policy Lessons, and Practical Guidelines

We have set out to study the nature, the different manifestations, and possible remedies for fiscal corruption. Corruption is present when public officials abuse their positions of public authority for private gain.

Corruption is, in the first place, a failure in ethics and moral standards of public officials. Thus, requiring strict adherence to a Code of Conduct and integrating ethics sensitization in the training, evaluation, and promotion of public officials should be considered a first step in the fight against corruption. But this is typically not enough. While corrupt behavior has other causes, which we still do not fully understand, to a large extent corrupt officials appear to behave in a very rational way by responding to incentives and opportunities, provided by existing fiscal institutions, to commit corrupt acts. Therefore, the design of effective anticorruption measures needs to take into account these rational responses to incentives and opportunities.

For convenience, we have organized the study around three main areas of fiscal policy and management: revenue collections, expenditure processes, and quasi-fiscal operations. For each of these areas, we have identified policy responses, from piecemeal to more general or programmatic, that have proven to be effective in combating corruption. Here we highlight the most prominent responses in each area.

First, there are policy responses that are effective in fighting corruption in all areas of fiscal management and policy. These include the introduction or strengthening of mechanisms to monitor officials, encouraging the cooperation from other public employees through whistle-blower protection plans, and the collection of anonymous reports. Laws for the mandatory disclosure of assets, effective prosecution and stringent penalties, and the reductions of wage differentials between the public and private sectors can also contribute to curbing corruption.

On the revenue side of the budget, it is important to focus on measures that reduce the number of tax evaders willing to exert pressure on tax officials and also reduce the potential gains from corruption and tax evasion, such as keeping tax burdens manageable and improving the fairness of the tax system.

Basic oversight mechanisms such as computerized paper trails, institutionalized routine cross-checks, internal and external audits, or measures that decrease the discretionary power of tax revenue officials can eliminate many opportunities for corruption. Other common-sense measures likely to decrease opportunities for corruption include the separation between officials responsible for the tax assessment, tax collection, and audits; rotation of staff; use of standardized and computerized systems of tax assessment and merchandise classification; use of presumptive tax regulations; and automatic mechanisms of tax audit selection, independent appeal courts; and of the existence of an ombudsman. Broader programmatic responses, such as the creation of "SARAs" and LTUs have also been proven to be effective in reducing corruption.

On the expenditure side of the budget, anticorruption design can be more complex due to the larger scope and the greater variety of avenues for corruption. But here again there are quite simple, common sense, and effective ways to fight administrative or petty corruption, such as public service spending controls, integrated treasury systems, transparent procurement processes, and the application of international standards for internal and external audits. Public Expenditure Tracking Surveys (PETS) have been quite useful for identifying the potential scope of corruption and mobilizing policy responses.

Controlling political corruption can prove to be a more difficult and subtle task. Nevertheless, active involvement by the parliament and parliamentarian anticorruption commissions, supreme external audit institutions, civil society organizations, and the investigative media have proven effective in controlling this type of corruption. In addition, opportunities for political corruption can be reduced by strengthening political institutions that promote political representation and electoral accountability. Large areas of the quasi-fiscal sector can face significant problems with corrupt practices. But here, too, there are practical steps that can be taken to reduce corruption incentives and opportunities. Corruption in the privatization of state assets can be reduced by decreasing the level of administrative discretion and bureaucratic clearances required in the process, and by increasing the transparency of the process through the public and open disclosure of information, valuation procedures, and results of the privatization process. Corruption and abuse of market regulation powers can be controlled by minimizing the number of market regulations, import controls, and so on. Corruption in the pricing of public utilities can be curtailed by promoting more independent regulatory agencies and by increasing the depth and scope of monitoring and auditing procedures. In the case of natural resource exploitation, the corruption stakes can be huge through the direct or indirect embezzlement of these revenues. Where democratic institutions are weak and parliamentary oversight and free media scrutiny are lacking, IFIs can be effective in exerting pressures on government leaders to disclose and enable external auditing of natural resource revenue accounts.

7.1. A few general lessons

Our understanding of the nature of fiscal corruption has improved significantly over the last decade but it is still limited in several ways. Similarly, our understanding of the relative effectiveness of policy responses and anticorruption strategies has also improved but is far from complete. With this note of caution we close this report with several preliminary lessons regarding the design of anticorruption strategies in developing and transitional countries.

7.1.1. Lesson 1: Fiscal corruption is a problem faced to different extents by every country

Corruption is a global phenomenon and it affects all countries without exceptions but in various degrees. Thus, it is not so important to free a country of corruption entirely, even if this were at all possible, but to introduce reforms and institutions that enable a country to fight and contain corruption where it arises. The realization that the effects of corruption do not stop at international borders and that the impact of corruption is felt not only by developing and transition countries but across the global economy, has led the international community to address corruption as a fundamental objective that goes beyond the notion of international aid, but also rather as a matter of global subsistence.

7.1.2. Lesson 2: Reducing corruption is not an irresolvable problem

An important conclusion of this study is that corruption is not an untouchable or irresolvable problem. While it is true that there are no easy solutions in combating corruption, we have uncovered in this book many practical instruments to fight different forms of corruption. In fact, some of the anticorruption responses have been quite successful in curtailing even the most entrenched forms of corruption. The recognition that corruption is neither untouchable nor an irresolvable economic governance problem signals a significant shift in attitudes toward this issue. As recently as the mid-1990s, the topic of corruption was taboo in a large sector of international policy circles. At that time, the prevailing notion was that corruption was primarily a domestic political problem and that the issue was outside the scope of international development efforts. Subsequent involvement of the IMF in developing a Code of Good Practices on Transparency; and the World Bank, USAID and other bilateral donors' engagement in anticorruption efforts, and in a variety of other governance issues, has signaled a sea of change in attitudes toward corruption.

7.1.3. Lesson 3: To be effective, it is important to understand the exact nature of the corruption challenge

Corruption is a problem that can be studied, at least in part, in objective and systematic ways, which can facilitate the design of effective policy responses and remedies. From the perspective of this study, and much of the existing literature, corruption may not be so much the result of a predetermined absence of ethics and morals in the public sector or society at large, but rather the result of conscious and rational decisions by agents responding to incentives and opportunities offered by a particular institutional framework. Several factors affect this decision, many of which can be conceptually modeled as a simultaneous system of incentives and opportunities to engage in corruption.

Corruption in the fiscal arena takes many forms, ranging from petty corruption by poorly paid public officials to grand corruption by wealthy, powerful, rent-seeking political operatives. Both forms of corruption are detrimental to economic growth and stability to different degrees. Anticorruption policies should target the specific incentives and windows of opportunity that motivate and enable these different forms of corruption.

7.1.4. Lesson 4: Good targeting is important because there are distinctive patterns of corruption across countries and regions

As this study uncovered, there are distinctive patterns of corruption across countries and regions although geographic regions around the world often share similar corruption problems. This presents potential challenges of contagion across countries but also opportunities for learning how to fight corruption. This also means that anticorruption strategies cannot be designed in a mechanistic way. Appropriate anticorruption design needs to recognize that corruption is a multifaceted phenomenon and that corruption in each country is likely to adopt different forms and nuances. Therefore, anticorruption strategies need to be adapted to the peculiarities of each country.

7.1.5. Lesson 5: Institutions matter and institutional reform is key in fighting corruption

This book has shown that the design of fiscal institutions is key for the presence (absence) of corruption. Other institutions of general governance, such as the rule of law and democratic representation are also key to containing corruption. Campaigns targeted to the introduction or reinforcement of anticorruption legislation and to promoting the independence of judicial systems are needed to increase the number of reported cases of corruption that end up prosecuted and penalized. Some key institutional reforms should aim to relax extremely high standards of proof for the prosecution, to authorize and support the investigation of corruption, to eliminate secrecy of bank account information, to eliminate immunity of senior political figures against corruption charges, to grant prosecutorial powers to audit institutions or anticorruption bureaus, and to promote the creation of bilateral and multilateral extradition agreements for corruption charges.

Other institutional reforms which may require longer periods of time to be effective in curbing corruption include the liberalization of markets, fiscal decentralization with functional and grass roots participation, the consolidation of democratic institutions and civil rights, and education in social ethics and moral standards.

7.1.6. Lesson 6: Successful anticorruption strategies require a comprehensive approach, sustained effort, and political support from the highest level

This study identifies a list of piecemeal anticorruption policies that are well-suited for quick implementation and which can attain outcomes in relatively short periods of time. Many of these have been proven to be quite effective, if not always long-lasting. A more permanent reduction of corruption is likely to require a sustained and comprehensive anticorruption strategy. Comprehensiveness means the active participation of different groups including the executive, the parliament and political opposition, citizen organizations, non-governmental organizations, the private sector, and often international organizations in the design and implementation of the anti-corruption strategy. Each and every one of these stakeholder groups executes a role that cannot be performed by the others. Each of these groups has also particular interests for which they should be held accountable by the other groups. Comprehensiveness also means the breadth and depth of the scope of the anticorruption strategy, from basic education programs, changes in laws and governance institutions, and so on. Anticorruption strategies should aim simultaneously at the incentives and the opportunities for corruption. Anticorruption policies targeting opportunities for corruption or the system of motivating factors alone are unlikely to be successful in curbing corruption. A double pronged approach should aim to control the opportunities of corruption by curative approaches based in enforcement and prosecution, while simultaneously using a preventive approach that attacks the roots of corruption by addressing the system of incentives embedded in the public sector. Hong Kong and Singapore are good examples of how much can be done with well-designed comprehensive strategies. Yet, both cases are small city–states with very unusual histories, which could be considered as outliers and may not reflect the challenges faced by a "typical" developing country.

To be successful, anticorruption efforts also need to be sustained over time. The international experience reviewed in this study shows that one of the most common causes of failure in anticorruption effort is the lack of continuity in effort once the strategy has been put into motion. In fact, sporadic efforts tend to be counterproductive as they undermine the credibility of future strategies. An important fact to keep in mind is that comprehensive anticorruption initiatives are costly and their sustainability greatly depends on the availability of resources to fund them. Ideally, anticorruption institutions should have long-term stable budgets that are independent of political influence.

Comprehensiveness and sustainability of effort are generally not sufficient for success. Anticorruption strategies need to be championed by the highest political offices in the country. This means the commitment of the office of the president and the entire government cabinet. Generating and keeping political will and momentum may be the most difficult of all these elements. The political class can get distracted (intentionally or not) after a while or may never be sufficiently motivated to provide support to the anticorruption strategy.

Political will to fight corruption can be generated or reinforced by different stakeholders' advocacy and pressure imposed on the others. Civil society organizations can be powerful advocates for an anticorruption commitment at the policymaking level. In some cases, IFIs can exert pressure or even impose explicit financing conditions, on the implementation of anticorruption reforms when political will is weak.

7.2. Some further reflections on the implementation of anticorruption policies

A thorough analysis of the causes and potential solutions for corruption is useful in order to understand the weaknesses that allow corruption to thrive in the fiscal structure of a country. It is equally important, however, to take into account a number of implementation issues, which go beyond the technical dimensions of anticorruption strategies. The same way that institutional deficiencies in a country can undermine the most suitable fiscal structure, it is important to identify the main flaws and causes of failure of anticorruption policies and be able to propose new courses of action in this regard.

Several important questions still remain to be fully answered in the current discourse on anticorruption policies. Which strategies have worked well, which have not worked so well, and which have not worked at all, and why? How can a "typical" developing country make sustainable headway toward reducing corruption? Finding answers to these important questions raises several difficulties. First, there is a methodological issue. Generally, it is difficult to categorize strategies by their degree of effectiveness because the ones that have been successful in some countries appear not to have worked in others. While empirical statistical methods can be helpful in the attempts to hold other things constant, applied practitioners have a much more difficult task because many other institutional details and country circumstances may affect the final outcome we observe. Nevertheless, practitioners often attempt to categorize some of the determinant factors in order to identify best strategies under a given institutional framework (i.e., expected effects of an Anticorruption Bureau given a strong, medium, or weak judiciary system, effects of wage increase under strong, medium, or weak monitoring, etc.). However, we need to be aware that the results of such exercises can be misleading. Careful observation of anticorruption strategies may reveal that failure is not necessarily a result of institutional deficiencies or design, but rather a result of flaws in the implementation process of the strategy itself or the lack of political will to carry through the strategy at the highest levels of government. In fact, in some cases those implementation flaws would seem to be the deliberate result of the lack of genuine will to reduce corruption levels due to the policy makers' own vested interests. Unfortunately, there are no objective and systematic ways to measure the degree of genuine political will to control corruption in a country. Therefore, empirical assessments and generalized observations can be subject to significant biases.

In order to make headway toward reducing corruption we may all agree that anticorruption strategies need to be sustainable, comprehensive, adequately implemented, and appropriately designed. But this may not be of enough practical help. We need to worry about other issues such as how to adapt the implementation of a strategy to the particular characteristics of developing countries or indeed, how to generate a genuine desire to fight corruption at the highest levels of government.

An important conclusion of this study has been that, even when the most sophisticated and sound anticorruption strategies and institutional structures are technically in place, their success depends critically on the details of their implementation and the de facto mechanisms that may bend or weaken the strategy to corrupt practices. Where these mechanisms have not been clearly identified, anticorruption efforts may prove futile. For example, it is unlikely that the establishment of an Anticorruption Monitoring Unit within the tax administration will reduce corruption levels if there are not additional monitoring mechanisms to ensure that this unit is not corrupted itself.[200] Similarly, it is hard to believe that an Anticorruption Bureau or Supreme Audit Institution will serve its purpose if their

---

[200] The obvious question becomes who guards the guard? Practically, a chain of guards cannot continue indefinitely. It would seem necessary that the ultimate guardian has a genuine or personal interest in controlling corruption. Civil society (ordinary citizens) and the private sector seem to be perfectly suited for this role since they are negatively affected by corruption and often dispersed enough to be bribed. But this is not easily made operational. Hong Kong seems to offer a good example of how to delegate this role to civil society. Hong Kong's Anticorruption Bureau has a special committee that receives complaints about their own officials and procedures from citizen's groups. A special department of community relations encourages the participation of the private sector and citizen groups in these activities. To close the circle of accountability, complaints and other information would need to be reviewed by the parliament and exposed widely by the mass media.

head and board are appointed by the executive branch. Often, these implementation "details" would seem to be overlooked. Thus, we need to ask not only whether a country does undertake a given anticorruption strategy or measure, but also whether they do it correctly.

In order to make headway toward reducing corruption, it is important to recognize the importance of the sustainability of the reform effort. The short-lived success of the SUNAT in Peru is one example. Failure in the sustainability of the reform effort has two main causes: (i) the absence of resources to maintain the program and (ii) the lack of political will to foster the program's implementation or maintain the process with rigor. The lack of adequate resources may be addressed by ensuring a minimum operational budget over a multiyear period for anticorruption agencies or programs rather than being subject to annual discussion. Of course, the assumption here is that the country can afford these programs or that foreign assistance is available. But it is the lack of political will to maintain the fight against corruption that is the most common cause of unsustainability and failure.

One problem with political will to fight corruption is that leadership in countries in which corruption is endemic is frequently weak and when it exists may quickly weaken over time. Therefore, the design of anticorruption policies should attempt to internalize this reality. How can this be done? As noted before in this study, political will against corruption can be supported by (or forced from) civil society's demands from the bottom up, or by donor organizations' suasion and pressure and by aid conditionality. A drawback of the first option is that those countries in which corruption is most deeply entrenched tend to be those in which citizens have less voice. For the second option, it may be practically impossible for donor organizations to control and monitor each and every aspect of the fiscal process of a country where corruption may occur. Hence, anticorruption conditionality from these agencies tends to rely on quite visible, but potentially superficial, measures such as the creation of an Anticorruption Bureau or a SARA. Under the absence of authentic political will to control corruption, the inevitable result of donors' conditionality can just end in cosmetic reforms which fulfill, at least on paper, the imposed conditions but that do not curtail corruption in any practical sense.

Thus, it becomes important to try to prevent this type of cosmetic reforms. Although there are no easy solutions for this problem, some policy alternatives should be explored. It seems obvious that the effectiveness of anticorruption institutions should be monitored and assessed by agents that are closest to the process. Suitable candidates for this role are the final users of public goods and public services. The problem, again, is that civil society's participation and voice tends to be low in highly corrupt countries. Donor institutions, on the other hand, have the voice to demand anticorruption efforts from governments of developing countries in exchange for financial aid, but do not have the necessary information to evaluate whether anticorruption measures are indeed effective or just cosmetic. When these strengths and limitations are put together, an anticorruption strategy that generates a coalition between international donors and civil society in highly corrupt countries becomes highly appealing. The difficulty with this type of coalition is that it can have very high transaction costs and that may be viewed by the country authorities as politically inadmissible inherence.

Other avenues need to be explored. Although more difficult to monitor and verify, international donors could base their aid conditionality on the effectiveness of anticorruption institutions rather than on their mere existence. The effectiveness of anticorruption institutions could be assessed by means of instruments of consultation such as surveys of taxpayers and final users of public services. Different tools such as Public Expenditure Tracking Surveys (PETS) and QSDS have already been used effectively in similar tasks, and thus, should be considered potentially useful tools for this purpose. The basic concept here is that perhaps the synergy between international donors and civil society can generate a control mechanism that "sees" through the eyes of civil society and "speaks" with the voice of donors and therefore be more effective in achieving meaningful anticorruption reforms.

In order to make headway toward reducing corruption it is also important to recognize the key role of completeness and comprehensiveness of the reform effort. Without one of the required pieces in place, the complete structure of the anticorruption strategy may become non-functional, with the effectiveness of all other components of the system greatly undermined. As we have seen, a system with particularly effective corruption detection capabilities through advanced monitoring mechanisms, effective watchdog agencies, and independent and effective audit institutions, becomes completely ineffective in the presence of an obsolete anticorruption legislation or if a corrupt judiciary cannot convert corruption charges into criminal prosecutions. We have seen other examples in the previous chapters of the interplay and interdependence of the different components of an anticorruption strategy. The key role of completeness and comprehensiveness in the reform effort is well-illustrated in the concept of National Integrity Systems. Assume a four-legged national integrity platform, where each of the legs is formed by a different type of pillars: (i) *institutional-pillars*, such as the judiciary, legal system, watchdog agencies, and the parliament; (ii) *actor-pillars*, such as civil society, private sector, and the media; (iii) *engine-pillars*, such as political will and financial donor pressure; and (iv) *public sector-pillars*, such as budgetary process, tax administration and so on. Using the same analogy as Langseth *et al.* (1997), when one of these pillars of the integrity system weakens, the others are overloaded, causing the platform to tilt and "the ball of sustainable anticorruption program to roll off." Keeping the foundations of the pillars sound requires paying attention to anticorruption measures that combat the incentives for corruption. Both types of strategies have been discussed in several parts of this book.

7.3. A practical guideline to the formulation of an anticorruption strategy

It would not be fitting to end this study without providing some more concrete guidance to policymakers all around the world facing the demanding task of designing effective anticorruption reform strategies. Space is limited and there is no point in repeating many of the findings and experiences reviewed in the body of this study. Instead, what we have in mind here is to provide a pragmatic guide and perhaps awaken the interest of policymakers fighting corruption to do further reading and study.

With all those considerations in mind, we believe that the first necessary step in an anticorruption strategy design is to evaluate the extent of corruption within the existing institutions and organizations, identify the types of corrupt practices affecting these institutions, and to evaluate the weaknesses of the anticorruption structure now in place, if there is any. This country-specific assessment and the careful consideration of national realities is the cornerstone for the development of an effective national anticorruption program.

The second step is to spend time and resources in planning. Even if it is not implemented as a package, the anticorruption strategy must define all the anticorruption elements and the interrelationships between all of them. Then an anticorruption implementation action plan should follow. This plan should contain the operational details of the strategy's implementation, such as the agents responsible for each specific task, the sequencing of proposed reforms, and the flow of resources to sustain the process. The anticorruption action plan should also make explicit the mechanisms and processes of coordination to ensure the cohesiveness of the strategy.

The third step is to gain as broad as possible political support and commitment to the anticorruption strategy. As we have amply illustrated in this book, leadership and political commitment are key for the success of anticorruption efforts. In order to maintain this political will it is important for the strategy to design formal channels of civil society's participation and programs to increase citizens' voice and general capability to demand greater accountability from their political leaders.

What are the concrete measures that can enter the anticorruption strategy? We are reminded again that the appropriate combination of anticorruption measures must be considered in relation to the specific context of each country, but starting from the more general institutional measures to the more concrete measures in fiscal policy and management, the following alternatives could be part of a national anticorruption strategy.

7.3.1. *Institutional framework*

7.3.1.1. *Watchdog agencies*

- *Anticorruption Bureau.* An independent anticorruption body can be responsible for the enforcement of anticorruption law and violations of public financial management laws and regulations, and also develop civil society and NGO's oversight capacity and awareness through means such as educational programs and technical training.[201]
- *Supreme Audit Institution.* There must be external ex-post auditing of the use of all fiscal resources during the budget execution process in order to control corruption. The independence of the national audit office is of utmost importance.
- *Ombudsman.* A separate office of the ombudsman can be instrumental in receiving and investigating corruption allegations that may be outside the scope or feasibility of the Supreme Audit Institution.

7.3.1.2. *Anticorruption legislation*

- *Financial disclosure laws.* Establishing a mandatory declaration of assets for public officials helps increase the probability of corruption detection. This legislation may shift the burden of proof from the prosecution to the defendant in illicit enrichment cases.
- *Codes of conduct-ethics.* A set of rules that define the standards of good behavior for public officials, ministers, and judges.
- *Party financing laws.* Regulations of political campaign financing such as contribution limits, campaign spending ceilings, and public disclosure of party campaign finances are required to reduce opportunities of lobbying and political corruption.
- *Whistle-blower protection legislation.* Protection from repercussions to those who denounce corrupt practices is vital in order to foster cooperation of public servants and ordinary citizens with watchdog agencies.
- *Electoral laws.* Electoral systems in which individuals vote for individual candidates (rather than vote for party lists) are less prone to corruption by making politicians accountable to their constituencies rather than to party platforms. Assuring a transparent voting system empowers citizens to vote corrupt leaders out of office.

---

[201] Anticorruption bodies and other watchdog agencies should respond primarily to the parliament and must be independent from the executive branch in order to avoid conflict of interests. Mechanisms of internal monitoring (based on measures such as the consultation of external agents and civil society) must be built in order to evaluate the agencies performance and ensure that they are not corrupted themselves.

7.3.1.3. The judiciary

- *Professionalization of the judiciary.* A judiciary system reform must ensure a transparent judicial appointment and promotion process and independence from political manipulation.
- Adequate remuneration for judges and court staff.
- *Modernization and restructuring of judicial procedures.* These included measures that may reduce opportunities for corruption, such as electronic recording of court files and standard mechanisms of case assignments among judges.
- *Systematic investigation of judicial corruption and reception of judicial corruption complaints.* The judiciary must be under the close oversight of watchdog agencies. Alternative mechanisms should be built in to make the judiciary also accountable to civil society and to collect and process allegations of judicial corruption.

7.3.1.4. Parliament involvement

- *Parliamentarian capacity building programs.* The parliament must develop their institutional capacity to analyze budget proposals and budget execution reports and investigate evaluations and audit reports. To this end a Parliament Fiscal Analysis Unit can provide specialized technical support in many of these areas.
- *Strengthen the interrelations between the Parliament, National Audit Institution and the Anticorruption Bureau.* The parliament must build in systematic procedures for the discussion and response to reports from these institutions.[202]
- *Promote international associations and networks of legislators.* International experiences and best-practices of effective oversight of the budget and endorsement of anticorruption legislation are valuable lessons for anticorruption policymaking.

7.3.1.5. Non-governmental support

- *Promote the creation of anticorruption coalitions outside government.* Citizens, NGOs, and the private sector can all be anticorruption champions.

---

[202] The parliament is the main responsible for holding the executive branch accountable of the budget formulation, and thus decrease opportunities for political corruption. It can do so by reviewing and discussing of audit work of the SAIs, reports from the Anticorruption Bureau and following steps toward corrective actions.

Coalitions of these groups may engage in activities such as the establishment of a Citizens Advocacy Office (CAO), conduct taxpayer surveys and public service surveys to promote dialogue between civil society and the government about corruption issues; increase public awareness of corruption in a country, and so on.

- *International donors' participation.* Donors can explore possibilities for supporting civil society and other national champions of corruption.

7.3.2. Fiscal system and management

7.3.2.1. The revenue side

- *Tax administration reform.* Important anticorruption measures within the tax administration include updating and modernizing tax agency procedures; restructuring the internal organization based in tax-function (as opposed to tax-type), limiting the discretionary power of tax officials; reducing number of clearances in computing tax liabilities and in the tax payment process, exploring the use of electronic filing and tax liability self-assessment.
- *Semi-autonomous revenue authority.* When properly implemented, this enclave approach to tax administration reform may make possible the depoliticization of tax officials, increased wage levels for tax officials, and the strengthening of internal monitoring mechanisms.[203]
- *Tax policy reform.* Reforms of the tax system can reduce opportunities for corruption by simplifying the tax system by reducing the number of discretionary tax incentives, exemptions, and deductions.

7.3.2.2. The expenditure side

- *Modern treasury systems.* Transparency of cash management and disbursement of resources for items authorized in the budget is required for the consistency between the budget formulation and the budget execution. The treasury must operate separately from the spending agencies. Discretionary power of treasury officials can be reduced by separating departments responsible for each budget execution stage (verification, payment authorization, etc.).

---

[203] Case experiences suggest that the enclave approach in the case of SARAs and LTUs relies heavily in the transparency and sustainability of a merit-based recruitment and the effectiveness of their internal monitoring units. Opportunities of patronage and capture of the merit-based recruitment are higher when the head of these institutions is appointed by the executive branch. Higher wages will only supplement bribes if they are not coupled by higher internal monitoring within these units. Additional monitoring mechanisms, such as taxpayer surveys and independent complaint units, should allow citizens to asses SARA's and LTU's performance and also oversee that the internal monitoring units are not corrupted themselves.

- *Financial management reform.* Having the basics right requires strengthening basic procedures of budget accounting, audit, and reporting. The public expenditure management system should take advantage of information technologies and IFMSs.
- *Public spending tracking systems.* The identification of leaks in the budget implementation stage, through means such as public expenditure tracking systems and QSDS can be useful in identifying problem areas.
- *Procurement system reform.* Establishing standardized procurement processes, ensuring maximum exposure and competition of foreign and national bidders, and satisfying international standards of procurement are key steps. Independent auditing of the procurement procedures should be conducted regularly and reviewed by parliament. E-procurement systems can be particularly useful if coupled with the necessary administrative capacity.
- *Civil service reform.* The professionalization and depoliticization of public servants, the reduction of turnover rates, merit-based recruitment and promotion of bureaucracy are key measures to reduce probabilities of corruption and patronage.
- *Comprehensive coverage of the budget.* The budgetary process should minimize the use of extra-budgetary and off-budget accounts in order to maximize transparency in the use of public resources.
- *Strategies that promote political representation and electoral accountability.* Broad political contestability decreases the opportunities of state capture. Relevant information regarding public spending, including parliament debates of the budget formulation, should be made available to the scrutiny of the ordinary citizen.

7.3.2.3. Intergovernmental fiscal structure

- *Decentralization of spending responsibilities and revenue sources.* Local governments' greater autonomy and increased accountability to citizens can be instrumental in reducing corruption.

What is the appropriate timing or sequencing of these reforms? Clearly, not all anticorruption steps and measures listed above can be applied simultaneously. There are some steps that need to be taken first to ensure the effectiveness of other subsequent steps. Some measures are actually alternative options to reach similar objectives, and others will not fit the institutional or constitutional context of specific countries.

Establishing an appropriate sequence for anticorruption reforms is not an easy task. Yet, it is possible to suggest some stages in the process, which could be of practical use. Strengthening the rule of law and the judiciary must be a primary objective. Assuring the enforcement of existing laws must precede the enactment of new anticorruption legislation. Similarly, ensuring the independence and the strengthening of the judicial system must precede the creation of additional watchdog agencies.[204] Initiatives to strengthen the rule of law must send a strong message that future anti-corruption measures will be enforced at the fullest extent.

A second stage could focus on promoting the enactment of new anti-corruption legislation supporting the existing institutional framework and building up the framework for future reforms.[205]

The next stage could focus on the establishment of new anticorruption institutions and organizations required to address the particular needs of the national anticorruption strategy. But, as we have seen from the inter-national experience a far-reaching anticorruption system does not result from unilateral initiatives of a central agency or ministerial committee, but from the sustained and coordinated participation of the entire government and other stakeholders.

---

[204] The logic of the sequence suggested is clear and also supported by the experience in several Southeastern European countries where new anticorruption legislation is rarely enforced leading to cynical expectations of future reforms (Tisne and Smilov, 2004).

[205] Several experiences reveal that new anticorruption measures and institutions should be implemented only once a supporting legislative and regulatory framework is in place.

References

AAA (2002). "BRAZIL: another presidential candidate accused of corruption". AAA Flash Publication, No. 463.

Abed, G., & S. Gupta (2002). *Costs of Corruption. World Bank 2000 and World Bank Development Report 2004*, p. 196.

Ablo, E., & Reinikka, R. (1999). *Do Budgets Really Matter? Evidence from Public Spending on Education and Health in Uganda, The World Bank, Policy Research Working Paper Series: 1926*. Washington, DC: The World Bank.

Acconcia, A., D'Amato, M., & Martina, R. (2003). *Corruption and Tax Evasion with Competitive Bribes, CSEF Working Papers 112*. Italy: Centre for Studies in Economics and Finance (CSEF), University of Salerno.

Ades, A., & Di Tella, R. (1997). National champions and corruption: some unpleasant interventionist arithmetic. *Economic Journal*, 107(443), 1023–1042.

Ades, A., & Di Tella, R. (1999). Rent competition and corruption. *American Economic Review*, 89(4), 982–993.

Ahlin, C.R. (2001). "Corruption: political determinants and macroeconomic effects". Working Paper 01-w26, Nashville, TN: Department of Economics, Vanderbilt University.

Ahmad, A. (2003). "Provision of primary health care in Bangladesh: an institutional". Paper presented at the conference on Development Research, Lund University, September 26.

Aidt, T. S. (2003). Economic analysis of corruption: a survey. *Economic Journal*, 113(491), 52.

Akerlof, G. A., & Yellen, J. L. (1990). The fair wage-effort hypothesis and unemployment. *Quarterly Journal of Economics*, 105(2), 255–283.

Alatas, H. S. (1986). *The Problem of Corruption*. Singapore: Times Books International.

Alesina, A., Devleeschauwer, A., Kurlat, S., & Wacziarg, R. (2003). "Fractionalization". *Journal of Economic Growth*, 8(2), 155–194.

Allen, R., Schiavo-Campo, S., & Columkill Garrity, T. (2004). *Assessing and Reforming Public Financial Management: A New Approach*. Washington, DC: World Bank.

Allen, R., & Tommasi, D. (eds.). (2001). *Managing Public Expenditure: A Reference Book for Transition Countries*. France: OECD.

Alm, J. (1998). Tax compliance and administration. In Hildreth, W. B., & Richardson, J. A. (eds.), *Handbook on Taxation*. (pp. 741–768). New York: Marcel Dekker, Inc.

Alm, J., Martinez-Vazquez, J., & Schneider, F. (2004). 'Seizing' the problem of the hard to tax. In Alm, J., Martinez-Vazquez, J., & Wallace, S. (eds.), *Taxing the Hard to Tax: Lessons from Theory and Practice*. (pp. 11–75). Amsterdam: Elsevier.

Aluko, M. E. (2003a). "Of pension and ghost workers". Retrieved February 4, 2004, from Dawodu.com, Website: http://www.dawodu.com/aluko69.htm

Aluko, M. E. (2003b). "Defense Ministry Discovers 24,000 Phantom Names in Pensions Audit August 30, 2003". Retrieved February 4, 2004, from Dawodu.com, Website: http://www.dawodu.com/aluko69.htm

Anderson, C. J., & Tverdova, Y. V. (2003). Corruption, political allegiances, and attitudes toward government in contemporary democracies. *American Journal of Political Science*, 47(1), 91–109.

Andreoni, J., Erard, B., & Feinstein, J. (1998). Tax compliance. *Journal of Economic Literature*, 36(2), 818–860.

Andrews, M., & Shah, A. (2004). Towards citizen-centered local budgets in developing countries. In Shah, A. (ed.), *Ensuring Accountability When There Is No Bottom Line. Handbook on Public Sector Performance Reviews.* , Vol. 1. Washington, DC: World Bank.

Andvig, J. C., & Moene, K. O. (1990). How corruption may corrupt. *Journal of Economic Behavior and Organization*, 13(1), 63–76.

Arikan, G. G. (2004). Fiscal decentralization: a remedy for corruption? *International Tax and Public Finance*, 11(2), 175–195.

Arze, F. J., Martinez-Vazquez, J., & McNab, R. (2003). "Fiscal decentralization and the functional composition of public expenditures". International Studies Program Working Papers 05-01, Atlanta: Andrew Young School of Policy Studies, Georgia State University. Retrieved from http://isp-aysps.gsu.edu/papers/ispwp0501.pdf

Azfar, O. (1999). "Are larger countries really more corrupt?", The World Bank, Policy Research Working Paper Series: 2470, Washington, DC: The World Bank.

Azfar, O., Meagher, P., & Kahkonen, S. (2001). *"Conditions for effective decentralized governance: a synthesis of research findings"*. Mimeo IRIS: University of Maryland, College Park, 2001.

Bac, M., & Bag, P. K. (1999). *Cost-Effective Control of Corruption in Public Offices*. Unpublished manuscript.

Baer, K., Benon, O. P., & Toro Rivera, J. A. (2002). *Improving Large Tax Payer's Compliance: A Review of Country Experience. IMF Occasional Papers N215*. Washington, DC: IMF.

Bagchi, A., Bird, R. M., & Das-Gupta, A. (1995). *An Economic Approach to Tax Administration Reform*. Toronto: International Centre for Tax Studies, University of Toronto.

Banfield, E. (1975). Corruption as feature of government organization. *Journal of Law and Economics*, 18(3), 587–695.

Bardhan, P. (1997). Corruption and development: a review of issues. *Journal of Economic Literature*, 35(3), 1320–1346.

Bardhan, P., & Mookherjee, D. (2000). Capture and governance at local and national levels. *The American Economic Review*, 90(2), 135–139.

Batley, R. (1999). The new public management in developing countries: implications for policy and organizational reform. *Journal of International Development*, 11(5), 761–765.

Batra, G., Kaufmann, D., & Stone, A. H. W. (2003). The firms speak: what the world business environment survey tells us about constraints on private sector development. In Fields, G. S., & Pfeffermann, G. (eds.), *Pathways out of Poverty: Private Firms and Economic Mobility in Developing Countries*. (pp. 193–214). Boston: Kluwer Academic, International Finance Corporation.

BBC (2000). "China to execute top official Monday". July 31, 2000, Retrieved on February 12, 2004 from http://news.bbc.co.uk/1/hi/world/asia-pacific/859263.stm

BBC (2001a). "Chirac's corruption battle". October 10, 2001. Retrieved June 13, 2004 from http://news.bbc.co.uk/1/hi/world/europe/1448471.stm

BBC (2001b). "Third arrest over South Africa's arms deal". November 16, 2001. Retrieved March 01, 2004 from http://news.bbc.co.uk/1/hi/world/africa/1659872.stm

BBC (2002). "Malawi corruption halts Danish aid". January 31, 2002. Retrieved February 2, 2004, from http://news.bbc.co.uk/2/hi/africa/1794730.stm

BBC (2003). "Former French PM starts corruption trial". September 29, 2003, Retrieved on April 2, 2004 from http://news.bbc.co.uk/1/hi/world/europe/3147874.stm

Beato, P., & Laffont, J.-J. (2002). Pricing monopoly segments of regulated industries in developing countries. In Beato, P., & Laffont, J.-J. (eds.), *Competition Policy in Regulated Industries: Approaches for Emerging Economies*. (pp. 147–163). Washington, DC: Inter-American Development Bank, distributed by Johns Hopkins University Press, Baltimore, MD.

Becker, G., & Stigler, G. (1974). Law enforcement, malfeasance and the compensation of enforcers. *Journal of Legal Studies*, 3(1), 1–18.

Becker, G. S. (1968). Crime and punishment: an economic approach. *Journal of Political Economy*, 76, 169–217.

Behrendt, A. (ed.) (2002). "Participatory assessment of key issues for Bolivia's decentralization process and strategy recommendations". *Santa Cruz for Sida*, Bolivia: Grupo Nacional de Trabajo en la Participación GNT-P.

Bejakovic, P. (2000). Assessment of the unofficial economy in selected economies. Proceedings of Rijeka School of Economics. *Journal of Economics and Business*, 18(1), 71–94.

Besley, T., & McLaren, J. (1993). Taxes and bribery: the role of wage incentives. *The Economic Journal*, 103(416), 119–141.

Bilello, S. (2001). "Disclosures of Peruvian media corruption stun even most jaded observers". Retrieved February 02, 2004, from Freedom Forum Website: http://www.freedomforum.org/templates/document.asp?documentID = 13381

Bird, R. (2001). *Subnational Revenues: Realities and Prospects*. Washington, DC: World Bank Institute.

Bird, R. (2003). *Administrative Dimensions of Tax Reform. International Tax Program, Paper 0302*. Canada: Institute for International Business Joseph L. Rotman.

Bird, R., Martinez-Vazquez, J., & Torgler, B. (2004). "Increasing tax effort in developing and transitional countries". Paper presented at The Challenges of Tax Reform in a Global Economy, May 24–25, Atlanta, GA.

Bird, R., & Oldman, O. (2000). *Improving Tax Payer Service and Facilitating Compliance in Singapore. PREM Notes. Public Sector 48*. Washington, DC: The World Bank.

Bird, R. M., & Casanegra de Jantscher, M. (1992). *Improving Tax Administration in Developing Countries*. Washington, DC: International Monetary Fund.

Blechinger, V. (2000). Corruption Through Political Contributions in South Korea, Report on Recent Bribery Scandals, 1996–2000. Berlin, Germany: Transparency International.

Bliss, C., & Di Tella, R. (1997). Does competition kill corruption? *Journal of Political Economy*, 105(5), 1001–1023.

Blumenthal, M., Christian, C., & Slemrod, J. (2001). Do normative appeals affect tax compliance? Evidence from a controlled experiment in Minnesota? *National Tax Journal*, 54(1), 125–136.

Boex, J., & Martinez-Vazquez, J. (2006). *Local Government Finance Reform in Developing Countries: The Case of Tanzania*. New York, NY: Palgrave-Macmillan.

Bohn, F. (2003). "A note on corruption and public investment: the political instability threshold". Retrieved March 04, 2004 from http://www.essex.ac.uk/economics/discussion-papers/papers-text/dp559.pdf

Boycko, M., & Shleifer, A. (1996). A theory of privatisation. *Economic Journal*, 106(435), 309–319.

Brennan, G., & Buchanan, J. M. (1980). *The Power to Tax: Analytical Foundations of a Fiscal Constitution*. Cambridge: Cambridge University Press.

Brennan, P. A., Mednick, S. A., & Jacobsen, B. (1996). Assessing the role of genetics in crime using adoption cohorts. In Bock, G. R., & Goode, J. A. (eds.), *Genetics of Criminal and Antisocial Behaviour*. Chichester: Wiley.

Broadman, H. G., & Recanatini, F. (2001). Seeds of corruption – do market institutions matter? *MOCT-MOST: Economic Policy in Transitional Economies*, 11(4), 359–392.

Brock, G. W. (2002). The new institutional economics. *Poverty, Wealth and Organization Series*, 39(Spring), 1–13.

Brunetti, A., & Weder, B. (2003). A free press is bad news for corruption. *Journal of Public Economics*, 87(7–8), 1801–1824.

Bull, M. J., & Newell, J. (2003). *Corruption in Contemporary Politics*. New York, NY: Palgrave-Macmillan.

Burgess, R., & Stern, N. (1993). Taxation and development. *Journal of Economic Literature*, 31(2), 762–830.

Business Week (2002). "The anticorruption coalition". February 2, 2002. Retrieved January 10, 2004 from Business Week Website: http://www.businessweek.com/magazine/content/02_02/b3765115.htm

Camerer, L. (1997). "Poverty and corruption in South Africa: government corruption in poverty alleviation programs". Retrieved March 20, 2004 from http://www.gov.za/reports/1998/poverty/corruption.pdf

Carney, G. (1998). "Conflict of interest: legislators, ministers and public officials". TI Working Paper, Transparency International.

Carrillo, J. D. (2000). Corruption in hierarchies. *Annales d'Economie et de Statistique*, 59, 37–61.

Caselli, F., & Morelli, M. (2004). Bad politicians. *Journal of Public Economics*, 88(3–4), 759–782.

CBS (2004). "Warrant for ex-Argentine Prez". April 20, 2004. Retrieved May 01, 2004 from http://www.cbsnews.com/stories/2004/04/20/world/main612826.shtml

Celarier, M. (1997). Privatization: a case study in corruption. *Journal of International Affairs*, 50(2), 531–543.

Chand, S. K., & Moene, K. (1997). *Controlling Fiscal Corruption. WP/97/100*. Washington, DC: International Monetary Fund.

China.Org.cn (2000). "Cheng Kejie executed for corruption". September 2000, Retrieved on February 10, 2004 from http://www.china.org.cn/english/2000/Sep/1804.htm

Chua, Y. T. (1999). *Robbed: An Investigation of Corruption in Philippine Education*. Quezon City: Philippine Center for Investigative Journalism.

CLAD (1998). "A new public management for Latin America". Retrieved from http://www.clad.org.ve/

Clarke, G. R. G., & Xu, L. C. (2004). Privatization, competition, and corruption: how characteristics of bribe takers and payers affect bribes to utilities. *Journal of Public Economics*, 88(9–10), 2067–2097.

CNN (2000). "China sentences 14 officials to death in graft case". November 9, 2000, Retrieved on February 10, 2004 from http://www.cnn.com/2000/ASIANOW/east/11/08/china.corruption/index.html

CNN (2002). "Italian judiciary attacks government". January 12, 2002. Retrieved February 10, 2004 from http://www.cnn.com/2002/WORLD/europe/01/12/italy.law/index.html

CNN (2004). "Polica toma pueblo peruano donde fue linchado el alcalde 27 de abril, 2004". Retrieved May 01, 2004 from http://www.cnnenespanol.com/2004/americas/04/27/peru.alcalde.ap/

Coalition 2000 (2005). "Anticorruption reforms in Bulgaria (2005-02-22)". February 22, 2005, http://www.anticorruption.bg/eng/coalition/about.htm

Cornwall, A. (2003). Whose voices, whose choices? Reflections on gender and participatory development. *World Development*, 31(8), 1325–1342.

Dehn, J., Reinikka, R., & Svensson, J. (2002). *Survey Tools for Assessing Service Delivery. Development Research Group*. Washington, DC: The World Bank.

Dehn, J., Reinikka, R., & Svensson, J. (2003). Survey tools for assessing performance in delivery. In Burguignon, & da Silva, P. (eds.), *Evaluating the Poverty and Distributional Impact of Economic Policies*. Washington, DC: World Bank.

Del Castillo, A. (2002). "Building corruption indexes. What do they really measure?", Working Paper No.119, Centro de Investigacion y Docencias Economicas (CIDE).

Della Porta, D. (2001). Los actores de la corrupcion: politicos de negocios en Italia. *Gestion y Analisis de Politicas Publicas*, 21, 23–34.

Della Porta, D., & Vannucci, A. (2005). "The governance mechanisms of corrupt transactions". In Lambsdorff, J., Graf, Taube, Markus, Schramm, & Matthias (eds.), *The New Institutional Economics of Corruption*. Oxford: Routledge.

Di Tella, R., & Savedoff, W. D. (eds.). (2001). *Diagnosis: Corruption: Fraud in Latin America's Public Hospitals*. Washington, D.C: IADB Press.

Di Tella, R., & Schargrodsky, E. (2003). The role of wages and auditing during a crackdown on corruption in the city of Buenos Aires. *Journal of Law and Economics*, 46(1), 269.

Dillman, B. (2001). Facing the market in North Africa. *Middle East Journal*, 55(2), 198–215.

Doig, A., & Theobald, R. (2000). *Corruption and Democratization*. London: Frank Cass.

Dye, K.M., & Stapenhurst, R. (1998). *Pillars of Integrity: The Importance of Supreme Audit Institutions in Curbing Corruption*. EDI/World Bank Institute. Reprinted in Williams *et al.* (2000), Vol. 4, Chapter 16.

Ensor, T. (2004). Informal payments for health care in transition economies. *Social Science and Medicine*, 58(2), 237–246.

Estela, M. (2000). "Strengthening the integrity of a tax collection agency: the case of Sunat Peru". Presented at the World Bank-Inter American Development Bank Seminar on Radical Solutions for Fighting Corruption in the Public Sector, November.

Eversole, R. (2003). Managing the pitfalls of participatory development: some insight from Australia. *World Development*, 31(5), 781–795.

Fisman, R., & Gatti, R. (2002a). Decentralization and corruption: evidence across countries. *Journal of Public Economics*, 83, 325–345.

Fisman, R., & Gatti, R. (2002b). Decentralization and corruption: evidence from U.S. federal transfer programs. *Public Choice*, 113(1–2), 25–35.

Fjeldstad, O. (2002). "Fighting fiscal corruption: the case of the Tanzania revenue authority". CMI Working Papers.

Fjeldstad, O., Kolstad, I., & Lange, S. (2003). *Autonomy, Incentives and Patronage: A Study of Corruption in the Tanzania and Uganda Revenue Authorities*. Bergen, Norway: Chr. Michelsen Institute.

Fjeldstad, O., & Tungodden, B. (2003). Fiscal corruption: a vice or a virtue? *World Development*, 31(8), 1459–1467.

Flatters, F., & Macleod, W. B. (1995). Administrative corruption and taxation. *International Tax and Public Finance*, 2, 397–417.

Frank, B., & Schulze, G. G. (1998). *How Tempting is Corruption? More Bad News About Economists*. Stuttgard: Department of Economics and Business, University of Hohenheim.

Fredriksson, P. G., Vollebergh, H. R. J., & Dijkgraaf, E. (2004). Corruption and energy efficiency in OECD countries: theory and evidence. *Journal of Environmental Economics and Management*, 47(2), 207–231.

Friedman, E., Johnson, S., Kaufmann, D., & Zoido-Lobaton, P. (2000). Dodging in the grabbing hand: the determinants of unofficial activity in 69 countries. *Journal of Public Economics*, 77(3), 459–493.

Gallagher, M. (1991). *Rent-Seeking and Economic Growth in Africa*. Boulder, CO.: Westview Press.

Gallagher, M. (2004). "USAID assistance to eliminate the payment bureaus and establish a modern government treasury and accounting system in Bosnia". Draft version.

Gallagher, M., & Bosnic, P. (2004). Toward an SME-friendly revenue system in Bosnia and Herzegovina. USAID Tax Administration Modernization Project (TAMP).

Ghura, D. (1998). "Tax revenue in Sub-Saharan Africa: effects of economic policies and corruption". IMF Working Paper, No. 98/135.

Giedion, U., Morales, L. G., & Acosta, O. L. (2001). The impact of health reforms on irregularities in Bogotá Hospitals. In Tella Di, & Savedoff (eds.), *Diagnosis: Corruption: Fraud in Latin America's Public Hospitals*. (pp. 163–168). Washington, DC: IADB press.

Giles, D. E., & Caragata, P. J. (1999). *The Learning Path of the Hidden Economy: The Tax Burden and Tax Evasion in New Zealand*. Reference Number EC/96461, New Zealand.

Glaeser, E. L., & Goldin, C. (eds.). (2006). *Corruption and Reform: Lessons from America's Economic History*. (p. 2006). Chicago: University of Chicago Press.

Glinkina, S. (1999). Russia's underground economy during the transition. In Feige, E. L., & Ott, K. (eds.), *Underground Economies in Transition: Unrecorded Activity, Tax Evasion, Corruption and Organized Crime.* (pp. 101–106). Aldershot, U.K.: Ashgate.

Global Witness (2004). "Time for transparency: coming clean on oil, mining and gas revenues". Global Witness Report, March.

Goel, R. K., & Rich, D. P. (1989). On the economic incentives for taking bribes. *Public Choice*, 61(3), 269–275.

Gokcekus, O., & Mookherjee, R. (2002). *Public Sector Corruption and Gender Perceptions of Public Officials from Six Developing and Transition Countries.* Washington, DC: The World Bank.

Golden, M. A., & Picci, L. (2005). Proposal for a new measure of corruption, illustrated with Italian data. *Economics and Politics*, 17(1), 37–75.

de Gonzales, A. M. (2000). *Reducing Corruption at the Local Level.* Washington, DC: World Bank Institute.

de Gonzales, A. M. (2001). La construccion de coaliciones para combatir la corrupcion. *Gestion y Analisis de Politicas Publicas*, 21, 157–162.

Gould, D. J., & Amaro-Reyes, J. A. (1983). *The Effects of Corruption on Administrative Performance.* Washington, DC: The World Bank.

Graeff, P. (2005). Why should one trust in corruption? The linkage between corruption, norms and social capital. In Lambsdorff, J. G., Taube, M., & Schramm, M. (eds.), *The New Institutional Economics of Corruption.* Oxford: Routledge.

Gray-Molina, E. P. de Rada, & Yañez, E. (1999). "Transparency and accountability in Bolivia: does voice matter?" Inter-American Development Bank Working Paper, No. R-381.

Groeneweg, S. (2001). *Three Whistleblower Protection Models: A Comparative Analysis of Whistleblower Legislation in Australia, United States and the United Kingdom.* PUBLIC Service Commission of Canada.

Grooger, J. (1991). Certainty vs. severity of punishment. *Economic Inquiry*, 29(2), 297–309.

Grossman, G. M., & Helpman, E. (1994). Protection for sale. *American Economic Review*, 84(4), 833–850.

Grossman, S., & Hart, O. (1986). The costs and benefits of ownership: a theory of vertical and lateral integration. *Journal of Political Economy*, 94, 691–719.

Gupta, S., Davoodi, H., & Alosno-Terme, R. (1998). "Does corruption affect income inequality and poverty?", IMF Working Paper 98/76, Washington, DC: International Monetary Fund.

Gupta, S., Davoodiand, S., & Tiongson, E. (2000). "Corruption and the provision of health care and education Services". IMF Working Paper, No. 00/116.

Gupta, S., de Mello, L., & Sharan, R. (2001). Corruption and military spending. *European Journal of Political Economy*, 17(4), 749–777.

Gurgur, T., & Shah, A. (2000). "Localization and corruption: panacea or pandora's box". World Bank Policy Research Working Paper Series, No. 3486.

Guriev, S. (1999). "A theory of informative red tape with an application to top-level corruption". New Economic School Working Paper, No. 99/007.

Harberger, A. C. (1962). The incidence of the corporation income tax. *The Journal of Political Economy*, 70(3), 215–240.

Hauk, E., & Saez-Marti, M. (2002). On the cultural transmission of corruption. *Journal of Economic Theory*, 107(2), 311–335.

Hellman, J. S., Jones, G., Kaufmann, D., & Schankeman, M. (2000). "Measuring governance corruption, and State Capture: how firms and bureaucrats shape the business environment in transitional economies". World Bank Policy Research Working Paper, No. 2312.

Henderson, J. V., & Kuncoro, A. (2006). "Sick of local government corruption? Vote Islamic". NBER Working Papers, No. 12110.

Herzfeld, T., & Weiss, C. (2003). Corruption and legal (In) effectiveness: an empirical investigation. *European Journal of Political Economy*, 19(3), 621–632.

Hettich, W., & Winer, S. (1988). Economic and political foundations of tax structure. *American Economic Review*, 78(4), 701–712.

Hettich, W., & Winer, S. (1999). *Democratic Choice and Taxation: A Theoretical and Empirical Analysis*. Cambridge: Cambridge University Press.

Hors, I. (2001). "Fighting corruption in customs administration: what can we learn from recent experiences?" OECD Development Centre Working Papers, No. 175.

Hors, I. (2003). "Anti-corruption instruments and the OECD guidelines for multinational enterprises". In: *Annual Report on the OECD Guidelines for Multinational Enterprises: Enhancing the Role of Business in the Fight Against Corruption*. (pp. 153–180). Paris: OECD.

Huang, H., & Shan-Jin, W. (2003). "Monetary policies for developing countries: the role of corruption". NBER Working Papers, WP#10093, Cambridge, MA: NBER.

Huntington, S. P. (1968). *Political Order in Changing Societies*. New Haven, CT: Yale University Press.

Huther, J., & Shah A. (1998). "Applying a simple measure of good governance to the debate on fiscal decentralization". World Bank Policy Research Working Paper No. 1894. Retrieved from SSRN website http://ssrn.com/abstract = 620584

Huther, J., & Shah A. (2003). *Anti-Corruption Policies and Programs: A Framework for Evaluation*. (Preliminary Version).

Hyun Yum, J. (2003). "Enhancing public procurement transparency through ICT". Paper presented at XI International Anti-Corruption Conference (IACC). Seoul, Korea.

Ibarra-Estrada, S. (2002). "E-procurement by Mexico's federal government". E-Government for Development Case Study, No. 14.

Jaen, M. H., & Paravisini, D. (2001). Wages, capture and penalties in Venezuela's public hospitals. In Di Tella, R., & Savedoff, W. D. (eds.), *Diagnosis Corruption*. Washington, DC: Inter-American Development Bank.

Jain, A. K. (ed.). (1998). *Economics of Corruption*. (p. 1998). Boston: Kluwer Academic Publishers.

Jain, A. K. (2001). Corruption: a review. *Journal of Economic Surveys*, 15(1), 71–121.

Johnston, M. (1986). The political consequences of corruption: a reassessment. *Comparative Politics*, 18(4), 459–477.

Johnson, S., Kaufmann, D., McMillan, D., & Woodruff, C. (2000). "Why do firms hide? Bribes and unofficial activity after communism". Journal of Public Economics, 76(3), 495–520.

Kang, B. (2000). "Anticorruption measures in the public procurement service sector in Korea". In: *Progress in the Fight Against Corruption in Asia and the Pacific*. Joint ADB-OECD Conference on Combating Corruption in the Asian and Pacific.

Kaufmann, D. (1997). "Corruption: the facts". Foreign Policy, Summer (1997). Retrieved December 20, 2003 from http://worldbank.org/wbi/governance/pdf/fp_summer97.pdf

Kaufmann, D. (2003). "Rethinking governance: empirical lessons challenge orthodoxy". World Bank Working Paper, Washington, DC: The World Bank.

Kaufmann, D., Kraay, A., & Mastruzzi, M. (2003). "Governance Matters III". World Bank Policy Research Working Paper 3106. Retrieved February 2004 from The World Bank Website: http://www.worldbank.org/wbi/governance/pubs/govmatters3.html

Kaufmann, D., Kraay, A., & Mastruzzi, M. (2006). *Governance Matters V. Aggregate and Individual Governance Indicators*. Washington, DC: The World Bank.

Kaufmann, D., Kraay, A., & Zoido-Lobaton, P. (1999). "Aggregating governance indicators". Policy Research Working Paper 2195, Washington, DC: The World Bank.

Kaufmann, D., & Siegelbaum, P. (1997). Privatization and corruption in the transition economies. *Journal of International Affairs*, 50(2), 419–458.

Kaufmann, D., & Wei, S.-J. (1999). "Does 'Grease Money' speed up the wheels of commerce?". National Bureau of Economic Research Working Paper 7093, Cambridge, MA.

Klitgaard, R. (1988). *Controlling Corruption*. Berkeley, CA: University of California Press.

Klitgaard, R. (1989). Incentive myopia. *World Development*, 17(4), 447–459.

Klitgaard, R. (1991). Gifts and bribes. In Zeckhauser, R. (ed.), *Strategy and Choice*. Cambridge, MA: MIT Press.

Klitgaard, R. (1995). "National and international strategies for reducing corruption". Paper prepared for the OECD International Symposium on Corruption and Good Governance, Paris, 13–14, March.

Klitgaard, R., MacLean-Abaroa, R., & Parris, H. R. (2000). *Corrupt Cities. A Practical Guide to Cure and Prevention*. Washington, DC: Institute for Contemporary Studies World Bank Institute.

Korean Herald (2001). "Combating corruption in Korea". May 19, 2001 Retrieved March 05, 2004 from http://kn.koreaherald.co.kr/SITE/data/html_dir/2001/05/19/200105190007.asp

Kpundeh, S. (1997). *Combating Corruption: An Assessment with International Cases*. Washington, DC: Management Systems International.

Kpundeh, S. J. (2001). The big picture: building a sustainable reform movement against corruption in Africa. In Johnston, M. (ed.), *Civil Society and Corruption: Mobilizing for Reform*. Lanham, MD: University Press of America.

Kronstadt, K. A. (2003). "Pakistan's domestic political developments: issues for congress". Retrieved February 2, 2004 from http://fpc.state.gov/documents/organization/29970.pdf

Lambsdorff, J. G. (2003). "Transparency international background paper to the 2003 corruption perceptions index, framework document". Retrieved March 7, 2004 from http://www.transparency.org/cpi/2003/dnld/framework.pdf

Lambsdorff, J. G., Taube, M., & Schramm, M. (2005). *The New Institutional Economics of Corruption*. Oxford: Routledge.

Langseth, P., Stapenhurstand, R., & Pope, J. (1997). "The role of a national integrity system in fighting corruption". *EDI World Bank Working Papers*, No. 400/142 E1976.

La Porta, R., Lopez-de-Silanes, F., Shleifer, A., & Vishny, R. (1998). Law and finance. *Journal of Political Economy*, 106(6), 1113–1155.

Leak, T. A. (1999). The experience of Singapore in combating corruption. In Stapenhurst, R., & Kpundeh, S. J. (eds.), *Curbing Corruption: Toward a Model for Building National Integrity*. (pp. 59–66). Washington, DC: World Bank.

Leff, N. H. (1964). Economic development through bureaucratic corruption. *The American Behavioral Scientist*, 8(2), 8–14.

Leite, C., & Weidmann, J. (1999). "Does mother nature corrupt? Natural resources, corruption, and economic growth". International Monetary Fund Working Paper 99/85, Washington, DC: IMF.

Lewis, M. (2000). *Who is Paying for Health Care in Eastern Europe and Central Asia*. Washington, DC: The World Bank.

Linster, B. C. (1994). Cooperative rent-seeking. *Public Choice*, 81(1–2), 23–34.

Litvack, J. I., Ahmad, J., & Bird, R. M. (1998). *Rethinking Decentralization in Developing Countries*, 2nd edition. Washington, DC: World Bank.

Malawi Anti-Corruption Bureau (2001). "News paper extract". Retrieved from http://chambo.sdnp.org.mw/ruleoflaw/acb/news-04.html

Mann, A.J. (2004). "Are semi-autonomous revenue authorities the answer to tax administration problems in developing countries?", Research paper for the project: Fiscal Reform in Support of Trade Liberalization. Retrieved from http://www.fiscalreform.net

Mann, A. J., & Smith, R. (1988). Tax attitudes and tax evasion in Puerto Rico: a survey of upper income professionals. *Journal of Economic Development*, 13(1), 121–141.

Manzetti, L., & Blake, C. (1996). Market reforms and corruption in Latin America: new means for old ways. *Review of International Political Economy*, 3(4), 662–697.

Martinez-Vazquez, J., & McNab, R. (2000). The tax reform experiment in transitional countries. *National Tax Journal*, 53(2), 273–298.

Martinez-Vazquez, J., Qiao, B., & Xu, Y. (2006). "Pocketing and deceiving: the behavior of the delivery agency in a donor-delivery". ISP Working Paper 06–13, Atlanta, USA: Andrew Young School of Policy Studies, Georgia State University.

Martinez-Vazquez, J., & Rider, R. (2005). Multiple modes of tax evasion: theory and evidence. *National Tax Journal*, 58(1), 51–76.

Matechak, J. P. (2002). "Fighting corruption in public procurement". Retrieved February 12, 2004 from Center for International Private Enterprise CIPE Website: http://www.cipe.org/publications/fs/articles/matechak.htm

Mauro, P. (1995). Corruption and growth. *Quarterly Journal of Economics*, 110(3), 681–712.

Mauro, P. (1996). "The effects of corruption on growth, investment, and government expenditure". IMF Working Paper 96/98, Washington, DC: International Monetary Fund.

Mauro, P. (1997). *Why Worry About Corruption? IMF Economic Issues*. Washington, DC: International Monetary Fund.

Mauro, P. (1998). Corruption and the composition of governments expenditure. *Journal of Public Economics*, 69, 263–279.

Mayville, W. (2003). *Codes of Ethics and Conduct in Revenue Administrations: What does International Practice Tell Us*. Washington, DC: The World Bank Tax Policy and Tax Administration Thematic Group.

McCarten, W. (2004). "Focusing on the few: the role of large taxpayer units in the revenue strategies of developing countries". Paper presented at The Challenges of Tax Reform in a Global Economy, May 24–25, Atlanta, GA.

McLure, C. (2000). *The Tax Assignment Problem: Conceptual and Administrative Considerations in Achieving Subnational Fiscal Autonomy*. Washington, DC: World Bank Institute.

Mendieta, V. (2001). Lucha contra la corrupcion en la Union Europea: El caso de España. *Gestion y Analisis de Politicas Publicas*, 21, 95–115.

Meseguer, C. (2002). "The diffusion of privatization in industrial and Latin America countries: what role for learning? Retrieved March 10, 2004 from http://galactus.upf.edu/giptsi/esf/papers/1privat.doc

Miles, M. A., Feulner, E. J., O'Grady, M. A., & Eiras, A. I. (2004). *Index of Economic Freedom 2004*. Washington, DC: Heritage Foundation/ Wall Street Journal.

Ministry of Finance Tanzania (2001). *Budget Execution Report: Budget for Fiscal Year 2001/2002*. Budget Performance July–September 2001.

Mixon, F. G., Laband, D. N., & Ekelund, R. B. (1994). Rent seeking and hidden in-kind resource distortion: some empirical evidence. *Public Choice*, 78(2), 171–186.

Mocan, N. (2004). "What determines corruption? International Evidence from Micro Data". NBER Working Papers, No. 10460.

Mokoro Ltd (2001). *"Sustainability of government revenue policy in Tanzania"*, DFID East Africa Report. Oxford: Policy Management Ltd.

Mookherjee, D. (1997). Wealth effects, incentives, and productivity. *Review of Development Economics*, 1(1), 116–133.

Mookjerjee, B., & Pung, I. P. L. (1992). Monitoring vis-a-vis investigation in enforcement of law. *American Economic Review*, 82, 556–565.

Muganda, A. (1995). "Tackling the corruption scourge in Tanzania: looking beyond the rhetoric". Paper presented at the Eastern and Southern African Universities Research Programme: Arusha, December 14–16, 1995.

Mundell, R. (1968). *Man and Economics*. New York: McGraw-Hill.

Musgrave, R. A. (1959). *The Theory of Public Finance: A Study in Political Economy*. New York: McGraw-Hill.

Myrdal, G. (1968). *Asian Drama*, Vol. II. New York, NY: Random House.

National Integrity Systems (2001). "Country study report: Jordan 2001". Transparency International Report.

New York Times (2004a). "French ex-premier is convicted of graft". In: Sciolino, E. (ed.), January 31, 2004, Saturday, Section A, Page 5, Column 1.

New York Times (2004b). "Angola set to disclose payments from big oil". by H. Timmons, May 13, 2004, Thursday, Business/Financial Desk, Section W, Page 1, Column 6.

Ngware, S.S.A. (1999). "An sssessment of people's participation in decision-making with reference to local authorities". Paper presented at the Workshop to Develop Strategies for a National Programme on Governance: Arusha, March 29–31, 1999.

OECD (1998). *Role of the Legislature*. Paris: OECD.

OECD (2003). *Fighting corruption what role for civil society? The experience of the OECD*. Paris: OECD.

Office of the High Representative (2004). *Newsletter – Economic Reform and Reconstruction Bosnia and Herzegovina*. Vol. 7(3), July 2004.

Ofosu-Amaah, W. P., Soopramanien, R., & Uprety, K. (1999). *Combating Corruption: A Comparative Review of Selected Legal Aspects of State Practice and Major International Initiatives.* Washington, DC: World Bank.

Olken, B. A. (2006). "Corruption perceptions vs. corruption reality". NBER Working Paper 12428, Cambridge, MA: NBER.

Osoro, N. E., Mpabngo, P. I., & Mwinyimvua, H. H. (1999). *Enhancing Transparency in Tax Administration in Tanzania.* Tanzania: University of Dar es Salaam, Department of Economics.

Paldam, M. (2001). Corruption and religion adding to the economic model. *Kyklos*, 54(2–3), 383–413.

Paoli, L. (2003). *Mafia Brotherhoods: Organized Crime, Italian Style.* New York: Oxford University Press.

Paul, C., & Wilhite, A. (1994). Illegal markets and the social costs of rent seeking. *Public Choice*, 79(1–2), 105–116.

Paul, S. (1995). *A Report Card on Public Services in Indian Cities: A View From Below.* Bangalore: Public Affairs Centre.

Pechlivanos, L. (2004). Self-enforcing corruption: information transmission and organizational response. In Lambsdorf, J. G., & Schramm, M. T. (eds.), *The New Institutional Economics of Corruption: Norms, Trust, and Reciprocity.* Oxford: Routledge.

Phongpaichit, P., Treerat, N., Chaiyapong, Y., & Baker, C. (2000). *Corruption in the Public Sector in Thailand: Perception and Experience of Households.* Bangkok: Political Economy Center, Chulalongkorn University.

Polinski, M., & Shavel, S. (1991). A note on optimal fines when wealth varies among individuals. *The American Economics Review*, 81(3), 618–621.

President's Office (United Republic of Tanzania) (1999). "The national anti-corruption strategy and action plan for Tanzania". Prevention of Corruption Bureau, Tanzania President's Office.

PriceWaterhouseCoopers (1998). *Tanzania Revenue Authority. Corporate Plan 1998/1999 to 2002/2003* (Appendix B: Taxpayer survey). Dar es Salaam (restricted distribution).

Probidad (2002). "Galera de corruptos latinoamericanos". Retrieved March 04, 2004 from http://probidad.org/regional/recursos/galeria/

Prud'homme, R. (1995). The dangers of decentralization. *The World Bank Research Observer*, 10(2), 201–220.

Ratiani, S. (2004). "Georgia corruption crackdown makes waves". CRN Report, No. 221, Institute for War and Peace Reporting.

Reinikka, R. (2001). *Recovery in Service Delivery: Evidence from Schools and Health Centers, Uganda's Recovery: The Role of Farms, Firms, and Government.* Washington, DC: World Bank.

Reinikka, R., & Svensson, J. (2002). "Assessing front line service delivery". Retrieved March 3, 2004 from World Bank/Development Research

Group Website: http://www.worldbank.org/wbi/governance/assessing/pdf/reinikka.pdf

Reinikka, R., & Svensson, J. (2003). "Survey techniques to measure and explain corruption". World Bank Working Paper.

Reinikka, R., & Svensson, J. (2004). Local capture: evidence from a central government transfer program in Uganda. *The Quarterly Journal of Economics*, 119(2), 679–705.

Reja, B., & Tavitie, A. (2000). "The industrial organization of corruption: what is the difference in corruption between Asia and Africa". Paper presented at the Annual Conference 2000 of the International Society for New Institutional Economics, Tbingen, September 2000.

Reuters (2002). "Angola: corruption undermines relief to Angola". Retrieved April 04, 2004 from http://support.casals.com/aaaflash1/busca.asp?ID_AAAControl = 8291

Rhodes, M. (1997). Financing party politics in Italy: A case of systemic corruption. In Bull, M., & Rhodes, M. (eds.), *Crisis and Transition in Italian Politics*. (pp. 54–80). London: Frank Cass.

Rogow, A., & Laswell, H. D. (1970). The definition of corruption. In Heidenheimer, A. J. (ed.), *Political Corruption: Readings in Comparative Analysis*. New York, NY: Holt, Rinehart and Winston.

Rose-Ackerman, S. (1978). *Corruption a Study in Political Economy*. New York: Academic Press.

Rose-Ackerman, S. (1999). *Corruption and Government: Causes, Consequences, and Reform*. Cambridge: Cambridge University Press.

Rosten, L. (1968). *The Joys of Yiddish*. New York, NY: McGraw Hill.

Russian Regional Report (1999). Bykov Allies with Zhirinovsky, Vol. 4, No. 33, September 1999.

Russian Regional Report (2002). New, But Transitional, Federation Council Starts Working, Vol. 7, Nos. 5–6, February 2002.

Ryan Hoover (2002). "Lesotho corruption trial: sole's applications dismissed". Retrieved March 1, 2004 from Africa Program, International Rivers Network. Berkeley, CA Website: www.odiousdebts.org/odiousdebts/index.cfm?DSP = content&ContentID = 6182

Salacuse, J. W. (1998). "Undertaking a direct foreign investment". In Streng, & Salacuse (eds.), *2002, International Business Planning: Law and Taxation-United States*, Vol. 6. CA: Matthew Bender.

Sang-Yool, H. (2000). "Recent reform of Korean tax administration – focused on measures for prevention of corruption". Paper presented at the Conference of Asia Pacific Forum on Combating Corruption, Seoul, Korea, December, 2000.

Santiso, C., & Belgrano, A. G. (2004). *Politics of Budgeting in Peru: Legislative Budget Oversight and Public Finance Accountability in Presidential Systems*. Washington, DC: Paul H. Nitze School of Advanced International Studies.

de Sardan, J. P. O. (1999). A moral economy of corruption in Africa? *Journal of Modern African Studies*, 37(1), 25–52.

SAS-Business Intelligence (2004). "Mission accomplished! The Philippines Bureau of Internal Revenue reduces federal deficit, improves tax collection processes with SAS, realizing 400 percent ROI". Retrieved in 2004 from http://www.sas.com/success/philippinesbir.html

Schaeffer, M. (2002). *Corruption and Public Finance*. Washington, DC: Management Systems International, USAID.

Scharpf, F. W. (1997). *Games Real Actors Play – Actor-Centered Institutionalism in Policy Research*. Oxford: Westview Press.

Schiavo-Campo, S. (ed.). (1999). *Governance Corruption and Public Financial Management*. (p. 1999). Manila, Philippines: Asian Development Bank.

Schiavo-Campo, S., & Tommasi, D. (eds.). (1999). *Managing Public Expenditures*. (p. 1999). Manila, Philippines: Asian Development Bank.

Schick, A. (2002). Can national legislatures regain an effective voice in budget policy? *OECD Journal on Budgeting*, 1(3), 9–36.

Schneider, F. (2003). *The size and development of the shadow economy around the world and the relaxation to the hard tax*. Working Paper, Linz, Austria: Johannes Kepler University.

Schriek (2004). "Tough line on graft in Georgia". Retrieved on January 26, 2005 from http://www.georgiaemb.org/DisplayMedia.asp?id = 303

Sedigh, S., & Muganda, A. (1999). The fight against corruption in Tanzania. In Stapenhurst, R., & Kpundeh, S. J. T. (eds.), *Curbing Corruption*. Washington, DC: The World Bank.

Segal, L. G. (2004). *Battling Corruption in America's Public Schools*. New York: Manhattan-Institute.

Shah, A., & Mathew, A. (2003). Toward citizen-centered local level budgets in developing countries. In Shah, A. (ed.), *Public Expenditure Analysis. Public Sector Governance and Accountability Series*. (pp. 183–216). Washington, DC: World Bank.

Shah, A., & Thompson, T. (2004). "Implementing decentralized local governance: a treacherous road with potholes, detours and road closures". World Bank Policy Research Working Paper 3353, June 2004, Washington, DC: the World Bank.

Shleifer, A. (1998). Origins of bad policies: control, corruption and confusion. In Baldassarri, M., Paganetto, L., & Phelps, E. S. (eds.), *Institutions and Economic Organization in the Advanced Economies: The Governance Perspective*. (pp. 239–259). New York, London: St. Martin's Press.

Shleifer, A., & Vishny, R. W. (1993). Corruption. *Quarterly Journal of Economics*, 108(3), 599–617.

Sigma (2002). "Candidates assessment reports". June 2002, Retrieved on March 5, 2004 from http://www.sigmaweb.org/libass/Candidates 0602_Intro.htm

Sigma (2003). "Bulgaria external audit assessment 2003". Retrieved on February 02, 2004 from http://www.sigmaweb.org/PDF/assessments/Candidates2002/BulgExtAud602.pdf

Silvani, C., & Baer, K. (1997). "Designing a tax administration reform strategy: experiences and guidelines, International Monetary Fund, IMF". Working Papers 97/30, Washington, DC: IMF.

Spector, B. I. (ed.). (2005). "Fighting corruption", *Developing Countries: Strategies and Analysis*. London, UK: Kumarian Press.

Sundet, G. (2004). *Corruption in Tanzania*. Monograph. Dar-es-Salaam.

Supreme Audit Institutions of the Central and Easter European Countries (2001). "Relations between supreme audit institutions and parliamentary committees". Retrieved January 07, 2004, from http://www.eca.eu.int/EN/sais/SAI_Parl_136.pdf

Swamy, A. V., Knack, S., Lee, Y., & Azfar, O. (2001). Gender and corruption. *Journal of Development Economics*, 64(1), 25–55.

Taliercio, R. (2000). "Administrative reform as credible commitment: the design, sustainability, and performance of semi-autonomous revenue authorities in Latin America", Unpublished dissertation. Cambridge: Harvard University.

Taliercio, R. (2002). *Designing performance: the semi-autonomous revenue authority model in Africa and Latin-America*. Mimeo (September), Washington, DC: World Bank.

Tanzi, V. (1995). Corruption: arm's-length relationships and markets. In Fiorentini, G., & Peltzman, S. (eds.), *The Economics of Organised Crime*. (pp. 161–180). Cambridge: Cambridge University Press.

Tanzi, V. (1997). *"Corruption in the public finances", 8th International Anti-corruption Conference*. Peru: Lima.

Tanzi, V. (1998a). Corruption and the budget: problems and solutions. In Arvind, K. J. (ed.), *Economics of Corruption*. Boston, MA: Kluwer Academic.

Tanzi, V. (1998b). Corruption around the world. *IMF Staff Papers*, 45(4), 559–594.

Tanzi, V., & Davoodi, H. (2000). Corruption, public investment and growth. In Tanzi, V. (ed.), *Policies, Institutions and the Dark Side of Economics*. (pp. 154–170). Cheltenham, U.K.: Elgar distributed by American International Distribution Corporation, Williston, VT.

Tanzi, V., & Davoodi, H. (2001). Corruption, growth and public finances. In Jain, A. K. (ed.), *The Political Economy of Corruption*. London: Routledge.

Tanzi, V., & Pellechio, A. (1995). "The reform of tax administration, International Monetary Fund", IMF Working Papers: 95/22, Washington, DC: IMF.

Tanzi, V., & Zee, H. (2000). "Tax policy for emerging markets: developing countries". *National Tax Journal*, 53(2), 223–299.

Terkper, S. E. (1994). International: improving the accountancy context of tax reform in developing countries. *Bulletin for International Fiscal Documentation*, 48(1), 21–32.

Terkper, S. (2003). Managing small and medium-sized taxpayers in developing countries. *Tax Notes International*, 29, 211–234.

Therkildsen, O. (2004). Autonomous tax administration in Sub-Saharan Africa: the case of the Uganda revenue authority. *Forum for Development Studies*, 31(1), 59–88.

Tirole, J. (1986). Hierarchies and bureaucracies: on the role of collusion in organizations. *Journal of Law Economics and Organization*, 2(2), 181–214.

Tisne, M., & Smilov, D. (2004). *From the Ground Up: Assessing the Record of Anticorruption Assistance in Southeastern Europe' Policy Studies Series*. Budapest: Centre for Policy Studies, Central European University.

Torgler, B. (2003). To evade taxes or not that's the question. *Journal of Socio Economic*, 32(3), 283–302.

Transparency International (1997). *TI Source Book*, 2nd edition. Berlin: Transparency International.

Transparency International (2001). *Global Corruption Report 2001*. Berlin: Transparency International.

Transparency International (2002). "Progress towards containment of forest corruption and improved forest governance". Forest Integrity Network.

Transparency International (2003). *Global Corruption Report 2003*. Berlin: Transparency International.

Transparency International (2004). *Global Corruption Report 2004*. Berlin: Transparency International.

Treisman, D. (2000). The causes of corruption: a cross-country study. *Journal of Public Economics*, 76, 399–457.

Tullock, G. (1967). The welfare costs of tariffs, monopolies and theft. *Western Economic Journal*, 5, 224–232.

Tumennasan, B. (2004). *"Fiscal decentralization, corruption, and investments"*. Georgia State University (Forthcoming).

USAID (1999). *A Handbook of Fighting Corruption. Center for Democracy and Governance*. Washington, DC: USAID.

USAID (2000). *USAID's Experience Strengthening Legislatures*. Washington, DC: Center for Democracy and Governance, USAID.

USAID (2001). "The Ghana democracy and governance of the USAID: strengthened democratic and decentralized governance through civic involvement". USAID mission in Ghana, Retrieved on June 4, 2004 from http://www.usaid.gov/mission/gh/democracy/background/index.htm

USAID (2002). "Think Tank helps Kyrgyz parliament make informed decisions". USAID Success Stories Archive April 2002.

Van Rijckeghem, C., & Weder, B. (2001). Bureaucratic corruption and the rate of temptation: do low wages in civil service cause corruption? *Journal of Development Economics*, 65(2), 307–331.

Vietnam News (2004). "Death sentence upheld in Embezzlement Case". Tuesday, April 6, 2004, http://vietnamnews.vnanet.vn/

Von Maravic, P. (2003). "How to analyze corruption in the context of new public management reform?", Paper Presented at the Study Group on Ethics and Integrity of Governance.

Wade, R. (1982). The system of administrative and political corruption: canal irrigation in South India. *Journal of Development Studies*, 18, 287–327.

Wade, R. (1985). The market for public office: why the Indian state is not better at development. *World Development*, 13(4), 467–497.

Waller, C. J., Verdier, T., & Gardner, R. (2002). Corruption: top down or bottom up. *Economic Inquiry*, 40(4), 688–703.

Warsta, M. (2004). *Corruption in Thailand. International Management: Asia*. Zurich: Asia Swiss Federal Institute of Technology Zurich.

Welch, D., & Fraemond, O. (1998). "The case-by-case approach to privatization: techniques and examples". World Bank Technical Paper, No. 403, Washington, DC: The World Bank.

Wittig, W. A. (2000). *A Framework for Balancing Business and Accountability within a Public Procurement System, Approaches and Practices of the United States and other Selected Countries*. Geneva, Switzerland: International Trade Center.

World Bank (1997). Helping Countries Combat Corruption. The Role of the World Bank. *PREM Notes Public Sector, 4*, Washington, DC: the World Bank.

World Bank (1999). An Anticorruption Strategy for Revenue Administration. *PREM Notes Public Sector, 33*, Washington, DC: The World Bank.

World Bank (2000a). *Anticorruption in Transition a Contribution to the Policy Debate*. Washington, DC: The World Bank.

World Bank (2000b). "Difficulties with autonomous agencies". Retrieved on March 4, 2004 from http://www1.worldbank.org/publicsector/civil-service/autonomous.html

World Bank (2000c). *Reforming Tax Systems: Lessons from the 1990s. PREM Notes Public Sector, 37*. Washington, DC: The World Bank.

World Bank (2000d). *Helping countries combat corruption: Progress at the World Bank since 1997*. Washington, D.C.: the World Bank, Poverty Reduction and Economic Management Network.

World Bank (2001a). *Strengthening Peru's Tax Agency. PREM Notes Public Sector, 60*. Washington, DC: The World Bank.

World Bank (2001b). *Salary Supplements and Bonuses in Revenue Departments. Report – August, 2001*. Washington, DC: The World Bank.

World Bank (2001c). *Indonesia: The Imperative for Reform – Brief for the Consultative Group on Indonesia. Report 23093-IND November, 2001.* Washington, DC: The World Bank.

World Bank (2002a). *Taming Leviathan: Reforming Governance in Bangladesh – An Institutional Review.* Dhaka: The World Bank.

World Bank (2002b). "Strengthening oversight by legislatures". PREM Notes, No. 74.

World Bank (2003a). "Nibbling at corruption and inefficiency in service delivery: a ten year retrospective on the Bangalore citizen report cards". World Bank Social Development Notes, No. 82.

World Bank (2003b). *World Bank Development Indicators 2003.* Washington, DC: The World Bank.

World Bank (2004a). "The costs of corruption". Website: News/Feature Stories (April 8, 2004).

World Bank (2004b). *WB programs courses: global organization of parliamentarians against corruption GOPAC.* Washington, DC: World Bank Institute.

World Bank (2004c). *WB Programs for Parliament: Overview of the Programs.* Washington, DC: World Bank Institute.

World Bank (2006). *Investing For Growth and Recovery. The World Bank Brief for the Consultative Group on Indonesia.* Washington, DC: The World Bank.

World Economic Forum (2003). *Global Competitiveness Report 2003–2004.* Oxford: Oxford University Press.

Yacoubian, M. (2001). "Popular unrest in Algeria: a significant challenge to stability". Retrieved February 04, 2004 from Policy Watch Website: http://www.washingtoninstitute.org/watch/Policywatch/policy-watch2001/542.htm

Yak, C.C. (1995). *Corruption Control: More Than Just Structures, Systems and Processes Alone. Resource Material Series No. 65. Sixth International Training Course On Corruption Control Visiting Experts Papers.* Singapore.

Yamamoto, H. (2003). *New Public Management: Japan's Practice, IIPS Policy Paper.* Tokyo, Japan: Institute for International Policy Studies.

Zipparo, L. (1999). Encouraging public sector employees to report workplace corruption. *Australian Journal of Public Administration,* 58(2), 83–93.

Subject Index

Lightning Source UK Ltd.
Milton Keynes UK
UKOW04n2136110314

227963UK00001B/58/P